Video Basics 7

The Wadsworth Series in Broadcast and Production

VIDEO BASICS 7

Herbert Zettl

CENGAGE
Learning·

Australia • Brazil • Japan • Korea • Mexico • Singapore • Spain • United Kingdom • United States

Video Basics 7

Source:

Video Basics, 7th Edition
Herbert Zettl - San Francisco State University
© 2013 Cengage Learning. All rights reserved.

Executive Editors:
 Maureen Staudt
 Michael Stranz

Senior Project Development Manager:
 Linda deStefano

Marketing Specialist:
 Courtney Sheldon

Senior Production/Manufacturing Manager:
 Donna M. Brown

Production Editorial Manager:
 Kim Fry

Sr. Rights Acquisition Account Manager:
 Todd Osborne

For product information and technology assistance, contact us at
Cengage Learning Customer & Sales Support, 1-800-354-9706

For permission to use material from this text or product,
submit all requests online at **cengage.com/permissions**
Further permissions questions can be emailed to
permissionrequest@cengage.com

This book contains select works from existing Cengage Learning resources and was produced by Cengage Learning Custom Solutions for collegiate use. As such, those adopting and/or contributing to this work are responsible for editorial content accuracy, continuity and completeness.

Compilation © 2012 Cengage Learning
ISBN-13: 978-1-285-12428-5

ISBN-10: 1-285-12428-6

Cengage Learning
5191 Natorp Boulevard
Mason, Ohio 45040
USA

Cengage Learning is a leading provider of customized learning solutions with office locations around the globe, including Singapore, the United Kingdom, Australia, Mexico, Brazil, and Japan. Locate your local office at:
international.cengage.com/region.
Cengage Learning products are represented in Canada by Nelson Education, Ltd.
For your lifelong learning solutions, visit **www.cengage.com/custom.**
Visit our corporate website at **www.cengage.com.**

Printed in the United States of America

Contents

About the Author

Edward Aiona

Herbert Zettl is a professor emeritus of the Broadcast and Electronic Communication Arts Department at San Francisco State University (SFSU). He taught there for many years in the fields of video production and media aesthetics. While at SFSU he headed the Institute of International Media Communication. For his academic contributions, he received the California State Legislature Distinguished Teaching Award and, from the Broadcast Education Association, the Distinguished Education Service Award.

Prior to joining the SFSU faculty, Zettl worked at KOVR (Stockton-Sacramento) and as a producer-director at KPIX, the CBS affiliate in San Francisco. While at KPIX he participated in a variety of CBS and NBC network television productions. Because of his outstanding contributions to the television profession, he was elected to the prestigious Silver Circle of the National Academy of Television Arts and Sciences (NATAS), Northern California Chapter. He is also a member of the Broadcast Legends of the NATAS Northern California Chapter.

In addition to this book, Zettl has authored *Video Basics Workbook, Television Production Handbook,* and *Sight Sound Motion.* All of his books have been translated into several languages and published internationally. His numerous articles on television production and media aesthetics have appeared in major media journals worldwide. He has lectured extensively on television production and media aesthetics at universities and professional broadcast institutions in the United States and abroad and has presented key papers at a variety of national and international communication conventions.

Zettl developed an interactive DVD-ROM, *Zettl's VideoLab 4.0,* published by Wadsworth/Cengage Learning. His previous CD-ROM version won several prestigious awards.

Preface

Camcorders, like cell phones and computers, change so fast that what you buy today may be obsolete tomorrow. Right? Well, considering how fast the mobile phone transformed into a pocket-sized high-definition camcorder and a sophisticated communication device that lets you talk to your friend while watching a YouTube movie, you may have a point. Does this mean that this technological advancement brought about a similar fundamental change in video production? No. The basic steps of moving from a good idea to a professional-looking video piece have pretty much remained the same, regardless of whether you use your old camcorder or the latest DSLR camera.

Video Basics is written in the spirit of helping you learn video production from the ground up so that your move from amateur to professional status will be relatively painless but maximally effective. A solid knowledge of the basics of video will also give you the confidence to go beyond the conventional—and to break the rules if necessary for the optimal clarification and intensification of a message.

Don't be bothered by the term *basics*. I was, so I will repeat with slight variations what I wrote in the preface of the previous *Video Basics* edition: Whenever I had to read a book that had "basics" in the title, I felt slightly put down before ever looking at what was in the book. I guess I took *basics* to mean I was automatically classified as inferior or, at best, unenlightened. This feeling grew even stronger when I thought I knew a little about the subject. Now I know better. *Basics* does not imply an evaluation of the reader but describes an essential prerequisite for helping someone acquire the necessary knowledge and skills to master a subject or an activity—such as video production. As a matter of fact, I now get annoyed when I try to learn the basics of a subject but find that many of the fundamental steps are left out.

The content of this book is streamlined so that it can be taught as well as learned in a single semester. Note, however, that reading even this text alone won't make you a hot-shot videographer. Much like learning how to play guitar or piano, video production requires considerable practice.

■ VIDEO BASICS 7 HIGHLIGHTS: DEFINITIONS

To avoid confusion about what is meant by some popular terms, the following definitions explain how the terms are used in this text. For specific definitions of these and other terms, consult the glossary at the back of this book.

Video

As in all previous editions, *video* is used throughout the text as a more inclusive term than *television*. Video encompasses the full range of today's electronically delivered moving images, from what we normally call "television" to corporate videos and productions done in media departments, to documentaries or digital filmmaking by individuals or a group of friends, to multimedia content and streaming video on the Internet.

Aesthetics

The term *aesthetics* does not refer to the theory of art or what is beautiful but rather to media aesthetics, which deals with the understanding and the control of light and color, two- and three-dimensional space, time/motion, and sound. The few descriptions of some of the basic aesthetic principles are not intended to detract from learning the technical aspects of production equipment but rather to facilitate their optimal application. Traditional media aesthetic factors such as lighting, picture composition, and shot sequencing are relatively independent of technological advances and therefore become the anchor of all successful video productions. How to compose an effective shot, choose the right music, or construct a successful sequence of close-ups must go hand-in-hand with learning the more technical aspects of video equipment.

Digital

Digital, which describes the nature of an electrical signal, has become a catchword for all types of video equipment, quality standards, and even production processes. To clarify some of the often-puzzling terminology of digital television and the various scanning systems, in this edition the scanning, sampling, and compression standards of digital television (DTV) and high-definition television (HDTV) are explored and their major differences are explained. Despite the lure of high-definition equipment, you will find that in many cases learning the actual operation of equipment and production processes is the same regardless of whether the equipment is a small consumer camcorder or a high-end HDTV one.

■ VIDEO BASICS 7 HIGHLIGHTS

To make full use of this text, you should be aware of some its special features. All are intended to help you learn a complex subject in an expeditious and affable way.

Chapter Grouping

To cover the broad spectrum of video production, this book is divided into six parts:

- ■ Production: Processes and People
- ■ Image Creation: Digital Video and Camera
- ■ Image Creation: Sound, Light, Graphics, and Effects

- Image Control: Switching, Recording, and Editing

- Production Environment: Studio, Field, and Synthetic

- Production Control: Talent and Directing

As you can see, the book describes how to move from an initial idea to an effective screen event regardless of whether you are doing a wedding video, a documentary, or large-screen digital cinema. It discusses the people normally involved in the production process, the major tools of video production, and how to use them to get the intended job done effectively and on time.

Key Terms

Each chapter's key terms appear at the beginning of the chapter, in the context of the text, and again in the extensive glossary. They are intended to prepare you for each chapter's terminology and serve as a quick reference as needed. The key terms are also identified in ***bold italic*** in the chapter text in the context in which they are defined.

You should make an effort to read the key terms before moving to the actual chapter text. There is no need to memorize them at this point—they merely serve as the first part of the pedagogical principle of redundancy. Hopefully, they will trigger an *aha!* response when you encounter them in context.

Key Concepts

The key concept margin notes emphasize each chapter's principal ideas and issues and are intended primarily as a memory aid. Once you learn a key concept, it should be easier for you to retrieve the rest of the related information.

Main Points

These summaries recap the chapter's most important points and key concepts. They do not represent a true précis—a precise and accurate abridgment of the chapter content—but are intended as a final reinforcement of the essential points. Beware of thinking that all you need to do is read the summaries. They are no substitute for the in-depth chapter content.

The following information is primarily directed to instructors who are already familiar with previous editions of *Video Basics*.

New to Video Basics 7

All chapters of this edition have been updated and, where necessary, the text streamlined and the concepts clarified. You may still find occasional references to analog processes and equipment. This is done only when comparing the two electronic principles or when a certain concept is better explained in the context of analog processes. The following list highlights some of the major changes in this edition:

- High-definition video (HDV) was eliminated because it has been replaced by true HDTV even in small consumer camcorders.

- Some of the content in chapter 3 (Image Formation and Digital Video) has been rearranged and some eliminated to make this admittedly demanding chapter as painless as possible for the reader.

- Super-HDTV scanning modes, normally used for digital cinema, are introduced.

- Digital single-lens reflex (DSLR) cameras and some mounting equipment are briefly discussed.

- Three-dimensional (3D) video is explained in chapters 4 (Video Camera) and 6 (Looking through the Viewfinder).

- Light-emitting diode (LED) lighting equipment and its studio use are added.

- Tapeless recording media and nonlinear editing are stressed throughout the text.

You should realize that while 3D video equipment is readily available, 3D production techniques are still in a great stage of flux. All of the past and present 3D productions show one thing: you cannot create effective 3D content by simply applying 2D production techniques, even if you use high-end 3D equipment. Whereas we all know that z-axis motion shots, which show objects hurling out of the screen toward the viewer, are quite effective, the assumption that we already know enough about 3D video production techniques to develop valid principles is simply false. For example, the so useful over-the-shoulder shot sequence is no longer effective when used in 3D video.

Such issues, however, should not prevent instructors or students from discussing 3D and undertaking some experimental productions that may speed up our understanding of what 3D video is all about. In fact, video production departments are the ideal platform for undertaking such production research.

■ SUPPORT MATERIALS

Video Basics 7 offers a wealth of support materials for both instructors and students. These thoroughly class-tested and highly praised print and electronic supplements are available to assist you in making the learning—and the teaching—experience as meaningful, enjoyable, and successful as possible.

For Students

As a student you can reinforce the text with three additional learning aids: *Video Basics 7 Workbook*, CourseMate for *Video Basics 7,* and *Zettl's VideoLab 4.0* DVD-ROM.

Video Basics 7 Workbook   The *Workbook* can test your retention and retrieval of video production basics. When doing the *Workbook* problems, try not to seek the answers in the text until you have finished a particular *Workbook* section. This way you will get a better idea of whether you have a sufficient grasp of a particular production process or piece of equipment so that you can apply it in a variety of contexts.

CourseMate for Video Basics 7   CourseMate for *Video Basics 7* includes an interactive eBook with highlighting, note taking and an interactive glossary, and interactive learning tools, including chapter tutorial quizzes, flashcards, and more. You can access CourseMate and other online resources at *www.cengagebrain.com*.

Zettl's VideoLab 4.0   The *Zettl's VideoLab 4.0* DVD-ROM lets you manipulate production equipment in a virtual studio or field environment and apply various production techniques from the text. For example, you can mix audio, frame shots, zoom in and out, create your own lighting effects, and have plenty of opportunity for editing. All you need is a laptop with a DVD slot.

WebTutor for Video Basics 7   WebTutor is a customized learning solution, keeping you connected to your textbook, instructor, and classmates.

For Instructors

For instructors, the following class preparation, classroom activity, and assessment materials are available.

Video Basics 7 Workbook   The *Workbook* can be used to test student retention and retrieval of video production basics and also serves as a primer for actual studio and field work. I have also successfully used the *Workbook* as a diagnostic tool for advanced production students. Having students do various in-class *Workbook* problems at the beginning of the semester (without the aid of the text) quickly reveals the strengths and weaknesses of their production knowledge and skills.

CourseMate for Video Basics 7   Cengage Learning's CourseMate for *Video Basics 7* reinforces course concepts with interactive learning, study, and exam preparation tools that support the printed textbook. See *www.cengage.com/coursemate*.

Zettl's VideoLab 4.0   Even if you lecture or conduct your lab activities in a studio, you may find it convenient, at least initially, to demonstrate some of the production techniques by first showing the class examples from the *Zettl's VideoLab* DVD. Such a primer seems to facilitate the use of equipment in an actual production or lab situation. *Zettl's VideoLab 4.0* now features Advanced Labs—challenging exercises designed to improve students' ability with the equipment and concepts introduced in the regular modules.

WebTutor for Video Basics 7   The WebTutor provides access to all of the content of this text's rich CourseMate and eBook from within a professor's course management system. CourseMate is ready to use as soon as you log on and offers a wide array of web quizzes, activities, exercises, and web links. Robust communication tools—such as a course calendar, asynchronous discussion, real-time chat, a whiteboard, and an integrated e-mail system—make it easy to stay connected to the course.

Instructor's Manual   The *Instructor's Manual for Video Basics 7 with Answer Key for Video Basics 7 Workbook* includes chapter notes with teaching suggestions and activities, multiple-choice questions, essay/discussion questions, and additional teaching resources. The manual also includes the answers to the exercises in the *Workbook*. Note that for the multiple-choice questions the correct answer is indicated by a > symbol and the page number where the specific problem is first discussed in the text.

ExamView® Computerized Testing   This testing aid lets you create or customize tests and study guides (both print and online) using the test bank questions from the online Instructor's Manual. ExamView offers both a Quick Test Wizard and an Online Test Wizard that guide you step-by-step through the process of creating tests. The "what you see is what you get" interface allows you to see the test you are creating on-screen exactly as it will print or display online.

If you are a qualified adopter of the text, you can order these resources through your local Wadsworth/Cengage representative. You may also contact the Wadsworth/Cengage Academic Resource Center at 1-800-423-0563 or get more information at *www.cengage.com/wadsworth.*

ACKNOWLEDGMENTS

As with the previous edition, I am indebted to Michael Rosenberg, publisher; Megan Garvey, development editor; and Rebecca Donahue, editorial assistant. Megan and her assistant were always available to quickly respond to my questions and requests.

Gary Palmatier of Ideas to Images and his team of superprofessionals translated my ideas into this book, as they have done so effectively for all of the previous editions. A big thank-you, Gary! We all—author and readers—benefit greatly from the brilliance and the diligence of my copy editor, Elizabeth von Radics. I am lucky to have someone of her caliber on my production team. Ed Aiona deserves special thanks for his impressive photographs. They help not only illustrate the equipment but also clarify specific concepts.

My gratitude also goes to Mike Mollett, proofreader; Medea Minnich, indexer; Christina Ciaramella of PreMedia Global, photo researcher; and Bob Kauser, Global Rights and Permissions Administration, Wadsworth/Cengage Learning.

I am grateful to the reviewers of the previous edition, all of whom made valuable suggestions: Dr. Nancy F. Kaplan, Hofstra University; Steven Mathena, Tri-County Technical College; Steven Middleton, Morehead State University; Ben Scholle, Lindenwood University; Lewis Trusty, Hawaii Pacific University; Randy Visser, Southern Maine Community College; and Kimberly Wells, Delta College.

As many times before, these colleagues of mine in broadcast education and the industry were always ready to help: Marty Gonzales, Hamid Khani, Steve Lahey, and Vinay Shrivastava of the Broadcast and Electronic Communication Arts Department at San Francisco State University; Rudolf Benzler, T.E.A.M. Lucerne, Switzerland; John Beritzhoff, Snader and Associates; Ed Cosci and Jim Haman, KTVU Oakland–San Francisco; Ed Dudkowski, Producer; Michael Eisenmenger of the Community Media Center of Marin; Elan Frank and Reed Maidenberg, Elan Productions; Professor Nikos Metallinos, Concordia University; and Professor Manfred Muckenhaupt, University of Tübingen. To all, a big thank-you!

This book could not have been done without the many volunteers who helped stage and modeled for the many photos in this edition: Socoro Aguilar-Uriarte, Karen Austin, Ken Baird, Hoda Baydoun, Clara Benjamin, Rudolf Benzler, Tiemo Biemüller, Gabriella Bolton, Michael Cage, William Carpenter, NeeLa Chakravartula, Andrew Child, Laura Child, Renee Child, Christine Cornish, Ed Cosci, David Galvez, Eric Goldstein, Poleng Hong, Michael Huston, Lauren Jones, Akiko Kajiwara, Hamid Khani, Philip Kipper, Fawn Luu, Orcun Malkoclar, Johnny Moreno, Anita Morgan, Tomoko Nakayama, Tamara Perkins, Richard Piscitello, Ildiko Polony, Robaire Ream, Kerstin Riediger, Joaquin Ross, Maya Ross, Algie Salmon-Fattahian, Heather Schiffman, Alisa Shahonian, Pria Shih, Jennifer Stanonis, Mathias Stering, Heather Suzuki, Julie Tepper, Takako Thorstadt, Mike Vista, Andrew Wright, and Arthur Yee.

My wife, Erika, gets a big hug for keeping me—and herself—in a good mood throughout the writing of this edition of *Video Basics*.

Herbert Zettl

I

Production:
Processes and People

Today it is possible for you to use your cell phone and a small laptop computer to create a documentary in high-definition video and sound that will garner you an Oscar nomination. Right? Well, there is always the chance that you get lucky—once. But as a professional in the video business, you must be much more consistent and produce high-quality programs on a more regular basis. To achieve this goal, you must understand not only how a specific piece of equipment works but also how to get from idea to video image efficiently and effectively—the whole production process. You must also learn to work with people—a team of experienced production experts—all of whom must collaborate to create a worthwhile program and bring it to its intended audience. This book will help you become such a professional.

Part I explores how the production process works and how to move systematically from the initial idea to the finished production with confidence and minimal wasted effort. You are also introduced to the standard technical and nontechnical production teams.

KEY TERMS

angle The particular approach to a story—its central theme.

field production Production activities that take place away from the studio.

medium requirements All personnel, equipment, and facilities needed for a production, as well as budgets, schedules, and the various production phases.

multicamera production The use of two or more cameras to capture a scene simultaneously from different points of view. Each camera's output can be recorded separately (iso configuration) and/or fed into a switcher for instantaneous editing.

postproduction Any production activity that occurs after the production. Usually refers to video editing and/or audio sweetening.

preproduction The preparation of all production details.

process message The message actually perceived by the viewer in the process of watching a video program.

production The actual activities in which an event is recorded and/or televised.

production model Moving from the idea to the program objective and then backing up to the specific medium requirements to achieve the program objective.

program objective The desired effect of the program on the viewer. The defined process message.

single-camera production All of the video is captured by a single camera or camcorder for postproduction editing. Similar to the traditional film approach. Also called *film-style*.

studio production Production activities that take place in the studio.

Production Process

Y ou are ready to roll. You've got a million ideas for shows, each of which is considerably better than what you ordinarily see on television. But how exactly do you get them out of your head and onto the screen? This step—the production process—is the core of all successful programs. It cannot be done intuitively; it must be learned. But don't be dismayed. This chapter provides you with a useful guide to moving from idea to image—your prizewinning masterpiece. It also explains the production phases and leads you through the preproduction steps. Finally, it helps you generate useful program ideas on demand and points you toward the ever-closer convergence of video and digital cinema productions, regardless of whether they are done as single- or multicamera productions in the studio or in the field.

▶ **PRODUCTION MODEL**
Organizing the details for moving from original idea to finished product

▶ **PRODUCTION PHASES**
Preproduction, production, and postproduction

▶ **IMPORTANCE OF PREPRODUCTION**
Moving from idea to script and from script to production details

▶ **PREPRODUCTION: GENERATING IDEAS ON DEMAND**
Brainstorming and clustering

▶ **PREPRODUCTION: FROM IDEA TO SCRIPT**
Program objective, angle, evaluation, and script

▶ **PREPRODUCTION: FROM SCRIPT TO PRODUCTION**
Medium requirements and budget

▶ **MEDIA CONVERGENCE**
Digital cinema and video and single- and multicamera use in the studio and in the field

◼ PRODUCTION MODEL

Don't be dismayed. A model is not a set of absolute rules; it is strictly a suggestion of how to approach and accomplish a difficult task. In this case it is meant to help you organize the many details necessary to move from the original idea to the finished product. The production model is not a foolproof system that works every time you use it but more of a road map for how to get from idea to screen image with the least number of detours.

The production model is based on the realization that the message that counts is not necessarily the one you start with but the one that is perceived by the viewer. This process is a bit like cooking: the final success of your undertaking is measured not by the ingredients you use (the initial idea) but whether your guests like the meal (the message actually received). Wouldn't it make sense, then, to start with an idea of how the meal should finally look and taste and then figure out what ingredients you need to make it?

This production model works on the same principle: once you have developed the initial idea, you move directly to what, ideally, you want the viewers to learn, feel, or do.[1] The **production model** suggests that rather than move from the initial idea to the production, you jump from the initial idea to a **program objective**—the desired effect on the viewer. Then and only then do you back up and decide on the medium requirements necessary to produce the intended communication effect. Because the final effect is the result of a process between what you present on-screen and what the viewer actually perceives, this all-important message is called the **process message**. SEE 1.1

As you can see, this model shows four distinct processes: (1) moving from the basic idea to the program objective (desired effect on the viewer) and the angle; (2) determining the necessary medium requirements in preproduction; (3) generating the program objective in the production phases; and (4) distributing the message (the production) to the target audience.

What happened to the process message? You won't really know what the actual process message is unless you observe a viewer watching your show and reacting to it. This is the weakest point in the production of video and broadcast communication. We rarely, if ever, know just what the actual process message is or how close the program objective came to the actual viewer impact.

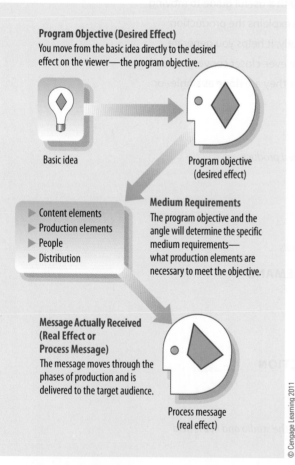

Program Objective (Desired Effect)
You move from the basic idea directly to the desired effect on the viewer—the program objective.

Basic idea

Program objective (desired effect)

- ▶ Content elements
- ▶ Production elements
- ▶ People
- ▶ Distribution

Medium Requirements
The program objective and the angle will determine the specific medium requirements—what production elements are necessary to meet the objective.

Message Actually Received (Real Effect or Process Message)
The message moves through the phases of production and is delivered to the target audience.

Process message (real effect)

© Cengage Learning 2011

1.1 PRODUCTION MODEL
The production model shows how to move from the show idea to the finished program with maximum efficiency.

1. This concept is based on the classic instructional design by Mager. See Robert Mager, *Preparing Instructional Objectives*, 3rd ed. (Atlanta: Center for Effective Performance, 1997).

Rating services estimate (more or less accurately) how many people are watching a particular show but not what they actually think, feel, or do while watching it. This is why smart producers of comedy series let a studio audience see each installment before it gets on the air. If a sure-fire joke does not generate audience laughter, it is rewritten on the spot or scrapped. `ZVL1` PROCESS→ Effect-to-cause→ basic idea | desired effect | cause | actual effect

Note: The `ZVL` icons point to related segments on the *Zettl's VideoLab 4.0* DVD-ROM. You can run each module when you see its cue in the text, or you may prefer to wait until you have finished reading the chapter and run all relevant modules at one time. The DVD-ROM is not an essential part of this book; it is meant to reinforce the text and to facilitate the transition from reading to actual practice.

◼ PRODUCTION PHASES

Over the years certain routines—production processes—have evolved that can facilitate the complex job of getting ideas translated into effective shows. These processes include chores that need to be done *before* the production, *during* the actual production activities, and *after* the production. In production lingo we call these the preproduction, production, and postproduction phases. `ZVL2` PROCESS→ Process introduction

Preproduction includes all the planning and coordination of details before the actual production activities.

Production starts when you open the studio doors and turn on the equipment or when you load your vehicle with the gear for a field production. In production you actually encode, or translate, the original program objective into a series of video segments. Production involves the medium requirements—the coordination of production and technical people and the operation of the production equipment.

In *postproduction* you select the best bits and pieces of the recorded event, enhance their picture and sound quality as necessary, correct some of the minor production mistakes, and assemble the shots and the scenes into a coherent whole—the video program. For complicated programs that require a great deal of editing, the postproduction phase may take as long as, or even longer than, the preproduction or production period. `ZVL3` PROCESS→ Phases→ production | postproduction

This chapter focuses on preproduction. The details of production and postproduction take up the rest of the book.

◼ IMPORTANCE OF PREPRODUCTION

In preproduction you develop the initial program idea, define the program objective, and select the people and the equipment necessary to translate your idea into effective video and audio images.

Meticulous preproduction is a key factor in maximizing your video production efficiency and effectiveness. There is a proven formula that you must not only remember but also always apply, even if the production you are doing is relatively simple: *the more attention you pay to preproduction, the more effective the production and postproduction phases will be.* Remember this advice especially when you are tired of organizing details and are itching to go on-location and start shooting. `ZVL4` PROCESS→ Phases→ preproduction

Normally, the preproduction activities require two distinct approaches: the move from idea to script and from script to production details.

■ PREPRODUCTION: GENERATING IDEAS ON DEMAND

All good productions start with a good idea. As obvious as this sounds, you may be surprised to find that one of the more difficult demands in professional video is coming up with good ideas consistently. Often the calendar or clock dictates when to be creative. Unfortunately, tight production schedules will not tolerate your waiting for divine inspiration. You must call on techniques that help you jolt your imagination even on a down day. Two well-known and effective devices for unlocking ideas are brainstorming and clustering.

Brainstorming

Brainstorming involves freeing your mind of the restrictions you impose on it because you feel, however unconsciously, that you have to think and say something that fits the situational framework and others' expectations. It is a form of "conceptual blockbusting" that ignores or breaks down traditional barriers to creative expression.[2]

Picture yourself for a moment as an observer of a brainstorming session of advertising people who are supposed to think of a "new approach to showing a family car that handles like a high-powered sports car." Six people sit in a circle; in the middle of the circle are two microphones and a small audio recorder. One of the people (P1 = person 1), who is also the team leader, starts with:

> P1: "Knock, knock!"
>
> P2: "Who's there?"
>
> P3: "Nobody. It's raining."
>
> P4: "Japanese calligraphy."
>
> P5: "Slick roads."
>
> P6: "Sports car–like handling."
>
> P1: "Bullet-like fast."
>
> P2: "Slalom ski race."
>
> P3: "Replaces space shuttle."
>
> P4: "Calligraphy of haiku poetry."

And so forth.

After a few more go-arounds, one of the participants gets annoyed at person 4, who consistently expanded on the theme of Japanese calligraphy and its aesthetic and spiritual meanings. Person 4, who works as a designer and is currently taking a workshop in Japanese calligraphy, defends herself by saying that this workshop opens up a whole new design world for her—poetry in motion. Some snickers. Person 1, the team leader, admonishes everybody that anything goes in brainstorming and that, initially, all ideas are equally valid. He reminds the idea team that there

---

2. See James L. Adams, *Conceptual Blockbusting,* 4th ed. (Cambridge, MA: Perseus, 2001).

should be no judgment passed as to the relevancy of the utterances, however far out they may initially seem. During the discussion period, person 4 says that she could easily paint a beautiful curvy wet road with one brush stroke on which the new red car could safely speed along. Bingo! This idea was finally translated into a highly successful car commercial: first you see the black road painted on the screen, then the red car moving fast, but safely, along the graceful curves of the shiny black road.

Although there should be no restrictions, successful brainstorming depends on a number of conditions:

- It is best done with several people.

- You start out with a general idea or related image (car commercial) and let everybody call out whatever springs to mind.

- It's important to let all minds roam freely and not evaluate or judge any of the ideas, however irrelevant they may seem.

- Document all ideas by audio-recording them or writing them down.

- In the review stage, recite the list of comments several times to discover novel connections.

If necessary, you can do brainstorming by yourself, but you will need some way of recording it or writing it down. One of the more popular solitary brainstorming techniques is clustering.

Clustering

In the middle of a piece of paper, write a single word that seems somehow central to your basic program idea or program objective and circle it. Now write down and circle another word that is somehow associated with your key word and connect the two. Write down other word associations and connect them to the last one circled.

In a short time, you will have created a cluster of words or ideas. Don't try to design a cluster or be logical about it. Work fast so that you will not be tempted to ponder your associations. Let your mind flow freely. When you feel that your ideas are exhausted, don't force yourself to find more connections or more-logical ones. The idea cluster seems to have a natural limit. You will most likely know when you have enough branches and it is time to stop. If one word or phrase is especially intriguing yet seems out of place, start a new cluster but leave the old one alone. Once you are at that point, look at the finished diagram and search for patterns. These patterns will inevitably reveal some novel connections and relationships that were not obvious before and can serve as springboards for the program objective (process message) and the medium requirements. SEE 1.2

As you can see, clustering is similar to brainstorming except that during clustering you create an immediate visual pattern that yields quite readily the major interrelationships of the various ideas.[3] But it is also much more restrictive than brainstorming. **ZVL5** PROCESS→ Ideas

> **KEY CONCEPT**
> Successful brainstorming and clustering depend on a free, intuitive, and noncritical flow of ideas.

---

3. Clustering as an idea-unlocking technique for writing was developed by Gabriele Lusser Rico in *Writing the Natural Way*, rev. ed. (Los Angeles: J. P. Tarcher, 2000).

1.2 CLUSTERING

Note that clustering starts with a central idea and then branches out in various directions. Clustering must be done quickly and uncritically; it is much like written brainstorming.

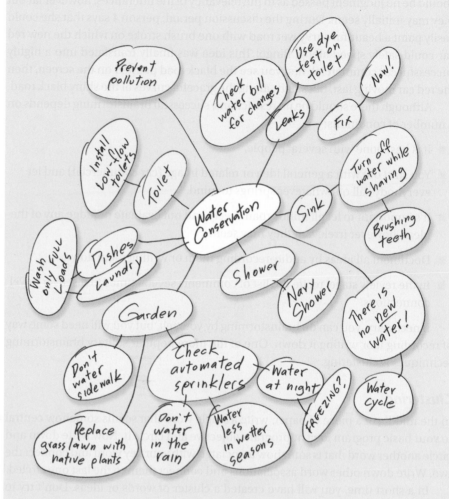

© Cengage Learning 2011

■ PREPRODUCTION: FROM IDEA TO SCRIPT

You must have some idea of what meal to prepare before starting to cook. The same is true in video production. Running around with your camcorder before deciding on what it is you want to tell your viewers is a wasteful activity at best. An effective production process depends on a fairly clear idea of what you want to communicate. As we all experience, however, most initial production ideas are rather vague and are rarely concise enough to serve as a definition of the desired communication effect—the program objective. This way of thinking is perfectly normal. As a matter of fact, you should weigh the potential effectiveness of several similar ideas before settling on a single one, but you should not move on to specific production details without first having a clear program objective.

For example, suppose you have just moved to Big City, and your daily commute prompts you to "do something about these crazy Big City drivers." You are certainly not ready at this point to plunge into production. Changing your idea to "do a documentary on the crazy Big City drivers" is no improvement. You need to think more about exactly what you want viewers to learn about becoming better drivers. The more precise your definition of the intended effect—the program objective—the easier it is to decide on the appropriate production format and the necessary procedures. `ZVL6` PROCESS→ Effect-to-cause→ basic idea

Program Objective

Exactly what is it that you want the audience to know, feel, or do? To "do something about these crazy Big City drivers" says little about what to do and how to go about achieving that "something." You need to construct a precise program objective.

Rather than tackle all the bad habits of the "crazy Big City drivers," you may want to isolate a single problem that is especially bothersome and that you consider important. As in most learning or persuasion tasks, specific objectives are usually more effective than general ones, and small steps are more easily managed and accomplished by the viewer than large ones. For instance, you may find that the misuse or nonuse of turn signals has become a serious threat to traffic safety. So, rather than address *all* the bad habits of Big City drivers, you can isolate a single objective: *Demonstrate to Big City drivers that turn signals help other drivers react to your changing directions and contribute to traffic safety.*

Once you have a clear program objective, you can start visualizing some possible approaches. Because you are a creative person, you come up with several good approaches to this video. But which one should you choose? What you now need is an effective angle. `ZVL7` PROCESS→ Effect-to-cause→ desired effect

Angle

In the context of designing a show, an **angle** is a specific approach to the story—a point of view of the event. Effective video programs often have an angle that is different from the usual treatment of the same subject and is more relevant to the viewer. Although the requirement of "finding an angle" has been abused by many newspeople in their attempts to sensationalize a basically uninteresting story, it is a valuable and positive way of clarifying and intensifying an event.

In our example one of the possible angles could be to show the terrible consequences of an accident that was caused by a driver who failed to signal his lane change. Or you may show the misuse or nonuse of turn signals from a bicyclist's point of view—one who has a hard time avoiding reckless drivers even during her relatively short ride to campus. You may find, however, that these drivers are not really reckless but simply absentminded or discourteous.

Isn't this now an entirely new angle on how to approach the turn signal problem? Yes, it is. Instead of telling Big City drivers that they are reckless and had better learn to use turn signals because it is the law, you may want to persuade them to be more courteous and helpful to one another and to the traffic around them. To accommodate and assist the less-than-perfect drivers, rather than accuse and attack them, may be a more effective angle for all sorts of traffic education. Instead of using threats as a means to make them use turn signals, you now appeal to their pride and self-esteem.

Unless you are the writer, you will find that scriptwriters often come up with a useful angle. Most writers will be happy to accept suggestions for an angle even if they later discover a better one.

Evaluation

Whatever angle you choose, always ask yourself two questions: *Is the proposed video worth doing?* and *Is it doable?* Despite your good intentions and desire to rival in your production the style of an elaborate Hollywood movie, you will not succeed unless you have the Hollywood budget and the production time to match. Money and time are production factors as real as cameras and microphones.

You will find that your clients—the school board, a big corporation, or a local cable channel—become more and more demanding. They expect you to come up with a superior product in an unreasonably short time for an unbelievably low budget. Give up right now? Not at all! But you may have to scale back your grand intentions and come up with ideas that are realistic, that is, that can actually be accomplished by you and your team and that will provide the client with the promised project on time and within budget.

Don't promise what you can't deliver. It is wise to accompany your creative leaps with the two reality factors: available time and money. You simply cannot do a million-dollar production if you have only $500 to spend. Or, if you have only four weeks to complete a show, don't attempt a production that requires on-location shooting in different parts of the world and two months of postproduction.

Script

You are now ready to write the script or hire a writer. You need a script, even if all it says is "no script." The script is an essential communication device among all nontechnical and technical production personnel. We discuss the various script formats in chapter 17. SEE 1.3

■ PREPRODUCTION: FROM SCRIPT TO PRODUCTION

In preproduction the script becomes the key for the actual production preparations. You must now translate the script into medium requirements, which include various people and production elements.

Medium Requirements

Normally, the **medium requirements** are expressed as workflow that includes selecting talent, determining technical and nontechnical personnel, and requesting studio or field facilities and equipment. SEE 1.4

As you can see in figure 1.4, the script now serves as the main guide for all further technical and nontechnical production requirements. As the producer your main preproduction contact will now be the director. Under your close supervi-

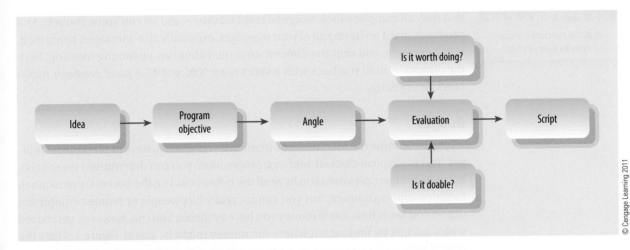

© Cengage Learning 2011

1.3 PREPRODUCTION: FROM IDEA TO SCRIPT

This preproduction phase involves the major steps that lead from idea generation to scriptwriting.

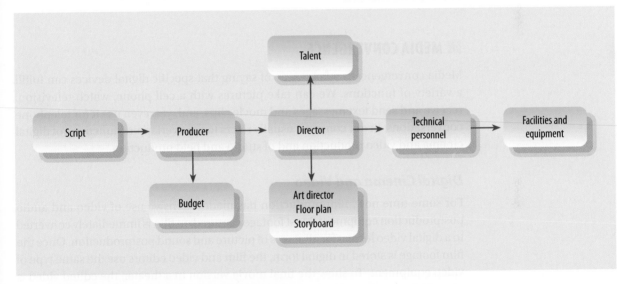

© Cengage Learning 2011

1.4 PREPRODUCTION: FROM SCRIPT TO PRODUCTION

This preproduction phase involves the major steps that lead from the script to the actual production process.

sion, the director chooses the talent, assigns the art director to design a set, and discusses with the technical supervisor the necessary personnel, facilities (studio, location, and postproduction facilities), and equipment (camera, lighting, audio, and video recorders).

Note that who does what in preproduction is not always as clear-cut as the figure implies. For example, you may find that sometimes the producer rather than the director will choose the talent or request a set design from the art director. This is all the more reason for you, the producer, to communicate frequently with all technical and nontechnical personnel involved in preproduction and to make sure

KEY CONCEPT

A good producer triple-checks everything.

that they all complete their assigned tasks on time—and let you know about it. As a producer, insist on having all of your messages, especially all e-messages, confirmed. If, for example, you sent the director an e-mail about an upcoming meeting, have the director e-mail you back with a short note: "OK, got it." *A good producer triple-checks everything.*

Budget

As you determine the medium requirements, you will also have to prepare the budget. This is a typical chicken-and-egg proposition: you can determine a reasonably accurate budget only when you have all the information on the necessary personnel, facilities, and equipment, but you cannot really hire people or request equipment unless you know how much money you have available. You can, however, get started with a budget by finding out where the money might be going. Figure 1.5 lists the typical general budget categories for a medium-sized video production. **SEE 1.5**

Although budgets are extremely important, we won't worry about money just yet but rather concentrate on how to make the video production process maximally efficient and effective.

▇ MEDIA CONVERGENCE

Media convergence is a fancy way of saying that specific digital devices can fulfill a variety of functions. We can take pictures with a cell phone, watch television, receive and send text messages and movie clips, and, yes, even use it for telephone conversations. In our context it usually refers to the overlapping functions of digital cinema and video production and of studio and field production.

Digital Cinema and Video

For some time now, film production has made extensive use of video and audio postproduction equipment. Most footage captured on film is immediately converted to a digital video format for all stages of picture and sound postproduction. Once the film footage is stored in digital form, the film and video editors use the same type of video equipment. To show the final movie version in a theater, the edited video is sometimes transferred back to film, mainly because many movie houses have not changed from traditional film projectors to digital ones. But many movie theaters are now using super-high-definition (HD) video projectors to show the video version without transferring it back to film.

The only part of traditional film production that has partially survived the digital video invasion is the camera. A few old-school filmmakers still insist (with some justification) that film delivers a softer, less in-your-face image than even the best digital cinema cameras.

But even this last holdout faces a serious challenge, if not inevitable defeat, from greatly improved digital cinema cameras. These super-HD digital cinema cameras not only rival or supersede the sharpness of the traditional film image but match other important characteristics, such as color fidelity, as well. You will read more about them in chapter 4.

1.5 BUDGET SAMPLE
This budget example shows the basic cost summary, which lists the essential preproduction, production, and postproduction categories. Such a summary is normally accompanied by a more detailed breakdown.

PRODUCTION BUDGET

CLIENT:
PROJECT TITLE:
DATE OF THIS BUDGET:
SPECIFICATIONS:

NOTE: This estimate is subject to the producer's review of the final shooting script.

SUMMARY OF COSTS	ESTIMATE	ACTUAL
PREPRODUCTION		
Personnel	————	————
Equipment and facilities	————	————
Script	————	————
PRODUCTION		
Personnel	————	————
Equipment and facilities	————	————
Talent	————	————
Art (set and graphics)	————	————
Makeup	————	————
Music	————	————
Miscellaneous (transportation, fees)	————	————
POSTPRODUCTION		
Personnel	————	————
Facilities	————	————
Recording media	————	————
INSURANCE AND MISCELLANEOUS	————	————
CONTINGENCY (20%)	————	————
TAX	————	————
GRAND TOTAL	————	————

Studio and Field Production

Up to now it has been convenient to divide the video production or film process into studio operations and field operations. After all, a ***studio production*** takes place in the studio, and a ***field production*** occurs outside of it—and you will certainly have to learn about both. But today more and more field techniques are brought into the studio, such as the use of a single handheld camera, highly flexible sound pickup devices, and low-powered lighting instruments for general, nondramatic lighting. Similarly, many field productions employ studio techniques, such as complex multi-camera and audio pickups of live sporting events and the relatively simple two- or three-camera setup of a wedding or charity fashion show in which each camera's output is recorded separately for later postproduction editing.

As you can see, this convergence of production techniques requires your thinking about not only whether to do your production in a studio or in the field but also whether it will be a ***single-camera production*** that produces all video for extensive postproduction (sometimes called film-style); a ***multicamera production*** in which each isolated, or iso, camera records simultaneously a different angle of the same event; or a multicamera setup for live transmission, in which the output of all cameras is fed into a switcher that allows the director to do instantaneous editing. **SEE 1.6–1.8**

This convergence means that you must be conversant with both systems, even if you later decide to concentrate on one or the other. Initially, you will find that starting with multicamera production—regardless of whether you work in the studio or outside of it—will make it easier for you to work in single-camera production later on. This is because when using two or more cameras simultaneously, you can actually see different camera angles side-by-side and how they cut together. In single-camera production, you see only one camera angle at a time and have to wait until the postproduction phase to find out whether they cut together smoothly during editing.

© Cengage Learning 2011

1.6 SINGLE-CAMERA (FILM-STYLE) APPROACH
In this production technique, only one camera is used to record all shots for postproduction.

1.7 MULTICAMERA SETUP IN ISO CONFIGURATION
In this setup several cameras are used to simultaneously record the same event from various viewpoints.

1.8 MULTICAMERA SETUP FOR SWITCHING
In this setup several cameras are used to feed their output to a switcher. The switcher enables its operator to select the appropriate shots and sequence them. This is also called instantaneous editing.

The big, largely unresolved convergence problem, however, is not a technical but an aesthetic one: How can we produce images and picture sequences that play equally well on a superlarge home theater screen and on a small cell-phone display, even if the phone happens to be smart? We elaborate briefly on this problem in chapter 6 in the hope that you will eventually help solve it.

M A I N   P O I N T S

▶ *Production Model*

The production model shows four distinct processes: (1) moving from the basic idea to the program objective (desired effect or process message) and the angle, (2) determining the necessary medium requirements, (3) generating the program objective, and (4) distributing the message (the production) to the target audience.

▶ *Production Phases*

The production phases are preproduction (planning and coordinating all production details), production (encoding the program objective into a series of video segments), and postproduction (selecting and sequencing the best video segments for a coherent video program).

▶ *Importance of Preproduction*

Preproduction is a key factor in maximizing video production efficiency and effectiveness.

▶ *Preproduction: Generating Ideas on Demand*

In video production, creativity means coming up with good ideas on a consistent basis on time and within budget. Two helpful methods are brainstorming and clustering. Both techniques demand a spontaneous and noncritical delivery of ideas.

▶ *Preproduction: From Idea to Script*

This preproduction step includes formulating a program objective, deciding on the angle, evaluating the entire concept, and writing the script.

▶ *Preproduction: From Script to Production*

This production phase concerns all medium requirements as well as the budget. It requires deciding on the nontechnical and technical personnel and on the facilities and the equipment for the actual production.

▶ *Medium Requirements*

The medium requirements include content elements (program objective, angle, and audience analysis), production and postproduction elements (equipment, facilities, and schedules), and people (talent and nontechnical and technical personnel).

▶ *Media Convergence*

The media convergence concerns the overlapping functions of digital cinema and video production and of studio and field production. Multicamera productions are sometimes instantaneously edited through switching and sometimes recorded as iso sources for postproduction. Single-camera productions usually resemble film production in shot acquisition and postproduction editing.

Z E T T L ' S   V I D E O L A B

For your reference or to track your work, the *Zettl's VideoLab* program cues in this chapter are listed here with their corresponding page numbers.

K E Y   T E R M S

EFP team Usually a three-person team consisting of the talent, a camcorder operator, and a utility person who handles lighting, audio, and/or video recording, and, if necessary, the microwave transmission back to the studio.

nontechnical production personnel People concerned primarily with nontechnical production matters that lead from the basic idea to the final screen image. Includes producers, directors, and talent. Also called *above-the-line personnel*.

postproduction team Normally consists of the director, a video editor, and, for complex productions, a sound designer who remixes the sound track.

preproduction team Comprises the people who plan the production. Normally includes the producer, writer, director, art director, and technical director. Large productions may include a composer and a choreographer. In charge: producer.

production schedule A calendar that shows the preproduction, production, and postproduction dates and who is doing what, when, and where.

production team Comprises a variety of nontechnical and technical people, such as producer and various assistants (associate producer and production assistant), director and assistant director, and talent and production crew. In charge: director.

technical personnel People who operate the production equipment, including camera operators, floor persons, and video and audio engineers. Also called *below-the-line personnel*.

time line A breakdown of time blocks for various activities on the actual production day, such as crew call, setup, and camera rehearsal.

Production Team: Who Does What When?

If you are a painter, you can do everything yourself: come up with the idea, buy the materials, prepare the canvas, struggle with form and color, and finally sign and date the finished work. You could even do the selling without other people involved. The entire creative process is under your control.

This is not the case with most video productions, unless you are simply video-recording your vacation adventures or working for a news department that uses VJs (video journalists). A VJ not only determines the best way to report a story but also does the camera work, the editing, and the voice-over narration. Although this is technically possible and saves money, it rarely results in a high-quality product.

Most professional video productions involve a group of people—a production team— with each member performing a clearly defined function.

This chapter focuses on what the people do and how they work together in standard video production.

▶ **PRODUCTION TEAMS**
The preproduction, production, and postproduction teams

▶ **PASSING THE BUCK**
What happens when production people do not work as a team

▶ **TAKING AND SHARING RESPONSIBILITY**
What happens when production people know their functions and work as a team

▶ **PRODUCTION SCHEDULE AND TIME LINE**
How to set up a production schedule and develop a realistic time line

▶ **PRODUCTION WORKFLOW**
How to move from one production activity to the next as efficiently as possible

You may best understand who does what by dividing the team into people involved in the preproduction, production, and postproduction phases. The preproduction team includes the people primarily involved with planning the production; the production team comprises the people who translate the ideas into actual video pictures and sound; and the postproduction people put together all the selected video clips, which contain the optimal video and audio segments, and give the whole production the final polish.

Some production people are involved in only one of these phases; others may be involved in all three. As you can readily see, no single individual has complete control over the entire creative process. Unlike the painter, you must learn to work as an effective team member, which means that you know exactly what is expected of you when assigned to a specific production position and also what everybody else is supposed to be doing. Once you know who is supposed to do what, when, and where, you can establish effective communication among the team members and let them know when specific tasks need to be done. A production schedule and a time line are essential in coordinating the different production steps and the efforts of all team members.

Regardless of whether you are a member of the preproduction, production, or postproduction team, you will find that some team members are more engaged and interested in what they are doing than others and that even the most conscientious team members have an off-day. But it is usually the weakest link in a chain that needs attention, not the strongest one. Rather than complain about the weak contributions of some team members, help them improve their performance. You must also get used to the idea that, in such a complex and high-pressure job as video production, occasional mistakes are inevitable. Fixing blame should then be done not to vindicate the other team members but to define the problem so that it can be avoided the next time.

The primary requisites for any kind of team are that all members respect one another and work for a common goal. A famous football coach and television commentator was once asked how to improve a team's sagging spirit and attitude. His answer: "By winning!" *Winning* in video production means enabling each team member to do his or her best to produce exceptionally good shows on a consistent basis.

■ PRODUCTION TEAMS

The size and the makeup of the production team depend on the scope of the production. As mentioned before, electronic news gathering (ENG) for simple stories can be done by a single person, the VJ, who simultaneously acts as reporter, camcorder operator, and editor/narrator. While financially profitable for the news operation, this one-person-band approach is very hard on the individual who is doing it, and the results are clearly uneven. Even relatively simple electronic field productions (EFPs) are usually done with three people. The *EFP team* consists of talent, camcorder operator, and a utility person who takes care of the lighting, audio, and, if necessary, additional video-recording devices. A big-remote telecast, such as a live sporting event, may keep 30 or more people very busy (see chapter 15).

The accompanying tables summarize the major *nontechnical production personnel* and *technical personnel* and their principal functions. **SEE 2.1 AND 2.2**

Sometimes the production people are divided into above-the-line and below-the-line personnel. These designations are not clear-cut and have more to do

2.1 NONTECHNICAL PRODUCTION PERSONNEL

PERSONNEL	FUNCTION
Executive producer	In charge of one or several programs or program series. Coordinates with client, station or corporate management, advertising agencies, investors, and talent and writer's agents. Approves and manages budget.
Producer	In charge of an individual production. Responsible for all personnel working on the production and for coordinating technical and nontechnical production elements. Often doubles as writer and director.
Line producer	Supervises daily production activities on the set.
Studio and field producers	In large operations, studio and field producers are assigned different producing responsibilities: the studio producer takes care of all studio productions, and the field producer handles all field productions.
Associate producer (AP)	Assists producer in all production matters. Often does the actual production coordination jobs, such as telephoning talent and making sure that deadlines are met.
Production assistant (PA)	Assists producer and director during the actual production. Takes notes of comments made by the producer or the director during rehearsals, which serve as a guide for the crew to fix minor production flaws before the final recording.
Director	In charge of directing talent and technical operations. Ultimately responsible for transforming a script into effective video and audio messages. In smaller operations also assumes the producer's responsibilities.
Associate, or assistant, director (AD)	Assists director during the actual production. Often does timing for director. In complex multicamera productions, helps to "ready" various operations (such as presetting specific camera shots or calling for a graphic effect).
Talent	Refers, not always accurately, to all performers and actors who regularly appear on video.
Actor	Someone who portrays someone else on-camera.
Performer	Someone who appears on-camera in nondramatic activities. Always portrays himself or herself.
Announcer	Reads narration but does not appear on-camera.
Writer	Writes video scripts. In smaller-station operations or in corporate video, the writer's function is often assumed by the director or producer or by somebody hired on a freelance basis.
Art director	In charge of the creative design aspects of show (set design, location, and graphics).
Music director/conductor	Responsible for music group in large productions, such as the band that plays on a variety show. Can also be the person who chooses all the recorded music for a specific show or series.
Choreographer	Determines all movements of dancers.

2.1 NONTECHNICAL PRODUCTION PERSONNEL *(continued)*

PERSONNEL	FUNCTION
Floor manager	Also called *floor director* and *stage manager.* In charge of all activities on the studio floor, such as setting up scenery, getting talent into place, and relaying the director's cues to the talent. In the field the floor manager is basically responsible for preparing the location for the shoot and for cueing all talent.
Floor persons	Also called *grips, stagehands,* and *facilities persons.* Set up and dress sets. Operate cue cards and other prompting devices. Sometimes operate microphone booms. Assist camera operators in moving camera dollies and pulling camera cables. In small operations also act as wardrobe and makeup people. Set up and ready all nontechnical facilities in the field.
Makeup artist	Does the makeup for all talent (in large productions only).
Costume designer	Designs and sometimes constructs costumes for dramas, dance numbers, and children's shows (in large productions only).
Property manager	Maintains and manages the use of set and hand properties, such as tables, chairs, and office furniture (set properties), and telephones, coffee cups, and flashlights (hand properties)—for large productions only. In smaller operations props are managed by the floor manager.

© Cengage Learning 2011

with who pays whom than who does what. In general, above-the-line personnel are people who do not operate any equipment; below-the-line people normally do. `ZVL1` PROCESS→ People→ nontechnical | technical

Let's find out who is normally involved in the three primary production stages: preproduction, production, and postproduction.

Preproduction Team

The primary responsibility of the **preproduction team** is to develop the idea for the video and plan its production so that the translation of idea to pictures and sound is as efficient as possible. For most standard EFPs, the preproduction team consists of the producer, the director, and sometimes the talent. In larger field and studio productions, the people involved in this initial idea-generating phase include the producer, writer, director, and scene designer or art director and sometimes the technical supervisor or the technical director.

The original idea may come from the corporate client ("Do a 10-minute video showing that the customer is our most precious commodity") or the producer ("Do a piece on your campus food service"), or it may come from a concerned citizen ("I would like to do a show on the pros and cons of timber clear-cutting"). Often specific show ideas, such as a particular angle for a commercial, are the product of several people's brainstorming.

Producer   Once the general idea is born, it is nurtured through all preproduction stages by the producer, who states the specific purpose of the show—the desired effect on the viewer (the program objective) and sometimes the process message

2.2 TECHNICAL PRODUCTION PERSONNEL

This category includes engineers who are actually engaged in engineering functions, such as installing and maintaining new electronic equipment; it also includes production people and technicians who operate such equipment.

PERSONNEL	FUNCTION
Chief engineer	In charge of all technical personnel, budgets, and equipment. Designs electronic systems, including signal transmission facilities, and oversees installations, day-to-day operations, and all maintenance.
Assistant chief engineer or technical supervisor	Assists the chief engineer in all technical matters and operations. Is often involved in preproduction activities of large productions. Schedules crews and participates in big-remote surveys.
Technical director (TD)	In charge of all technical setups and operations during a production. Does the actual switching in a studio production. Often acts as technical crew chief.
Lighting director (LD)	In charge of studio and field lighting; normally for large productions only.
Director of photography (DP)	Carryover from film production. Takes care of lighting and camera operation in single-camera productions.
Camera operators	Also called *videographers* and *shooters*. Operate studio and field cameras. Sometimes also do lighting.
Video operator (VO)	Also called *video engineer* and *shader*. Adjusts the camera controls for optimal camera pictures (also called *shading*). Sometimes doubles as maintenance engineer.
Video-record operator	Operates video recorders (VRs) during the production. In small field productions, the audio technician doubles as VR operator.
Video editor	Operates video-editing equipment. Often makes creative editing decisions as well.
Sound designer	In charge of creating the sound track of a complex production, such as a drama, commercial, or large corporate assignment.
Audio engineer	Often called *audio technician*. In charge of all audio operations in production and, in the absence of a sound designer, in postproduction. Sets up microphones and operates audio console during the show.
CG operator	Operates the character generator (CG), a computer dedicated to the creation of letters and numbers in various fonts.
Maintenance engineer	A true engineering position. Maintains all technical equipment and troubleshoots during productions.

© Cengage Learning 2011

(the message that the viewer actually perceives while watching the show). The producer also prepares a budget for the entire production.

As soon as the budget has been approved, you, as producer, need to hire and coordinate all additional personnel, equipment, and production activities. You or your associate producer (AP) will then devise a production schedule that indicates who is to do what and the times when the assigned tasks should be completed. This calendar is essential for coordinating the activities of all the people involved in the production.

Writer   The next step is writing the script. The writer interprets the program objective into a video production and writes down what he or she wants the viewers to see and hear. This production step is obviously crucial. It often determines the production format, such as instructional show, interactive multimedia show, or documentary, and the style and the quality of the production. Like the production schedule, the script serves as the guide for all further production activities.

Scripts are almost always revised several times. Sometimes the original content isn't accurate and needs some corrections. At other times the words sound too stilted and pedantic when actually spoken, or there may be some shots that are unnecessary or too difficult to produce. For all of these reasons, good video writers do not come cheaply. Settle on a fee before the delivery of the script. (There are various script samples in chapter 17.)

Director   The director translates the script into specific video and audio images and often selects the necessary production crew and equipment. In large productions, such as a drama for digital cinema, the director is greatly aided in this translation process by a storyboard artist (see figure 12.15). The sooner the director is brought onboard in preproduction, the better. The director may work with the writer early on, for example, to ensure the most effective interpretation of the program objective. He or she may even help the writer with the basic approach, such as changing the original idea of producing a brief instructional video into an interactive multimedia experience, or a documentary into a dramatic format, or a company president's address into a town hall–type forum. The director can also define or change the angle or help with ideas about the specific environment in which the event is to take place.

When directing an electronic field production or a big remote, the director is part of the survey team (see chapter 15).

Art director   The art director uses the script and the director's comments for the set design or specific location for the show. He or she is also in charge of decorating the set and designing the graphics, such as the titles for a show. The art director must create an environment that fits the overall style of the show and that facilitates the anticipated production procedures. Even the most beautifully designed set is useless if there is not enough room for camera movement and microphones or if it cannot be properly lighted. In digital cinema and large video productions, the production designer is responsible for these activities and normally assigns to the art director specific jobs, such as designing the set.

For normal studio productions, the art director prepares a floor plan, which is a diagram of scenery, stage properties (tables and chairs), and set dressings (wall hangings, lamps, and plants) drawn on a grid. (See chapter 14 for a more detailed discussion of the floor plan.) The floor plan is an important preproduction guide for the director and, for large productions, the lighting director (LD), audio engineer, and floor manager as well. With a good floor plan, these people can visualize the principal shots and place the cameras, lights, and microphones accordingly. The floor manager needs the floor plan to set up and dress the studio set.

Technical director   The preproduction team may also include a technical director (TD), or technical supervisor, especially if the production is a live telecast of a special event, such as a parade or the dedication of a new building. The TD can determine ahead of time the major technical facilities necessary for the proposed production.

Small production companies and television stations often combine roles. The functions of the producer and the director, and even the writer, might be carried out by a single person—the producer-director; and the floor manager might also act as art director and property manager.

Large productions may include on the preproduction team a graphic artist, a costume designer, a sound designer, and a choreographer. **ZVL2** PROCESS→ Phases→ preproduction

Production Team

Most routine EFPs are accomplished by a three-person *production team:* the talent, the camcorder operator, and a utility person who takes care of audio, lighting, recording, and transmission. If you use two cameras for a multicamera shoot, you have to add a second camcorder operator. In single-camera EFPs that are more ambitious, the camera operator may also take care of the lighting; this dual job is carried out by the director of photography (DP)—a carryover from film production.

In most multicamera productions, the production team is considerably larger. The nontechnical members include the producer and various assistants—associate producer and production assistant (PA)—the director, the associate or assistant director (AD) if it is a complex show, and the talent. Whereas the major part of the producer's job is in preproduction, in the actual production phase it is the director who is heavily involved. Sometimes there are several producers for a show series: a producer who arranges the budget and negotiates with talent, and a line producer, who supervises the daily activities on the set or in the studio. Some productions have a studio producer who is responsible for the studio segments of a show and a field producer who takes care of the segments video-recorded outside the studio.

The production crew, which comprises technical and nontechnical production personnel, normally includes the floor manager and floor persons (grips or utility persons), the technical director, camera operators, the lighting director, video and audio engineers, the video-record operator, the CG (character generator) operator, and the video operator (VO), who adjusts the cameras during the production for optimal video output. Large productions add an engineering supervisor and a maintenance engineer as well as various costume people, a property manager, makeup artists, and hairdressers. **ZVL3** PROCESS→ Phases→ production

Postproduction Team

The *postproduction team* is relatively small and normally consists of a video editor and the director. The editor will try to make sense of the various video-recorded segments and put them in the order indicated by the script. The director will guide the editor in the selection and the sequencing of shots. If you, as the director, have a good editor and a detailed script, you will have relatively little to do. You may want to see a rough-cut, or an "off-line" editing version, before you give the editor the go-ahead to prepare the final "on-line" video recording. If the project requires complicated special effects or the selection of unusual shots, you may have to sit with the editor throughout the process to select most of the shots and determine their sequence.

Complex postproduction may also include extensive manipulation of sound, called audio sweetening. It consists of remixing, adding, or replacing small or large portions of the original sound track and can take more time and effort than editing pictures. Major sound postproduction is done by a sound designer.

Most producers do not get involved in postproduction, at least not until the first rough-cut is done. Some producers cannot stay away from the editing room, however, and get intimately involved in every decision. Such fervor is, despite all good intentions, not always appreciated by the editor and the director. **ZVL4** PROCESS→ Phases→ postproduction

■ PASSING THE BUCK

Let's visit a television studio to watch the video recording of a visiting rock group.

When you arrive at the studio well before the scheduled start time, the production is already in the wrap-up stage. Neither the musicians nor the production people look too happy. The PA tells you that the recording session had been pushed ahead three hours because of the band's tight schedule. It becomes obvious that the session did not go as planned. There are small groups of people on the studio floor engaged in lively discussions. Let's listen in on what they are saying.

In one group, the band manager is complaining about poor scheduling and the "static look" of the show, and the lead singer is kvetching about the "bad sound." The executive producer tries to appease the band members, while the producer accuses everybody of not communicating with him. The director defends his overall visual concept and personal style and accuses the musicians of not understanding the "true nature of video." The band manager mutters something about the sloppy contract and the lack of coffee during rehearsals.

Some crew and band members vent their frustrations about technical problems. They argue about which microphones should have been used and where they should have been placed and about light levels that were much too uneven for good pictures. The LD counters by saying that she had practically no time for adequate lighting, mainly because she lost three hours of setup time. The musicians complain that the sound levels were too low, while the camera operators say that the music was too loud for them to hear the director's instructions in their headsets. They felt lost, especially because the director had not briefed them ahead of time on what shots to get.

The floor manager and his crew wonder aloud why they had no floor plan. It would have saved them from having to move the heavy platform on which the band performed from place to place until the director was finally satisfied with its location.

Everyone seems to be passing the buck and blaming everybody else for the production problems. What could have been done to minimize or avoid these issues? Before reading on, write down the complaints of the band and the production members and, by referring to figures 2.1 and 2.2, try to figure out who on the production team was directly responsible for the various problems.

Ready? Now compare your notes with the following recommendations.

Situation: The video-recording session was pushed ahead by three hours because of the band's tight schedule.

> ***Responsibility:*** Producer. He should have coordinated the band's schedule more carefully with his production schedule. Moving up a shooting schedule by three hours forces the crew to work unreasonably fast and causes stress. Most seriously, it reduces, if not eliminates, valuable rehearsal time.

Situation: The band's manager complains about poor scheduling and the "static look" of the show. The lead singer is unhappy with the sound as recorded.

> ***Responsibility:*** Again, the producer is responsible for scheduling and should have double-checked with the band manager about exactly when the band would be available for the studio production. The "static look" complaint is aimed at the show's director; and the "bad sound" is directed at the audio technician, who chose the type and the position of microphones and did the sound mixing. Ultimately, the TD is responsible for all technical processes, including the sound pickup and mixing. The producer should have brought together the lead singer, band manager, and audio technician in the preproduction phase to discuss the sound requirements. The producer should also have arranged for the band manager to meet with the director to discuss the visual requirements and the overall look of the performance. The director could then have discussed his ideas about the "true nature of video" with the band manager. Even if the initiative did not come from the producer, the director and the audio technician should have pressed for such a meeting. Obviously, there was little communication among the members of the production team. The blame for the sloppy contract goes to the band manager and the executive producer, and the PA should have arranged for coffee.

Situation: The choice of microphones and their placement is being challenged. The band members complain that the sound levels of the foldback—during which the sound as mixed was played back to the band members—were too low. The camera operators could not hear the director's instructions because of the music's high volume and were without direction.

> ***Responsibility:*** The type of microphones used and their placement is clearly the responsibility of the audio technician. Again, despite the drastically reduced setup time, a prerecording meeting with the key members of the band could have prevented most of the sound problems, including the low playback levels. The director or TD should have anticipated the intercommunication problems between the director and the camera operators. Even the best intercom headsets

will not function when used close to high-volume sound sources such as the speakers of a rock band. The director could have minimized this problem by meeting with the camera operators ahead of time to discuss the principal shots for each camera.

Situation: The light levels were too uneven for good pictures.

Responsibility: The LD is responsible for the uneven light levels. Her excuse is that she lost three full hours of setup time and that she had no floor plan with which to do even the most rudimentary preproduction planning. She could have contacted the director during the preproduction stage, however, or at least two days before the production, and asked about the floor plan and the lighting requirements for the show. In addition, when time is tight it is more sensible to illuminate the set with a generous amount of overall light rather than with highly specific light beams in limited areas. This would have made the lighting more even. (See chapter 8 for lighting techniques.)

Situation: The floor manager and his crew lacked a floor plan, which resulted in needlessly moving a heavy platform.

Responsibility: A floor plan would have told the floor crew the exact location of the platform on which the musicians perform. It would also have helped the LD decide on the basic lighting setup and the director on the basic camera positions. The lack of a floor plan is a direct result of poor communication among the preproduction team and, therefore, the ultimate responsibility of the producer. The director should have consulted the art director about the set and the floor plan during preproduction and then asked the art director why the floor plan was not done according to schedule. The TD, LD, and floor manager should have asked the director for the floor plan before the actual production date.

As you can see, a production team can operate successfully only when each member knows his or her assignment and all members are in constant communication with one another during the preproduction and production phases. Just as with team sports, if a single member of the production team makes a major mistake, the show goes down despite the superior performance of everyone else. Thorough preproduction could have averted many of these problems.

> **KEY CONCEPT**
>
> Know the functions and the responsibilities of each member of the nontechnical and technical production staffs.

TAKING AND SHARING RESPONSIBILITY

Fortunately, a subsequent visit to an elaborate multicamera EFP of an MTV segment turns out to be a much more satisfying experience than our studio encounter.

When you get to the location of the MTV shoot, you find a whole section of the street already blocked off by local police, and you have to show your pass. You see action everywhere. The audio technician and his assistants are adjusting the loudspeakers, and the camera operators are checking out some shots. You are greeted by the floor manager and introduced to the producer and the director. Despite the bustling activity, the producer seems amazingly calm and takes time out to explain the concept of the MTV segment: the lead singer drives an old Cadillac convertible down the street to a stop sign, where the dancers mob his car.

Some of the dancers are already practicing their routine, while others are coming out of a large trailer that serves as the talent's makeup and dressing room. Everybody seems relaxed, and you sense purpose and competence in what each team member is doing.

The director checks the time line (the schedule for the production day), posted by the trailer, and asks the floor manager to call for a run-through. There is instant activity: the dancers take their positions, the car is moved to the starting point, the camera operators get their opening shots, and the audio people start the sound track playback. So far as you can tell, the run-through goes very smoothly; the crew and the talent also seem happy with the outcome. Nevertheless, the director calls for a brief meeting of crew and talent to discuss some production problems.

The PA reads the notes that were dictated to him by the producer and the director during the run-through:

- ◼ "Dancers in the back can't hear the music."

- ◼ "Johnny [the lead singer driving the Cadillac] can't see the mark."

- ◼ "Shadows on him are too harsh when the car stops."

- ◼ "Need a tighter shot of Johnny."

- ◼ "We should be looking up at Johnny, not down on him."

- ◼ "Johnny is sweating too much. Light reflects off his nose."

- ◼ "Lots of dirt in the dancing area."

- ◼ "We can see audio cables in the background."

- ◼ "Some dancers are blocking Johnny on a close-up."

Which people would you ask to take care of these minor production problems? Let's look at the notes again.

"Dancers in the back can't hear the music."

Correction by the audio engineer.

"Johnny can't see the mark."

This means that Johnny can't see the mark on the curb that tells him exactly where to stop the car. The mark has to be moved to the stop sign.

Correction by the floor manager.

"Shadows on him are too harsh when the car stops."

Correction by the floor crew under the direction of the LD.

"Need a tighter shot of Johnny."

Correction by the director and, ultimately, the camera operator.

"We should be looking up at Johnny, not down on him."

The producer looks at the director. She turns to the specific camera operator.

Correction by the director and, ultimately, the camera operator.

"Johnny is sweating too much. Light reflects off his nose."

The director looks at the makeup artist. This problem has nothing to do with lighting.

Correction by the makeup artist.

"Lots of dirt in the dancing area."

Correction by the floor manager and the floor crew.

"We can see audio cables in the background."

The audio engineer says that he will take care of it.

Correction by the audio assistant and the floor persons.

"Some dancers are blocking Johnny on a close-up."

Correction by the director and the choreographer.

After this brief meeting, the director calls for a 15-minute reset break during which the production crewmembers go about correcting the problems. After the reset the director checks the time line and calls for another run-through. The following three hours are taken up by more rehearsals, two more such brief production meetings (often called "notes"), and several takes. The floor manager calls for a wrap (the completion of all production activities) a half-hour ahead of schedule.

Unlike the studio show of the rock band, this MTV field production was obviously well prepared in preproduction. During production the members of the technical and nontechnical staffs knew what they had to do, how to communicate constructively, and how to share responsibilities. The notes meetings were an effective and efficient way to identify major and minor production problems and to ensure that the appropriate people took care of them. Some directors in complex productions schedule as much as one-third of the total rehearsal time for notes and resets.

■ PRODUCTION SCHEDULE AND TIME LINE

Like the script, a production schedule is essential to proper production coordination. It shows the specific dates for preproduction, production, and broadcast. Although the terms *production schedule* and *time line* are sometimes used interchangeably, they are quite different from each other and fulfill different functions. The **production schedule**, compiled by the producer, is the overall calendar for a production, which can span weeks. The **time line**, on the other hand, is usually drawn up by the director and shows the allotted time segments for a single production day.

Here is an example of a production schedule for a 15-minute studio interview with the president of City College.

INTERVIEW PRODUCTION SCHEDULE

March 1	Confirmation by college president.
March 2	First preproduction meeting. Interview format ready.
March 4	Second preproduction meeting. Script ready. Floor plan ready.
March 5	All facilities requests due, including set and prop requests.
March 9	Production. Studio 1.
March 10	Postproduction, if any.
March 14	Air date (broadcast).

Note the four-day lead-time from the due date for all facilities requests (March 5) to the actual production date (March 9). This lead-time is necessary to ensure that the studio and all facilities requested are available.

The time line for the actual production is much more detailed and breaks a single production day into blocks of time for specific activities. As you recall from the MTV field production, the director, floor manager, and PA periodically checked the time line to see whether the production was on schedule. Following is the director's time line for the interview of March 9, as indicated on the producer's production schedule.

TIME LINE: MARCH 9—INTERVIEW (STUDIO 1)

8:00 a.m.	Crew call
8:30–9:00 a.m.	Technical meeting
9:00–11:00 a.m.	Setup and lighting
11:00 a.m.–12:00 p.m.	Meal
12:00–12:15 p.m.	Notes and reset
12:15–12:30 p.m.	Briefing of guest in Green Room
12:30–12:45 p.m.	Run-through and camera rehearsal
12:45–12:55 p.m.	Notes
12:55–1:10 p.m.	Reset
1:10–1:15 p.m.	Break
1:15–1:45 p.m.	Video recording
1:45–1:55 p.m.	Spill
1:55–2:10 p.m.	Strike

Let's examine more closely each of the time line's activities.

Crew call   This is the time when all production crewmembers (floor manager and assistants, TD, LD, camera operators, audio people, and other equipment operators) are expected to show up and start working.

Technical meeting   This meeting includes the principal nontechnical and technical people: producer, director, interview host, PA, floor manager, TD, LD, and audio engineer. The director briefly explains the program objective and how she expects the show to look (simple interview set, bright lighting, fairly tight shots of the college president). This meeting is also to double-check all technical facilities and the scenery and props.

Setup and lighting   According to the floor plan, the setup is relatively easy for the floor manager and his crew. The lighting is routine and does not require any special effects. The two hours allotted should be sufficient for both activities.

Meal   It is important that everybody be back from lunch at exactly 12:00 p.m., which means that everyone has to be able to leave the studio at exactly 11:00 a.m., even if there are still minor setup and lighting details remaining. Minor adjustments can be made during the reset time.

Notes and reset   If there are no major setup and equipment problems, the period set aside for notes may be considerably shorter. The available time can then be spent on a more leisurely reset: fine-tuning the lighting, moving a plant that may interfere with the person in front of it, cleaning the coffee table, and so forth.

Briefing of guest   While the production crew is getting ready for the first run-through and camera rehearsal, the producer, the interview host, and the PA (and sometimes the director) meet with the college president in the Green Room to go over the program concept. The Green Room is a small, comfortable room specifically set up for such a briefing.

Run-through and camera rehearsal   This run-through is to familiarize the guest with the studio environment and procedures, to check on the camera shots, and to rehearse the show's opening and closing. It is intentionally brief to keep the guest as fresh as possible. Because of severe time constraints, news interviews are normally not rehearsed. The producer may brief the guest during camera setup and lighting.

Notes and reset   The run-through and camera rehearsals will inevitably reveal some minor problems with the lighting or audio. The floor manager may ask the makeup person to straighten the president's tie and put a little makeup on his forehead to hide the perspiration.

Break   Even when working on a tight schedule, it is important to give the talent and the crew a brief break just before the production. This will help everybody relax and separate the rehearsal from the actual video recording.

Video recording   The time allotted allows for a few false starts or closings. The fewer takes there are, however, the fresher the interview will be.

Spill   This is a grace period to fix things that went wrong unexpectedly. For example, the director might use this time to redo the introduction by the host because the president's name was inadvertently misspelled in the opening titles.

Strike   This activity does not refer to a protest by the crew but to the clearing of the studio of all scenery, properties, and equipment.

Such a detailed time line is especially important for an electronic field production. The EFP schedule normally includes additional items, such as loading and unloading equipment and transportation to and from the remote location.

Once you have a production schedule and a time line, you must stick to them. The best schedule is useless if you don't observe the deadlines or the blocks of time designated for a specific production activity. Experienced producers and directors move on to the next segment according to schedule, regardless of whether they have accomplished everything in the previous segment. If you ignore the time limits too often, your schedule becomes meaningless. **ZVL5** PROCESS→ Phases→ production

As you can see, knowing the functions of every member of the production team and coordinating them according to a precise schedule are essential to effective and efficient video productions.

> **KEY CONCEPT**
> Establish a realistic production schedule and time line and stick to them.

■ PRODUCTION WORKFLOW

Regardless of whether you work for a small independent video company or a television network, you cannot avoid hearing about production workflow. Like other such buzzwords, *workflow* has a variety of meanings. At the most basic level, workflow is how to move from one production activity to the next as efficiently as possible. This process may be as simple as adding transitions and effects to an edited video sequence, or as complex as receiving daily news stories from a number of sources and processing them for multiple newscasts.

An efficient workflow may also require establishing and maintaining effective communication channels. For example, the video editor in Seattle may want to show you, the producer, a specific editing sequence before continuing; the client and her sales staff in Houston would like to see some shots of the product they are advertising so that they can give you some feedback on how it should look; and the executive producer in New York may want to see the rough-cut before allocating more money for the project. Fortunately, in the age of web streaming and smartphones, you can send and receive text, video, and audio files with incredible speed from anywhere in the world. There are companies that specialize in such workflow communication, which can even automate routine channels. They can analyze your workflow needs, assist you in streamlining your workflow, and send high-quality pictures and sound files to the right people at the right time. **SEE 2.3 AND 2.4**

2.3 BASIC WORKFLOW

The basic workflow moves from the script to production and from there to postproduction; it requires reliable feedback channels.

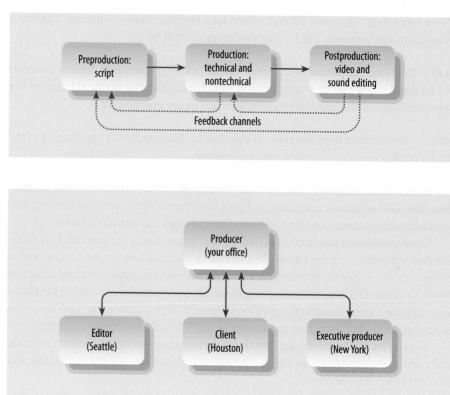

2.4 WORKFLOW COMMUNICATION

The key to a smooth workflow is a multidimensional communication system. All production personnel and other related agencies have access to optimally efficient two-way channels.

KEY CONCEPT

Efficient production depends on a reliable workflow.

The efficiency of your workflow is measured by the speed and the reliability of your communication channels and how fast you can move from one activity to the next with a minimum of errors and wasted effort.

MAIN POINTS

▶ **Team Members**

The members perform nontechnical and technical functions. Nontechnical people do not normally operate equipment; technical people do. The nontechnical people are also called above-the-line personnel; the technical people, below-the-line personnel.

▶ **Preproduction Team**

These people plan the production. This team normally includes the producer, writer, director, art director, and, occasionally, technical director (TD). Small production companies or television stations often combine preproduction functions to be carried out by a single person, such as producer-director, producer-writer, and video journalist (VJ). Larger productions employ additional preproduction personnel, such as an associate director (AD), a sound designer, and a choreographer.

▶ **Production Team**

An ENG (electronic news gathering) "team" may consist of a single VJ, who not only reports the story but also operates the camera and does the postproduction editing.

The typical EFP (electronic field production) team comprises the talent, a camcorder operator, and a utility person. Larger field and studio productions employ a much larger team. It may include the producer and various assistants, such as associate producer (AP) and production assistant (PA); the director and the associate director (AD); and the talent. The production crew usually includes the floor manager and floor persons (grips or utility persons), technical director, camera operators, lighting director (LD), video operator (VO), audio engineer, video-record operator, and CG (character generator) operator. In preproduction the producer is in charge of coordinating the various people and production details; in the production phase, the director is in charge.

▶ *Postproduction Team*

This team normally consists of the director, the editor, and, in complex productions, a sound designer who remixes the sound track. The director and occasionally the producer guide the editor in the selection and the sequencing of shots.

▶ *Production Schedule and Time Line*

A production schedule, prepared by the producer, is a calendar that shows the major preproduction, production, and postproduction activities. A time line, drawn up by the director, shows a breakdown of time blocks for a single production day.

▶ *Production Workflow*

An effective workflow helps you move from script to screen as efficiently as possible. The key factor is fast and reliable communication channels that connect all decision-making people of the production process.

Z E T T L ' S V I D E O L A B

For your reference or to track your work, the *Zettl's VideoLab* program cues in this chapter are listed here with their corresponding page numbers.

PART II

Image Creation:
Digital Video and Camera

After having learned what video production is all about and who does what in producing a program, shouldn't you be able to run out and finally create a knock-your-socks-off movie or documentary? Not quite yet. You must exercise a bit more patience and realize that mastering the art of video capture includes a healthy dose of technical know-how. Before you embark on an ambitious production, learning the technical basics of video, the workings of a video camera, and how to use the camera to capture compelling images will save you time, money, and especially nerves.

Even if a camera's automated features enable you to produce acceptable images, there are many instances in which the automatic video controls work against rather than for you. You probably notice that when you photograph your friends against a bright window, they appear as silhouettes or, at best, look woefully underexposed. As a professional, you need to know how to override the camera's automatic features when the circumstances or your artistic intentions require that you go beyond the default settings.

Part II covers the basics of how an electronic image is formed—a prerequisite to understanding how to use a camera to its fullest technical and artistic potential.

KEY TERMS

aperture Iris opening of a lens; usually measured in *f*-stops.

beam splitter Optical device within the camera that splits the white light into the three additive primary light colors: red, green, and blue.

camcorder A portable camera with the video recorder built into it.

camera chain The camera and the associated electronic equipment, consisting of the power supply, sync generator, and camera control unit.

camera control unit (CCU) Equipment, separate from the actual camera, that allows the video operator to adjust the color and brightness balance before and during the production.

CCD Stands for *charge-coupled device*. One of the popular imaging devices in a studio camera or camcorder.

chrominance channel Contains the RGB video signals or some combination thereof. Also called *color*, and *C, channel*.

CMOS Stands for *complementary metal-oxide semiconductor*. A high-quality imaging device similar to a CCD.

DSLR camera Stands for *digital single-lens reflex camera*. Basically a still-photo camera that can also produce video footage. It has an optical viewfinder that permits viewing through the lens for still pictures. In the video mode, it switches to an electronic image.

ENG/EFP camera Highly portable, high-end self-contained camera without a built-in video recorder used for electronic field production.

fast lens A lens that permits a relatively great amount of light to pass through at its largest aperture (lowest *f*-stop number). Can be used in low-light conditions.

focal length With the lens set at infinity, the distance from the iris to the plane where the picture is in focus. Normally measured in millimeters or inches.

f-stop The scale on the lens, indicating the aperture. The larger the *f*-stop number, the smaller the aperture; the smaller the *f*-stop number, the larger the aperture.

iris Adjustable lens-opening mechanism. Also called *lens diaphragm*.

luminance channel Contains the black-and-white part of a video signal. It is mainly responsible for the sharpness of the picture. Also called *luma*, or *Y, channel*.

sensor A solid-state imaging device in a video or digital cinema camera that converts the optical image into electric energy—the video signal. Also called *CCD, chip*, and *CMOS*.

slow lens A lens that permits a relatively small amount of light to pass through (relatively high *f*-stop number at its largest aperture). Requires higher light levels for optimal pictures.

viewfinder A small video screen or flat-panel display on a camera that shows the black-and-white or color picture the camera generates. The flat-panel displays are also called *monitors*.

zoom lens Variable-focal-length lens. All video cameras are equipped with a zoom lens.

zoom range How much the focal length can be changed from a wide shot to a close-up during a zoom. The zoom range is stated as a ratio, such as 20:1. Also called *zoom ratio*.

Video Camera

Your friend brags about the new digital camcorder he just purchased. It has a three-chip sensor that allows video capture in both a 4 × 3 and a 16 × 9 aspect ratio, a fast 15:1 optical zoom lens with image stabilization, a high-resolution viewfinder, and a foldout color LCD monitor. Audio is captured with a built-in stereo microphone, but he can also attach an external one. The camcorder uses large-capacity memory cards to record 720p or 1080i high-definition (HD) video, and it connects to the computer with an HDMI or USB cable. He encourages you to get the same model because it produces superior video and audio and is especially well suited for nonlinear editing. But how do you know that these features really justify the relatively high price of the camcorder?

This chapter helps you answer this question. You will also learn how a video camera works as well as the relative advantages of various camera types and systems.

▶ **BASIC CAMERA FUNCTION AND ELEMENTS**
   Function, lens, beam splitter and imaging device, video signal processing, and viewfinder and monitor

▶ **TYPES OF CAMERAS**
   Camcorders, ENG/EFP cameras, studio cameras, DSLR cameras, digital cinema cameras, and 3D camcorders

▮ BASIC CAMERA FUNCTION AND ELEMENTS

Whether digital or analog, and regardless of their size, cost, and quality, all video cameras operate on the same basic principle: they transduce (translate) the optical image that the lens sees into a corresponding video picture. More specifically, the camera converts an optical image into electrical signals that are reconverted by a television receiver into visible screen images.

Function

To fulfill this function, each video camera needs three basic elements: the lens, the imaging device, and the viewfinder. **SEE 4.1**

The lens selects a portion of the scene at which you point the camera and produces a sharp optical image of it. The camera contains a beam splitter and an imaging device that convert the optical image of the lens into weak electric currents, which are amplified and further processed by a variety of electronic components. The viewfinder and the foldout monitor reconvert these electrical signals into video pictures of the lens-generated scene. **SEE 4.2**

To explain this process, we start with how a lens operates and sees a particular portion of a scene, then we move on to how the beam splitter and the imaging device work, and finally to how the video signal is reconverted into a video picture by the television receiver. Why bother with knowing all this, especially since most

4.1 BASIC CAMERA ELEMENTS

The video camera has three main elements: the lens, the imaging device, and the viewfinder.

© Cengage Learning 2011

© Cengage Learning 2011

4.2 FUNCTIONS OF THE CAMERA

The video camera translates the optical light image as seen by the lens into a corresponding picture on the screen. The light reflected off an object is gathered and transmitted by the lens to the beam splitter, which splits the white light into red, green, and blue (RGB) light beams. These beams are then transformed by the imaging device (sensor) into electric energy, which is amplified and processed into a video signal. It is then reconverted into video pictures by the viewfinder and the monitor.

camcorders have automatic functions that can produce pretty good pictures and sound? The problem is that such automatic functions produce good pictures and sound only under ideal conditions. But what are ideal conditions? And what can you do when conditions are less than ideal? Knowing the basics of how a camera works will help you decide when and how to override the automatic functions to produce optimal video. It will also aid you in understanding how other production elements such as lighting must be manipulated to meet the requirements of the camera. Most importantly, such knowledge will help you become a video professional. **ZVL1** CAMERA→ Camera introduction

Lens

Lenses determine what cameras can see. They are classified by *focal length*, which is a technical measure of the distance from the iris inside the lens to the plane behind the lens where the projected image is in focus. This measurement assumes that the lens distance calibration is set at infinity (∞). This distance is normally given in millimeters (mm); thus a still camera can have a 24mm or a 200mm lens. Lenses can also be classified by how wide a view you get from a specific camera position. A wide-angle lens (short focal length) gives a relatively wide vista. A narrow-angle lens (long focal length) gives a relatively narrow vista with the background greatly magnified.

The optical quality of the lens determines to a great extent how good the video picture will look. Regardless of the quality of the camcorder itself, a good lens is one of the principal prerequisites for good pictures. This is why the lenses for high-end cameras can cost many times more than your entire camcorder, including its built-in lens.

Focal length The *zoom lens* on a camera can change from a short-focal-length, or wide-angle, position to a long-focal-length, or narrow-angle, position and back in one continuous move. A short-focal-length zoom position gives you a wide-angle view: you can see more than with a lens in the narrow-angle position. To bring a zoom lens into the extreme-wide-angle position, you need to zoom all the way out. You will see a relatively large portion of the scene in front of you, but the middle- and background objects look quite small and therefore far away. **SEE 4.3**

Zooming all the way in puts the zoom lens in a long-focal-length, or narrow-angle, position. The zoom lens will now give a much narrower, but enlarged, view of

4.3 WIDE-ANGLE VIEW
The wide-angle lens shows a wide vista, with the faraway objects looking quite small.

Herbert Zettl

Herbert Zettl

Herbert Zettl

4.4 NARROW-ANGLE VIEW
The narrow-angle, or telephoto, lens shows only a narrow portion of the scene, with the background objects appearing much larger relative to the foreground objects than in a wide-angle view. The tugboats now look much closer together.

4.5 NORMAL VIEW
The normal lens shows a vista and a perspective that are similar to what we actually see.

the selected scene. Because the narrow-angle lens functions similarly to binoculars, it is also called a telephoto lens. **SEE 4.4**

When you stop a zoom in the middle of the zoom range (between the extreme-wide-angle and narrow-angle positions), you are more or less in the normal lens position. The angle of view of a normal lens approximates what you would see when looking directly at the scene. **SEE 4.5**

Because the zoom lens offers a great variety of focal lengths between its extreme-wide-angle and narrow-angle positions, it is also called a variable-focal-length lens. **ZVL2** CAMERA→ Zoom lens→ focal length

Zoom range   The *zoom range*, also called zoom ratio, refers to how close a view you can achieve when zooming in from the farthest wide-angle position to the closest narrow-angle position. The higher the first number of the ratio, the closer you can get to the object from the farthest wide-angle position. A 20:1 zoom lens lets you narrow the field of view (your vista) 20 times when zooming in from the farthest wide-angle position to the closest narrow-angle position. In practical terms you can move in to a pretty good close-up from a wide-angle shot. The 20:1 zoom ratio can also be indicated as 20×. **SEE 4.6**

Small camcorder lenses rarely go above an optical zoom ratio of 20:1. Most studio lenses have a zoom ratio of between 15:1 and 30:1. A 30× zoom gets you a good close-up without moving the camera in even a large studio. Field cameras, however, need much greater zoom ranges. Covering sports or other outdoor events demands lenses with zoom ratios of 40:1 or even 60:1. With such a lens, you can zoom in from a wide shot of the entire football field to a close-up of the quarterback's face. The large zoom range is necessary because these cameras are usually relatively far from the event. Instead of moving the camera closer to the event, as is possible with a camcorder, the zoom lens must bring the event closer to the camera that might be positioned on top of the sports stadium. Unfortunately, the higher the zoom ratio, the larger the lens gets. A 60:1 field lens is quite a bit larger and certainly heavier than the camera to which it is attached.

Edward Aiona

Edward Aiona

4.6 MAXIMUM WIDE-ANGLE AND NARROW-ANGLE POSITIONS OF A 10:1 ZOOM LENS
A 10× zoom lens can narrow the angle of view by 10 times. It appears to bring a portion of the scene closer to the camera.

The focal length of a lens influences not only the field of view (how close or far away an object seems) but also how far apart objects appear to be. (You will learn more about these and other aspects of framing and perception in chapters 5 and 6.)

Digital zoom   There is a great difference between an optical zoom and a digital zoom. In an optical zoom, the elements inside the lens change its focal length. In a digital zoom, the center of the digital image is gradually magnified; we perceive this gradual magnification as the image coming closer. The problem with digital zooms is that the enlarged image becomes progressively less sharp and eventually displays oversized pixels that look like tiles of a mosaic. Inevitably, a digital zoom-in to a fairly tight shot produces a slightly fuzzy image. An optical zoom does not influence the sharpness of the picture, which is why optical zooms are preferred.

Lens speed   This term refers to how much light can pass through a lens to the imaging device. A ***fast lens*** can let a relatively great amount of light pass through; a ***slow lens*** is more limited in how much light it can transmit. In practice a fast lens allows you to produce acceptable pictures in a darker environment than does a slow lens. Fast lenses are therefore more useful than slow ones, but they are also larger and more expensive.

You can tell whether a lens is fast or slow by looking at its lowest f-stop number, such as $f/1.4$ or $f/2$ (see figure 4.7). The lower the number, the faster the lens. A lens that can open up to $f2$ is pretty fast; one that can't go below $f4.5$ is quite slow.

Lens iris and aperture   Like the pupil of your eye, all lenses have an ***iris*** that controls the amount of light transmitted. In a bright environment, your iris contracts to a smaller opening, restricting the amount of light passing through; in a dim environment, it expands to a larger opening, admitting more light.

The lens iris, or lens diaphragm, operates in the same way. Like your pupil, the center of the iris has an adjustable hole, called the ***aperture***, that can be made large or small. The size of the aperture controls how much light the lens transmits. When there is little light on a scene, you can make the aperture bigger and let more light through. This is called "opening the lens" or "opening the iris." When the scene is

4.7 IRIS CONTROL RING

The *f*-stop calibration is printed on a ring that controls the iris opening, or aperture, of the lens. The *C* on the control ring of this lens refers to *cap,* which means the iris is totally closed, letting no light pass through the lens, thus acting like a physical lens cap.

Iris control ring with *f*-stops

Edward Aiona

well illuminated, you can make the aperture smaller, or "close down" the lens, to restrict the light going through. You can thus control the exposure of the picture so that it looks neither too dark (not enough light) nor too washed out (too much light).

Now you can explain a fast or slow lens in more technical terms: a fast lens transmits more light at its maximum aperture than does a slow one. **ZVL3** CAMERA→ Exposure control→ aperture

KEY CONCEPT

The lower the *f*-stop number, the larger the aperture and the more light is transmitted. A fast lens has a low minimum *f*-stop number (such as *f*/1.4).

f-stop   We measure how much light is transmitted through the lens with the help of the **f-stop**. Normally, lenses have a ring at their base with a series of *f*-stop numbers (such as 1.4, 2.8, 4, 5.6, 8, 11, 16, and 22) printed on it that controls the iris opening. **SEE 4.7** You won't find such numbers on many studio camera lenses, however. Studio lenses are encased in a protective cover, so you couldn't see the markings even if they were on the lens. Camcorders usually display the *f*-stop numbers in the viewfinder menu.

KEY CONCEPT

The higher the *f*-stop number, the smaller the aperture and the less light is transmitted. A slow lens has a relatively high minimum *f*-stop number (such as *f*/4.5).

When you turn the ring so that *f*/1.4 lines up with the indicator, you have "opened" the lens to its maximum aperture; it now transmits as much light as it possibly can. When you turn the ring to *f*/22, the lens is "stopped down" to its minimum aperture, letting very little light pass through. Notice that the *f*-stop numbers mean just the opposite of what you would expect: The lower the *f*-stop number, the larger the aperture and the more light is transmitted. The higher the *f*-stop number, the smaller the aperture and the less light is transmitted. **SEE 4.8** **ZVL4** CAMERA→ Exposure control→ *f*-stop

Auto-iris   Most camcorders enable you to choose between the manual iris control and an automatic iris feature. The auto-iris adjusts the aperture electronically to its optimal setting. The camera reads the light level of the scene and tells the auto-iris to open up or close down until the resulting picture is neither too dark nor too light. Such an automated feature is not without drawbacks, however. The problem is that the camera does not know which part of the picture you want properly exposed. If you are video-recording a brief field interview, with the reporter and her guest standing in front of a white sunlit building, the auto-iris will adjust the aperture to bring down the glare of the white building while ignoring the two people standing in front

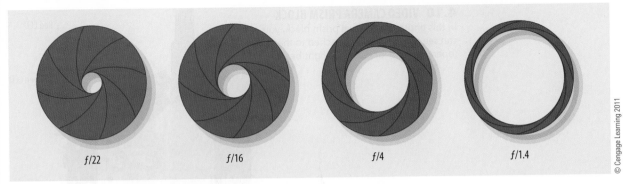

f/22   f/16   f/4   f/1.4

© Cengage Learning 2011

4.8 *f*-STOP SETTINGS
The higher the *f*-stop number, the smaller the aperture and the less light is transmitted by the lens. The lower the *f*-stop number, the larger the aperture and the more light is transmitted by the lens.

of it. The result will be a perfectly exposed background but woefully underexposed people in the foreground. A similar problem can occur in reverse when you try to frame a scene with dark tree branches in the foreground and a bright, snowcapped mountain in the far background. The automatic iris will dutifully lighten up the dark foreground objects (the tree branches), thereby overexposing the mountain in the background. You will end up with nicely detailed branches in the foreground that frame a uniformly bright background. Most likely, you will have lost the mountain.

Beam Splitter and Imaging Device

A second main system within the camera comprises the beam splitter and the imaging device, usually called the sensor, which transduces light into electric energy. **ZVL5** CAMERA→ Camera introduction

Beam splitter   The ***beam splitter*** consists of a series of prisms and filters locked into a prism block. **SEE 4.9** Its function is to separate the ordinary white light of the lens-projected image into the three primary light colors—red, green, and blue (RGB)—and

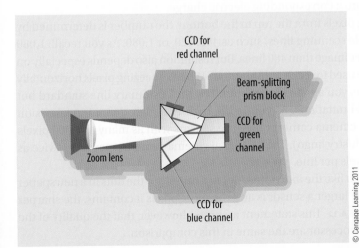

Zoom lens

CCD for red channel

Beam-splitting prism block

CCD for green channel

CCD for blue channel

© Cengage Learning 2011

4.9 BEAM-SPLITTING PRISM BLOCK
The prism block contains prisms and filters that split the incoming white light into its three basic light colors—red, green, and blue—and direct these beams to their corresponding CCDs.

4.10 VIDEO CAMERA PRISM BLOCK

In this photo of an actual prism block, you can see the three CCDs attached to the port (opening), one for each RGB light beam.

Red CCD

Green CCD

Blue CCD

Sony Electronics, Inc.

to direct these light beams at their corresponding sensors. Most larger camcorders use three sensors: one for the red beam, one for the green beam, and one for the blue beam. Each of the three sensors is solidly attached to the prism block. **SEE 4.10**

Sensor   The ***sensor,*** also called a chip, is an imaging device that transduces light into an electrical charge, which, after processing, makes up the video signal. The most common sensor in video cameras is the ***CCD*** (charge-coupled device). Higher-end cameras or camcorders use the more refined ***CMOS*** chips. You will find them exclusively in DSLR (digital single-lens reflex) cameras and digital cinema cameras. One of the great operational advantages of a CMOS sensor over a CCD is that the CMOS uses less battery power.

> **KEY CONCEPT**
>
> The CCD converts the light variations of an image into electric energy—the video signal.

Both types of sensors basically consist of a solid-state silicon chip containing thousands or even millions of light-sensing pixels that are arranged in horizontal rows (representing each scanning line) and vertical stacks (representing the number of scanning lines). This is quite an accomplishment considering that most chips in video cameras are no larger than your thumbnail. Each pixel can translate the light energy it receives into a corresponding electric charge.

When counting pixels from the top to the bottom, the number is determined by the number of visible scanning lines, such as 480, 720, or 1,080. As you recall, 1,080 lines produce a better image than 480 lines. But resolution also depends especially on how many pixels are used for each scanning line. When squeezing pixels horizontally onto a scanning line, you are no longer bound by the customary line standard but simply by technical limitations. As you recall, high-end high-definition television (HDTV) and digital cinema cameras may use sensors with as many as 4,000 pixels per line ("4K" in industry lingo). The 8K digital cinema cameras may have twice as many horizontal pixels per line. **SEE 4.11**

All pixels function like the individual tiles in a mosaic or the dots in a newspaper photo. Generally, the larger a sensor is and the more pixels it contains, the sharper the image will be. **SEE 4.12** This statement assumes, however, that the quality of the lens and the signal processor are the same in this comparison.

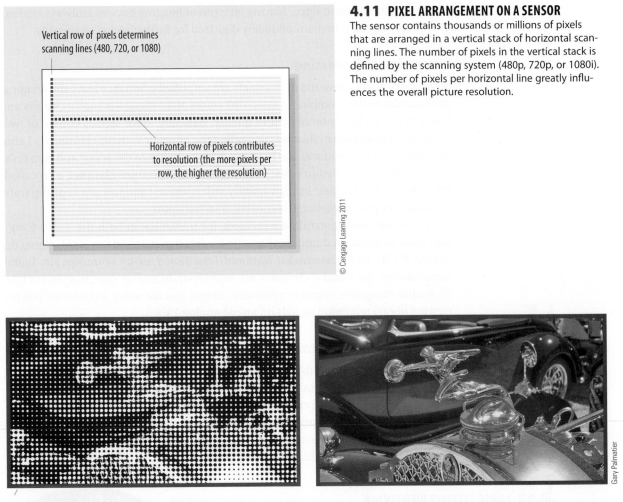

4.11 PIXEL ARRANGEMENT ON A SENSOR

The sensor contains thousands or millions of pixels that are arranged in a vertical stack of horizontal scanning lines. The number of pixels in the vertical stack is defined by the scanning system (480p, 720p, or 1080i). The number of pixels per horizontal line greatly influences the overall picture resolution.

Vertical row of pixels determines scanning lines (480, 720, or 1080)

Horizontal row of pixels contributes to resolution (the more pixels per row, the higher the resolution)

© Cengage Learning 2011

Gary Palmatier

4.12 PICTURE RESOLUTION

The picture on the right is composed of more pixels than the one on the left. It has a higher resolution and looks sharper. The more pixels a CCD contains, the higher the resolution of the video image.

High-quality cameras usually contain three CCDs—one for each of the RGB light beams as delivered by the beam splitter. Many smaller camcorders and, paradoxically, the very high-end digital cinema cameras, however, have just a single chip. In this case the incoming white light is divided by an RGB-striped filter into the three primary colors, which are then processed as individual signals by the single CCD or CMOS. Although single-chip camcorders can produce as sharp a picture as three-chip cameras, their color fidelity is generally inferior. The big advantage of a single-chip camcorder is that it is small, lightweight, and relatively inexpensive—important considerations when aiming at a large consumer or prosumer market.

The single chip in DSLR and digital cinema cameras is quite large and, as just mentioned, contains a vast number of horizontal and vertical pixels; but such sensors are neither practical nor necessary for standard camcorders, whose output will probably not be projected on giant movie screens.

Note that the video signal leaving all types of imaging devices is always analog. This analog signal is then immediately digitized for further signal processing.

Video Signal Processing

Signal processing—how the RGB signals are amplified when they leave the imaging device and how they combine to match the colors of the scene—is another significant factor in producing optimal picture quality. Basically, color signals consist of two channels: a **luminance channel**, also called the luma, or Y, channel (*lumen* is Latin for "light"), which produces the black-and-white image of the scene and is mainly responsible for the picture's sharpness; and a **chrominance channel**, also called the color, or C, channel. In high-quality video, these channels are kept separate throughout signal processing, recording, and transport.

In the old analog standard television, for transmission both the Y and C signals must be combined into a composite analog signal, called the NTSC signal or, simply, NTSC. (*NTSC* stands for *National Television System Committee.*) In digital transmission, the Y and C channels are kept separate and no such translation into an analog composite signal is necessary, unless you are using a converter box for viewing digital television signals on an old analog TV set.

Viewfinder and Monitor

The **viewfinder** is a movable tubelike device attached to the camera. It shows a black-and-white or color image of what the camera sees. The flat-panel LCD display, which is attached to the camera or can be folded out, is called the monitor. Because the small eyepiece viewfinder often produces a sharper picture than the standard foldout monitor and does not wash out in sunlight, most camcorder operators prefer the viewfinder over the foldout monitor. **SEE 4.13**

**4.13 LARGE-EYEPIECE VIEWFINDER
AND FOLDOUT LCD MONITOR**
This camera has a relatively large viewfinder and an LCD foldout monitor that give the operator great flexibility in camera handling. Such flat-panel displays can wash out in bright surroundings.

Viewfinder

High-definition flat-panel color monitor

Panasonic Broadcast

VariZoom

4.14 LCD MONITOR ATTACHED TO CAMCORDER
To optimize the handling of a large camcorder, you can attach a flat-panel monitor to the camcorder handle. This way you can frame a shot while carrying the camera close to the ground.

Some large camcorders have high-resolution color viewfinders but no foldout flat-panel monitor. If used in electronic field production, many camera operators opt to connect the camera's video output to a larger, independent, high-resolution monitor panel. **SEE 4.14** This detachable flat-panel display is mounted on a flexible arm, or "hot shoe," which lets you see the camera output even while taking the camcorder off your shoulder for certain shots. Note that all flat-panel monitors tend to drain the camera battery significantly faster than the built-in viewfinder, and they are worthless if the sun shines on them.

■ TYPES OF CAMERAS

Although their functions often overlap, we can distinguish among six types of video cameras: shoulder-mounted (large) and handheld (small) camcorders, ENG/EFP (electronic news gathering/electronic field production) cameras, studio cameras, DSLR cameras, digital cinema cameras, and 3D camcorders.

Camcorders

As pointed out before, a ***camcorder*** (for *cam*era and re*corder*) is a portable video camera with its recording device attached to it or built-in. The large ones are usually called shoulder-mounted camcorders, and the small ones are called handheld camcorders. Of course this classification should not prevent you from carrying your large camcorder in your hand or carrying one of your larger handheld ones on your shoulder. The very small point-and-shoot camcorders, which fit into a shirt pocket, can under good conditions produce excellent video and audio. **SEE 4.15–4.17**

KEY CONCEPT
A camcorder has its video recorder built-in.

Canon

Panasonic

4.15 HIGH-END HANDHELD CAMCORDER

This small high-end HDTV camcorder has three CMOS sensors, an 18× optical zoom lens, and two professional (XLR) microphone inputs. It records in all HDTV standards, with a variable frame rate on CF (compact flash) memory cards.

4.16 SHOULDER-MOUNTED CAMCORDER

This large camcorder has three high-density MOS (metal-oxide semi-conductor) sensors (an improved CMOS-type sensor), a 17× zoom lens, and four separate audio channels. It can hold two P2 memory cards for continuous variable-frame-rate HDTV recording.

The recording device in a camcorder is either some kind of tapeless device, such as a memory card, a hard drive, or an optical disc, or, in older models, a videotape recorder (VTR). The tapeless recording devices are described in more detail in chapter 11.

Except for the pocket-sized models, all other camcorders—shoulder-mounted and handheld—have at least two audio inputs: one is normally used for the camera mic, and the other is for an additional, external microphone. In small camcorders the camera mic is built-in. Larger models have two jacks (inputs) that let you plug in specific mics (see chapter 7). Many high-end camcorders have provisions for plugging in a wireless microphone receiver, which makes the use of an external receiver expandable when wireless mics are used.

Most camcorders also have a camera light for illuminating small areas during ENG or to provide additional illumination. Note that if you run the camera light off the camcorder's battery, the battery will run down considerably faster; it's best to use a separate battery pack for the light.

Some high-end camcorder models have provisions to send their video and audio signals to a satellite.

Quality difference When you compare the pictures your friend took with his digital camcorder to a similar scene shot with an expensive and much larger and heavier camcorder, you will probably not see much difference in how the pictures

4.17 POINT-AND-SHOOT CAMCORDER

This pocket camcorder can record 720p or 1080p HD video and superior stereo audio, all on an SD (Secure Digital format) memory card. It displays audio-recording levels on the monitor and has additional input and output jacks for a variety of external devices.

Samson Technologies Corp.

look. Why, then, do you still see professional ENG shooters lugging around heavy camcorders on their shoulders? One of the main reasons is that television stations are reluctant to dump a perfectly fine camera that they purchased for a hefty price not too long ago. But there are also some technical advantages to using the larger camcorder for critical shoots.

The single-most important difference between large and standard small camcorders is that the small cameras have a built-in zoom lens that cannot be exchanged. When using a large camcorder or a DSLR camera, however, you can choose the lens that best suits your purpose. For example, you can use a very-wide-angle lens when shooting in confined quarters, such as the inside of an automobile, or a lens that lets you get a close-up view from far away. Additionally, the lens of a large ENG/EFP camcorder has better optics (high-quality lens elements) and a smoother zoom mechanism. Large camcorders also have more manual video and audio controls for overriding the automatic ones, robust recording devices, and usually a better processing system with better color sampling that ensures faithful colors even when shooting in low-light conditions.

But don't worry: even if you don't have a shoulder-mounted ENG/EFP camcorder, you can still produce professional-looking video footage. You will find that shooting good video depends more on what shots you select and how you frame them than on the technical specifications of the camcorder. (The discussion in chapter 6 about looking through the viewfinder will help you achieve maximally effective shots.)

ENG/EFP Cameras

The basic difference between an ENG/EFP camera and a camcorder is that the ENG/EFP camera does not have a built-in video recorder (VR) but must feed its output via cable to a stand-alone VR. Like a camcorder, the ***ENG/EFP camera*** is self-contained, but it can be, and often is, connected with a camera cable to a remote control unit (RCU) and an external recording device. Why use an RCU when the camera is basically self-contained and has automatic controls?

4.18 ENG/EFP CAMERA CONNECTED TO RCU AND EXTERNAL VIDEO RECORDER
This high-end ENG/EFP camera has no built-in video recorder but is connected to a remote control unit and from there to a high-capacity hard drive or studio VTR for high-quality recording.

First, although an ENG/EFP camera is capable of running on batteries, it is often better to power it with an external source. External power frees you from worrying about battery life during a long shoot or a live pickup. Second, in situations where optimal pictures are critical, the RCU allows the video operator (VO) to override the camera's automatic circuits and tweak the settings for optimal performance under a variety of shooting conditions. This way the camera operator can pay full attention to composing effective shots. **SEE 4.18** Third, because the director can see on a monitor what the camera operators see in their viewfinders, he or she can give them the necessary instructions over the intercom headsets while the multicamera event is in progress. All of these production advantages considerably outweigh the slight disadvantage of having the cameras tethered to a remote truck or a temporary video control. The ENG/EFP camera is now operating much like a highly portable studio camera.

Studio conversion of ENG/EFP camera   Because ENG/EFP cameras are considerably cheaper and easier to handle, they are often used in place of studio cameras, even if they can't quite match the quality. To adapt an ENG/EFP camera to studio conditions, you replace the small viewfinder with a larger one, attach a faster lens (lower maximum f-stop number) that has a zoom range more appropriate for studio dimensions (15× or 20×), affix cables for focus and zoom controls, and install a frame and mounting devices for a tripod or studio pedestal. Unless the PL (private line or phone line) is wireless, an intercom connection box must be attached to the mounting frame. **SEE 4.19**

Studio Cameras

The large HDTV cameras you normally find in television studios are, appropriately enough, called studio cameras. They are built to produce exceptionally good pictures under a variety of conditions. They usually contain a high-quality (fast) zoom lens, three high-density CCDs or CMOS chips as sensors, extensive signal-processing equipment, and a large, high-definition viewfinder.

Studio cameras are usually bulky and too heavy to be maneuvered without the aid of a pedestal or some other kind of camera mount. What makes the equipment

High-quality
ENG/EFP camera

Ikegami

4.19 STUDIO CONVERSION OF ENG/EFP CAMERA
Converting a high-quality ENG/EFP camera for studio use usually requires adding a large viewfinder, a faster lens with a zoom range appropriate for the studio size, cables that allow zooming and focusing from the operator's position, and a frame and mounting devices for a tripod or studio pedestal.

so heavy is not necessarily the camera itself but the large zoom lens and, typically, the teleprompter attached to it. **SEE 4.20** Studio cameras are used for such programs as news, interviews, game shows, music and dance spectaculars, and of course soap operas. These cameras are also taken on big remotes, such as football games and parades. For this function they are equipped with higher-ratio zoom lenses (40× or even 60×) and mounted on field dollies or heavy-duty tripods (see chapter 5).

Wherever studio cameras may be located, they are always connected by cable to their CCUs (camera control units) and to other essential equipment, such as the sync generator and the power supply. These three elements constitute what is called the camera chain.

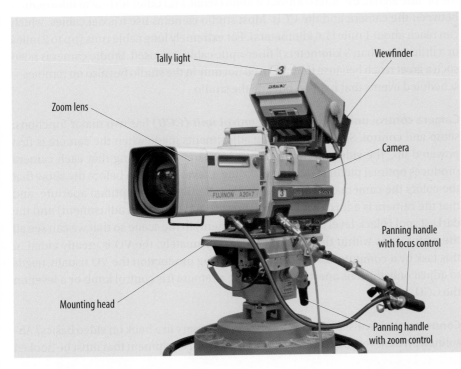

Tally light

Zoom lens

Viewfinder

Camera

Mounting head

Panning handle with focus control

Panning handle with zoom control

FUJINON A20×7

Edward Aiona

4.20 STUDIO CAMERA
Studio cameras normally use three high-density CCDs or CMOS chips and a variety of picture-enhancing electronic circuits. This studio camera uses a high-quality 25× zoom lens and a large 9-inch high-definition viewfinder. Most studio cameras also have a teleprompter attached, which makes the whole camera head considerably heavier than an ENG/EFP camera or camcorder.

4.21 STANDARD CAMERA CHAIN

The standard camera chain consists of the camera head (the actual camera), the power supply, the sync generator, and the CCU.

Camera chain The standard ***camera chain*** consists of four parts: the camera itself, the power supply, the sync generator, and the camera control unit. SEE 4.21

As the front part of the camera chain, the camera itself is called the camera head. It cannot function by itself without the other parts of the chain. The power supply feeds the electricity to the camera head through the camera cable. Unlike ENG/EFP cameras or camcorders, studio cameras cannot be powered by batteries.

The sync generator produces the uniform electrical pulse that is necessary to synchronize the scanning of the video pictures in all cameras used in a multicamera telecast. This pulse also keeps in step the scanning of a variety of other equipment, such as viewfinders, video monitors, and video recorders.

Camera cable The camera cable carries the power to the camera and transports the picture signal, the intercommunication signal, and other technical information between the camera and the CCU. Most studio cameras use triaxial cables, which can reach about 1 mile (1.6 kilometers). For extremely long cable runs (up to 2 miles or a little more than 3 kilometers), fiber-optic cables are used. Studio cameras need such a great reach because they are used not only in the studio but also on remotes—scheduled events that happen outside the studio.

Camera control unit The ***camera control unit (CCU)*** has two major functions: setup and control. Setup refers to the adjustments made when the camera is first powered up. The video operator, who is in charge of ensuring that each camera produces optimal pictures during recording, makes sure even before the show that the colors the camera delivers are true, that the iris is at its optimal aperture, and that the camera is adjusted for the brightest spot (white-level adjustment) and the darkest spot (black-level or pedestal adjustment) in the scene so that we can see all the major steps within this contrast range. Fortunately, the VO is greatly aided in this task by a computerized setup panel. During production the VO usually needs to adjust only the lens aperture, by moving a remote iris control knob or a lever on the CCU. SEE 4.22

Connectors Is a discussion of connectors necessary in a book on video basics? Absolutely. Whenever you work with several pieces of equipment that must be hooked

Waveform monitors (for brightness adjustment) and vector scope (for color adjustment)

Monitors showing preview or line video

Operation of video controls:

Iris control adjusts exposure (reduces glare or lightens shadows)

Adjusts all luminance (grayscale) steps together

Video controls for 10 cameras

Herbert Zettl

4.22 CAMERA CONTROL UNIT

The CCU has a variety of controls with which the video operator can continuously monitor and adjust picture quality. The remote version of a CCU is called an RCU.

BNC   S-video   RCA phono   HDMI   FireWire   USB

Edward Aiona

4.23 STANDARD VIDEO CONNECTORS

The standard video connectors are the BNC, S-video, RCA phono (also used for audio), HDMI, FireWire, and USB 2.0 or 3.0 connectors. Adapters enable you to interconnect all of them in various configurations.

together to form a video or audio system, you need the appropriate cables and especially the right connectors; and despite careful preproduction, many productions have been delayed or even canceled because the connectors for camera or audio cables did not fit. Though you may hear production people call all connectors "plugs," regardless of whether they represent the male or female part of the connector, it is more precise to call the male part of the connector a plug and the female part a jack.

The most widely used video connectors are the BNC, S-video, RCA phono, HDMI, and FireWire (IEEE 1394). Some systems allow you to use a USB 2.0 or USB 3.0 cable to transfer video. **SEE 4.23** (The standard audio connectors are shown in figure 7.26.) A variety of adapters let you change from one plug to another, such as from a BNC to an RCA phono, but don't rely on them. An adapter is strictly a makeshift solution and always presents a potential trouble spot.

Canon

4.24 DSLR CAMERA

This still-photography digital single-lens reflex camera can be used for video recording when switched to the movie mode. Because of the superior sensor and exchangeable lenses, DSLR cameras are also adopted for digital cinema production.

DSLR Cameras

The digital single-lens reflex cameras used for video capture are still-photo cameras that have the capability to record motion sequences, much like a regular camcorder. Basically, a DSLR camera lets you capture motion at the traditional 24 frames per second (fps) or at 30 fps. The advantages of DSLR cameras for video capture are their very large CMOS sensor, which delivers superior HD footage, great color, and surprisingly brilliant pictures in low-light conditions. Best of all, you can use all of the lenses available for still photography.

The disadvantage is that DSLR cameras are basically designed for normal photographic work of still shots. Unless you use an external monitor, you need to have the camera right in front of you so that you can see its video display on the back. Because when shooting in the video mode you see an electronic image rather than an optical one, bright sunshine will render the DSLR monitor pretty much useless. The duration of a shot is also quite limited, as is the total recording time. One of the most serious disadvantages is in audio. Most models accept only a mini plug for an external microphone instead of the professional XLR plug (see chapter 7), and you cannot monitor audio with headphones.

To make a DSLR camera functional as a camcorder, you need all sorts of attachments, such as camera supports, an external video recorder, and an external mixer and recorder for high-quality sound. By the time you add all of these extras, you could get an excellent camcorder for the same price. **SEE 4.24**

Digital Cinema Cameras

Digital cinema cameras are highly specialized super-HDTV video cameras or camcorders that contain ultra-high-quality imaging devices (either high-density CCDs or CMOS chips or a single custom-made CMOS-like sensor with 2,000 ["2K"] or more pixels per horizontal scanning line), viewfinders and flat-screen monitors with high-resolution images, and various attachments that are adapted from standard film cameras. One of the most useful electronic features for filmmaking with the digital cinema camera is its variable frame rate, which permits a change from 24 fps scanning (modeled after the standard film frame rate) to a slower rate for fast-motion effects, called undercranking, or a higher rate for slow-motion effects, called overcranking. Though it seems paradoxical, you need fewer frames per second than the normal speed to accelerate the screen action and more frames to slow it down.[1] **SEE 4.25**

Although far from being ideal for motion picture production, the small DSLR cameras have caught the fancy of some filmmakers. One reason is because these

---

1. See Herbert Zettl, *Sight Sound Motion: Applied Media Aesthetics,* 6th ed. (Boston: Wadsworth, 2011, pp. 265–68.

cameras produce dazzling images. The more expensive ones have a large CMOS sensor and let you mount any type of high-quality lens.

The small size of a DSLR camera should be a great advantage because you can point the camera in any direction. This is true so long as you don't have to see the viewfinder in the back. In most cases, however, you must always hold the camera in front of your nose, usually with partially outstretched arms. This is as awkward as is it tiring, especially for longer takes. The various camera mounting devices will not make it easier to get unusual angles unless you twist and bend your body to keep the viewfinder in sight. The small size is also a problem when trying to use the camera for long, smooth dolly and tracking shots. Other problems lie in the audio area. The built-in mics and the jacks for external mics are simply not sufficient for high-quality audio recording. Nevertheless, when used for standard photographic work, these cameras can deliver stunning still images and bursts of several still images, which cannot be matched by even a good-quality camcorder.

Fortunately, you don't need such cameras to produce your documentary or short movie. Many documentaries and even feature films have been shot with so-called consumer camcorders and successfully shown in motion picture theaters. It is, after all, your creativity and aesthetic judgment that make for a good film rather than high-end equipment. Yes, you knew that all along, but it is worth repeating from time to time, especially if you feel that you would rather upgrade your equipment than rewrite your script.

The Arri Group

4.25 DIGITAL CINEMA CAMERA
This super-high-definition electronic cinema camera contains a large 2K+ sensor and records video and audio on high-capacity memory cards. It offers a 4 × 3 or 16 × 9 aspect ratio and a variety of frame rates, including the digital movie favorite of 24 fps.

3D Camcorders

Pushed by equipment manufacturers and 3D movies, three-dimensional video is trying to find its way into independent video productions. The current problem is that the equipment has clearly outrun its proper use. The basic principle of 3D image projection is based on the fact that our two eyes see a scene from slightly different angles. When superimposed by our brain, the two offset images result in a stereo image that reinforces all the other 3D cues we get even when looking at it with only one eye. Wouldn't we then need two cameras as substitutes for our two eyes for 3D vision? Yes, indeed.

To capture 3D video, you can use two small identical camcorders mounted next to each other on a 3D rig, or a single camcorder housing with a twin lens. Each lens sends its image to its own camera recording device, such as a high-capacity SD (Secure Digital format) card. **SEE 4.26** Just like the stereo audio left and right channels, which are mixed by our brain into a single, multidimensional sound image, the 3D video camera records simultaneously a left-eye channel and a right-eye channel.

4.26 3D CAMCORDER

This small 3D camcorder has two cameras with a CMOS sensor for each. Both cameras and twin lenses are built into a single housing. Both the left-eye camera and the right-eye camera record HDTV signals (1080 and 720) on their own large-capacity internal memory device or on twin SD cards. You can view the 3D images on the foldout monitor without glasses.

The two video channels are then mixed by our brain into a single 3D stereoscopic visual image.

In some camera setups, both lenses are pointed straight ahead so that what they see will always be slightly offset. Other types of 3D camera rigs allow the lenses of the two cameras to be toed-in to a certain degree, which means that they can be panned slightly toward each other so that their divergent views will at one point converge and perfectly overlap. All 3D camera setups have provisions to change the distance between their lenses. We discuss the perception of 3D images further in chapter 6.

MAIN POINTS

▶ **Basic Camera Elements**

These are the lens, the beam splitter and imaging device, and the viewfinder and monitor.

▶ **Lenses**

Lenses are classified by the focal length (short and long), angle of view (wide and narrow), and speed (largest aperture expressed in the lowest f–stop). The zoom lens has a variable focal length. The zoom range is stated as a ratio, such as 20:1 or 20×. A 20:1 lens can show the angle of view 20 times narrower than the extreme-wide-angle position with the background magnified.

▶ **Lens Iris and Aperture**

One quality factor of the lens is determined by its speed, that is, the maximum aperture, or iris opening. A fast lens lets a relatively large amount of light pass through; a slow lens, relatively little. A fast lens is better than a slow one. The specific aperture is indicated in f-stops. The lower the f-stop number, the larger the aperture and the more light is transmitted. A fast lens has a low minimum f-stop number (such as $f/1.4$). The higher the f-stop number, the smaller the aperture and the less light is transmitted. A slow lens has a relatively high minimum f-stop number (such as $f/4.5$).

▶ **Beam Splitter and Imaging Device**

These devices change the light of the optical image as produced by the lens into electric charges of various strengths. The beam splitter divides the light that comes through the lens into red, green, and blue (RGB) light beams. The imaging device, usually called a sensor, is attached to the beam splitter and transduces the colored light beams into electric charges, which are then further processed into the video signal.

▶ *Types of Cameras*

Camera types include small handheld and large shoulder-mounted camcorders—portable cameras with the recording device attached or built-in; ENG/EFP cameras, which are high-end, shoulder-mounted field cameras; high-definition television (HDTV) studio cameras, which with a different lens are also used in the field; DSLR (digital single-lens reflex) cameras; super high-definition digital cinema cameras, and 3D camcorders.

▶ *Camera Chain*

The studio camera chain consists of the camera head (the actual camera), the power supply, the sync generator, and the camera control unit (CCU). A camcorder contains the entire camera chain plus the recording device.

▶ *Connectors*

The most widely used video connectors are the BNC, S-video, RCA phono, HDMI, FireWire (IEEE 1394), and USB 2.0 and 3.0.

▶ *DSLR and Digital Cinema Cameras*

DSLR cameras are designed for still photography. Because of their large HD sensors, which produce superior images, DSLR cameras are occasionally used for filmmaking. Digital cinema cameras are highly specialized super-HDTV cameras or camcorders that produce extremely high-resolution pictures. All have large sensors and are also equipped with high-resolution viewfinders and other attachments carried over from film.

▶ *3D Camcorders*

To produce three-dimensional footage, you need to capture the event with either two identical camcorders mounted side-by-side, or a camera with twin lenses, which records what one lens sees on a left-eye channel and what the other lens sees on a right-eye channel.

Z E T T L ' S   V I D E O L A B

For your reference or to track your work, the *Zettl's VideoLab* program cues in this chapter are listed here with their corresponding page numbers.

KEY TERMS

arc To move the camera in a slightly curved dolly or truck.

calibrate the zoom lens To preset a zoom lens to stay in focus throughout the zoom.

cant To tilt the camera sideways.

crane To move the boom of the camera crane up or down. Also called *boom*.

dolly To move the camera toward (dolly in) or away from (dolly out) the object.

jib arm A small camera crane that can be operated by the cameraperson.

mounting head A device that connects the camera to its support. Also called *pan-and-tilt head*.

pan To turn the camera horizontally.

pedestal To move the camera up or down using a studio pedestal.

shutter speed A camera control that reduces the blurring of bright, fast-moving objects. The higher the shutter speed, the less blurring occurs but the more light is needed.

studio pedestal A heavy camera dolly that permits raising and lowering the camera while on the air.

tilt To point the camera up or down.

tongue To move the boom with the camera from left to right or from right to left.

tripod A three-legged camera mount. Also called *sticks*.

truck To move the camera laterally by means of a mobile camera mount. Also called *track*.

white-balance To adjust the color circuits in the camera to produce white color in lighting of various color temperatures (relative reddishness or bluishness of white light).

zoom To change the focal length of the lens through the use of a zoom control while the camera remains stationary.

Operating the Camera

et's watch a tourist who is itching for something interesting to shoot with his brand-new camcorder. He quickly takes aim at one of the towers of the Golden Gate Bridge, tilts his camera up to the top, zooms in, zooms out again, tilts down to the bay just as a freighter passes below, zooms in on the containers, zooms out again, tilts up to the rail where some seagulls have perched, zooms in on one of the more aggressive birds that refuses to stay in the frame, and finally zooms out to catch a passing jogger, who waves at him.

Although such camera handling may be good exercise for the arm and the zoom mechanism, it rarely results in satisfactory footage. Such unmotivated camera motion produces images that seem restless and unsettling for anyone except, perhaps, the person who shot them. The tourist would have done much better had his camera been mounted on a tripod.

When operating a handheld camcorder, you are virtually unrestrained in moving the camera. But when the camera is mounted on a tripod, its movements become much more restricted. Initially, you will probably feel that a tripod constrains your artistry and that it is much better to handhold the camera so long as it is not too heavy. After some experience with camera operation, however, you will discover that it is actually easier to operate the camera and control picture composition when the camera is mounted on some kind of support. In fact, the art of operating a camera is not as dependent on its electronic design or basic operational controls as it is on its size and especially on how it is mounted.

This chapter explores basic camera movements and operation and how they can be accomplished.

▶ **BASIC CAMERA MOVEMENTS**
   Pan, tilt, cant, pedestal, dolly, truck, arc, crane, tongue, and zoom

▶ **CAMERA MOUNTS AND HOW TO USE THEM**
   Handheld and shoulder-mounted cameras, tripods, special camera mounts, and the studio pedestal

▶ **OPERATIONAL FEATURES**
   Focusing, adjusting shutter speed, zooming, and white-balancing

▶ **GENERAL GUIDELINES**
   Checklists for camcorders, ENG/EFP cameras, and studio cameras

◼ BASIC CAMERA MOVEMENTS

The various camera mounts are designed to steady the camera and help you move it as smoothly and easily as possible. To understand the features and the functions of camera mounting equipment, you should first learn about the major camera movements. The terms are the same regardless of whether the camera is carried on your shoulder or mounted on a tripod, a studio pedestal, or some other camera support.

There are nine basic camera movements: pan, tilt, cant, pedestal, dolly, truck, arc, crane, and tongue. Sometimes zoom is included in the major camera movements, although the camera itself does not normally move during a zoom. **SEE 5.1**

Pan   To *pan* is to turn the camera horizontally, from left to right or from right to left. To pan right means to swivel or move the camera clockwise so that the lens points more to the right; to pan left means to swivel or move the camera counterclockwise so that the lens points more to the left.

Tilt   To *tilt* is to make the camera point up or down. A tilt up means to point the camera gradually up. A tilt down means to point the camera gradually down.

Cant   To *cant* is to tilt the camera sideways. You can cant the camera either left or right. When you cant right, the horizon line will be slanted uphill; its low point will be screen-left, its high point screen-right. Canting left will produce the opposite effect. Canting is easy with the handheld or shoulder-mounted camera, but you cannot cant a camera supported by a standard camera mount.

Pedestal   To *pedestal* is to elevate or lower the camera on the center column of a tripod or studio pedestal. To pedestal up you crank or pull up the center column, thereby raising the camera. To pedestal down you crank or pull down the center column, lowering the camera. This motion puts the camera into different vertical positions, which means that the camera sees the scene as though you were looking at it from the top of a ladder or while kneeling on the floor. You can "pedestal" a handheld camera by simply raising it slowly above your head or lowering it to the ground.

Dolly   To *dolly* is to move the camera toward or away from an object in more or less a straight line by means of a mobile camera mount. When you dolly in, you move the camera closer to the object; when you dolly out or dolly back, you move the camera farther away. With the handheld or shoulder-mounted camera, you simply walk the camera toward or away from the scene. Some directors call this "dollying" in or out, even though the camera is not mounted on a dolly; others simply ask you to get closer or back up.

Edward Aiona

Truck To *truck,* or *track,* is to move the camera laterally by means of a mobile camera mount. When you truck right or truck left, you move the camera mount to the right or left with the camera lens pointing at a right angle to the direction of travel. If you want to follow somebody walking on a sidewalk, you would truck with the camera alongside on the street, with the lens pointing at the person. Tracking often means the same as trucking. Sometimes tracking refers simply to a moving camera's keeping up with a moving object. With a handheld or shoulder-mounted camera, you walk parallel to the moving object while keeping the camera pointed at it.

Arc To *arc* is to move the camera in a slightly curved dolly or truck movement. To arc left means that you dolly in or out in a camera-left curve, or you truck left in a curve around the object. To arc right means that you dolly in or out in a camera-right curve, or you truck right in a curve around the object. With the handheld or

5.2 CAMERA-FAR PERSON PARTIALLY BLOCKED
In this over-the-shoulder shot, the camera-near person partially blocks the camera-far person.

5.3 ARC CORRECTS BLOCKED SHOT
By arcing left you can properly frame the camera-far person.

shoulder-mounted camera, you simply walk in a slight arc while pointing the lens at the scene. Arcing is often required to reveal more of the camera-far person in an over-the-shoulder shot when the camera-near person is blocking or nearly blocking our view of the camera-far person. **SEE 5.2 AND 5.3**

Crane   To *crane*, or *boom*, is to move the camera up or down on a camera crane or jib arm. A crane is a large and bulky device that can lift the camera and its operator, and sometimes a second person (usually the director), up to 30 feet aboveground in one impressive sweep. The crane itself is moved by a driver and an assistant. A jib arm is a simpler crane that can be handled by a single camera operator (as shown in figure 5.21). To crane up or boom up means to raise the boom with the attached camera; to crane down or boom down means to lower the boom and the attached camera. Simply holding a small camcorder or DSLR camera high above your head and then swooping it down close to floor level will not duplicate the feeling of a crane motion; unless you are 10 feet tall, there is simply not enough height difference between the extreme high and low camera positions to simulate a crane motion.

Tongue   To *tongue* is to move the whole camera from left to right or from right to left with the boom of a camera crane or jib arm. When you tongue left or right, the camera usually points in the same general direction, with only the boom swinging left or right. Tonguing creates an effect similar to a truck except that the horizontal arc of the boom with the camera is usually much wider and can be much faster. Tonguing is often combined with a boom-up or boom-down movement.

The crane and tongue movements are somewhat of a special effect. Even if you have access to a crane, use such extreme camera movements sparingly and only if they contribute to the shot's intensity.

Zoom   To *zoom* is to change the focal length of a lens through the use of a zoom control while the camera remains stationary. To zoom in means to change the lens gradually to a narrow-angle position, thereby making the scene appear to move closer to the viewer; to zoom out means to change the lens gradually to a wide-angle position, thereby making the scene appear to move farther away from the viewer.

Although the effect of a zoom is the object's moving toward or away from the screen rather than the camera's moving into or out of the scene, the zoom is usually classified as one of the camera "movements." **ZVL1** CAMERA→ Camera moves→ dolly | zoom | truck | pan | tilt | pedestal | try it

■ CAMERA MOUNTS AND HOW TO USE THEM

You can support a camera in four ways: by carrying it with your hands or on your shoulder, with a tripod, with special camera mounting devices, and with a studio pedestal. They all influence greatly, if not dictate, how you operate the camera.

Handheld and Shoulder-Mounted Camera

We have already mentioned that the small, handheld camcorder invites excessive camera motion. You can point it easily in any direction and move it effortlessly, especially if it has a foldout monitor. Although such high mobility can be an asset, it is also a liability. Too much camera movement draws attention to itself and away from the scene you want to show. Unless the camera has a built-in image stabilizer to absorb minor camera wiggles, you will find it difficult to avoid some wobbling during a long uninterrupted shot. When zoomed in all the way (with the lens in the narrow-angle, or telephoto, position), it is almost impossible to avoid some shaking and unsteadiness in the handheld shot.

To keep the handheld camera as steady as possible, support the camera in the palm of one hand and use the other hand to support the camera arm or the camera itself. **SEE 5.4**

With a foldout monitor, press your elbows against your body and use your arms as shock absorbers. Avoid operating the camera with your arms outstretched, which invites annoyingly quick pans and tilts. Inhale and hold your breath during the shot. The lack of oxygen will obviously limit the length of the shot, and that is probably a good thing. Shorter shots that show a variety of viewpoints are much more interesting than a long one with constant panning and zooming. Handheld camera mounts can reduce the wobbles of small camcorders (see figure 5.18). When using your arms as a camera mount, bend your knees slightly when shooting or, better, lean against a sturdy support, such as a building, wall, parked car, or lamppost, to increase the camera's stability. **SEE 5.5**

If you or the event moves, keep the lens in the wide-angle position (zoomed out) to minimize camera wiggles. When using a DSLR camera with a wide-angle lens, watch that your fingers are not in front of the lens, blocking part of the shot. If you need to get closer to the scene, stop the video recording, walk closer to get the tighter shot, and start to record again. If you need to zoom, work the zoom controls gently during the shot. For a relatively long take without a tripod, try to find something stable on which to place the camera, such as a table, park bench, or the roof or hood of a car.

Edward Aiona

5.4 HOLDING THE SMALL CAMCORDER
Hold the camcorder with both hands, with the elbows pressed against the body.

5.5 STEADYING THE CAMERA OPERATOR
Leaning against a support will steady both camera operator and camera.

5.6 PANNING THE CAMCORDER
Before panning, point your knees toward the end of the pan, then uncoil your upper body during the pan.

When moving the camera, do it smoothly. To pan the camera, move it with your whole body rather than just your arms. Point your knees as much as possible to where you want to end the pan, while keeping your shoulders in the starting position. During the pan your upper body will uncoil naturally in the direction of your knees and will carry the camera smoothly with it. **SEE 5.6** If you do not preset your knees, you will have to coil your body rather than uncoil it when panning, which is much harder to do and usually results in jerky camera motion.

When tilting the camera (pointing it up or down), try to bend forward or backward at the waist as much as possible while keeping your elbows against your body. As with a pan, your body motion makes the tilt look smoother than if you simply moved your wrists to point the camera up or down.

When walking with the camera, walk backward rather than forward whenever possible. **SEE 5.7** While walking backward you will lift your heels and walk on the balls of your feet. Your feet rather than your legs will act as shock absorbers. Your body, and with it the camera, will tend to glide along rather than bounce up and down.

For unconventional shots you can tilt the camera sideways, raise it above your head, and shoot over the people or other obstacles in front of you, or you can lower it close to the ground to get some low-angle views. Most regular viewfinders can be adjusted (at least tilted up and down) so that you can see what you are shooting

5.7 WALKING BACKWARD

Walking backward rather than forward makes it easier to keep the camera steady.

5.8 SHOULDER-MOUNTED CAMCORDER

When carrying the camcorder on the shoulder, one hand slips through a strap attached to the lens, leaving the fingers free to operate the zoom control. The other hand steadies the camera and operates the focus ring.

during such maneuvers. The foldout monitor offers a great advantage in such situations, especially if you find that the only way to get a good shot is to hold the camera high above your head and aim the lens more or less in the direction of the event. The foldout monitor still enables you to see the shot the camera is getting.

One of the problems when using a DSLR camera is that you need to keep it in front of your eyes to see what you are shooting. You can keep track of your shot only if you connect the camera to an external monitor. In normal lighting conditions, the foldout monitor of a small camcorder displays crisp color images; in bright light, however, you can see nothing or, at best, only a very dim image. In such situations, you may find that you might get usable shots by simply pointing the camera in the general direction of the event without ever looking at the monitor.

Larger camcorders that are too heavy to be handheld for long are best supported by the shoulder. Although the shoulder-mounted camera is slightly more restrictive than the handheld camcorder, the basic moves are much the same. **SEE 5.8** When carrying the camcorder on your shoulder, you need to adjust the viewfinder to fit your prominent (usually right) eye. Some camera operators keep the left eye open to see where they are going; others prefer to close it and concentrate on the viewfinder image. Most viewfinders of large camcorders can be flipped over for the left eye, and there are lenses with straps and zoom operating controls for the left hand.

Tripod-Supported Camera

Unless you are running after a breaking news story, the best way to keep the camcorder or ENG/EFP camera steady and the movements as smooth as possible is to support it on a ***tripod***, called "sticks" in production lingo. A good tripod, or some other similar mount, should be lightweight but sturdy enough to support the camera during pans and tilts. Its collapsible legs must lock securely in place at any extension

5.9 TRIPOD WITH SPREADER
The tripod has three adjustable legs that are sometimes secured by a spreader.

Spreader

Vinten

point and should have rubber cups and spikes at the tips. The rubber cups prevent the tripod from slipping on smooth surfaces, as do the spikes on rough surfaces.

Most professional tripods come with a spreader, a triangular base mount that locks the tips in place and prevents the legs from spreading no matter how much weight is put on them. Some spreaders come as part of the tripod. **SEE 5.9**

Some tripods have a center column that enables you to elevate and lower a small camcorder without having to adjust the tripod legs. Unless the camcorder is very small, such columns may not be sturdy enough for smooth shots, especially when the column is fully extended. All good tripods have a leveling bubble at or near the top ring so that you can ensure that the tripod is level.

Camera mounting head   One of the most important parts of a tripod is its camera *mounting head*. This device, also called the pan-and-tilt head, permits smooth pans and tilts. It also lets you attach the camera and remove it from the tripod quickly. Many mounting heads have an additional leveling bubble so that you can easily adjust the head even if the tripod is on uneven ground.

Most big tripod mounting heads have a load limit of 30 to 45 pounds—ample to hold even a large camcorder and a teleprompter. These days the problem is not whether the mounting head can support a heavy camera but whether it can function smoothly with a small, lightweight camcorder. Even with a midsized camcorder, use a mounting head with a rating of 10 pounds or below. If the weight rating of the

Quick-release plate

Panning handle

Tilt lock

Bogen Imaging, Inc.

5.10 MOUNTING HEAD WITH PANNING HANDLE
The mounting head permits smooth pans and tilts for a small camcorder. Its pan-and-tilt mechanism can be adjusted to various degrees of drag and can be locked.

mounting head is much higher than the actual weight of the camera, even the lowest drag position will be too tight for smooth pans and tilts.

All mounting heads have similar basic controls. You move the mounting head (and with it the camera) with the attached panning handle. **SEE 5.10** Lifting the handle makes the camera tilt down; pushing it down makes the camera tilt up. Moving the panning handle to the left pans the camera to the right; moving the handle to the right pans the camera to the left. *Right* and *left* always refer to where the camera lens is supposed to point, not to movement of the panning handle.

To prevent jerky, uneven movements, a mounting head must provide a certain degree of drag, or resistance, to panning and tilting. The pan and tilt drags can be adjusted to fit the weight of the camera and your personal preference. A small camcorder needs a lighter drag adjustment than does a large camcorder. Now you know why the weight rating for cameras is important: the heads for large camcorders have a much higher minimum drag than is necessary or even desirable for small camcorders.

The mounting head also has pan and tilt lock mechanisms that prevent the camera from moving horizontally or flopping forward or backward when unattended. Lock the mounting head every time you leave the camera unattended, no matter how briefly. Never use the drag mechanism to lock the camera.

> **KEY CONCEPT**
>
> Lock the mounting head every time you leave the camera unattended. Don't use the drag mechanism to lock the camera.

Quick-release plate   This mechanism consists of a small rectangular plate that attaches to the bottom of the camera. The quick-release plate makes it easy to attach a camcorder in a balanced position. This feature is especially useful when you want to take the camera off the tripod to run after a new shot and then reattach it quickly when returning to the tripod position. You simply slide the camcorder into the plate receptacle on the mounting head, and it is locked in place and ready to go without your having to rebalance its weight (see figure 5.10).

When switching from a handheld to a tripod-supported camera, you will initially find that the tripod severely restricts your use of the camera. You can no longer run with the camera, lift it above your head, shoot from close to ground level, cant it, or swing it through the air. You are limited to panning and tilting and, if there is a center column, a rather modest camera elevation. So why use a tripod?

- The tripod steadies the camera, whether you are zoomed in or out.

- Pans and tilts are much smoother than with a handheld camera.

- The tripod prevents you from moving the camera excessively—a positive rather than a negative factor in good camera work.

- Mounting the camera on a tripod is less tiring than carrying it on your shoulder or in your hand.

Tripod dolly   To dolly or truck with a tripod-mounted camera, you must put the tripod on a three-caster dolly, which is simply a spreader with wheels. **SEE 5.11** With the casters in a freewheeling position, you can dolly, truck, and arc. Most professional dollies let you lock the casters in position for straight-line dollying. Be sure to check that the floor is smooth enough for an "on-air" move while the camera is "hot," or operating. When moving the tripod dolly, you usually push, pull, and steer with your left hand while guiding the panning handle and the camera with your right hand.

When a camera or camcorder is connected to a camera cable, you must adjust the cable guards so that the cable does not get wedged under the dolly casters. It is also a good idea to tie the cable to one of the tripod legs so that it is not pulled by its connector. **SEE 5.12**

Field dolly   When dollying on a rough surface, such as gravel or grass, you need to mount the tripod on a field dolly—a platform supported by four wheels with pneumatic tires. The steering mechanism works like the one you may remember

5.11 TRIPOD DOLLY
The tripod can be mounted on a three-wheel dolly, which permits quick repositioning of the camera.

Cable guards

5.12 CABLE GUARDS
Cable guards prevent the dolly wheels from running over the camera cable. They must be close enough to the studio floor to push the cable aside.

Vinten, Inc.

Bogen Imaging, Inc.

from your red Radio Flyer wagon: a large handle turns the front wheels in the desired direction and lets you pull or push the entire platform. **SEE 5.13**

To operate the camera, you can stand on the dolly or walk alongside while the dolly operator pushes or pulls it along the dolly path. When the surface is especially rough, you can underinflate the tires to make the trip smoother. Many dollies are homemade and constructed from parts readily available in hardware stores.

Special Camera Mounts

Special camera mounts range from beanbags, skateboards, and wheelchairs to heavy Steadicam mounts. This is an area in which you can put your imagination and creativity to work.

Homemade devices   A simple beanbag, made from a pillowcase filled with foam packing peanuts, can serve as a reasonably good device for mounting a camcorder on the hood of a car or on bicycle handlebars. Professional "beanbags" are filled with a very flexible synthetic material that adjusts to the shape of the camera yet remains highly shock absorbent. **SEE 5.14**

Mounting a small camcorder on a skateboard and pulling it along a smooth surface can give you an interesting low-angle dolly shot. And a wheelchair or shopping cart is a cheap but effective device for transporting camera operator and camcorder for a long tracking shot. If the floor is smooth, such tracking shots can rival the ones done with a much more expensive studio pedestal.

5.13 FIELD DOLLY
The field dolly has a platform with four pneumatic tires that supports the tripod-mounted camera and the camera operator.

5.14 BEANBAG AS CAMERA MOUNT
A pillowcase filled with foam packing peanuts cradles the camera and prevents minor wiggles. Professional beanbags are filled with a flexible synthetic material.

5.15 STUNT BAR

This extendable bar lets you lower the camcorder close to the ground for low-angle shots or raise it above your head for high-angle shots. Note that it does not absorb camera wobbles.

Handheld camera mounts   A variety of handheld stabilizers allow you to carry a small camcorder with one or both hands and keep the shot relatively steady so long as you don't jump up or down.

A simple yet highly effective handheld camera mount consists of an extendable bar to which you can attach the camera. This bar allows you to lower the camera close to the ground for from-below-eye-level shots or to raise it above your head while walking, running, or sitting in a shopping cart for low-angle tracking shots. You keep track of what the camera sees by looking at the foldout monitor. Note, however, that such a device will not absorb any camera wobbles. **SEE 5.15**

When using a DSLR camera for still shots, you can easily support it in the palm of one hand while adjusting focus and activating the shutter release with the other. When recording video, however, you need some kind of support to keep the camera steady during the shot. One useful device is the monopod, which is simply an extendable pole onto which the camera is mounted. Other useful supports for a small camera are the single- or double-handled plate and the lightweight brace that rests on your shoulder. **SEE 5.16** For a pocket camcorder, you can use a miniature tripod with flexible legs, or you can mount it on a flexible arm that can be attached with a suction cup to smooth surfaces. **SEE 5.17**

If you want the shots to appear wobble-free while you are running with the camera, you need a stabilizer. Once you have used one a few times and practiced operating the camera while walking or running, you will be surprised by how smooth your shots look. But don't be tempted to tell your whole story while running with the camcorder! **SEE 5.18**

5.16 DSLR SUPPORTS

A The single handgrip facilitates the movement and the operation of a DSLR camera.

B The dual handlebar facilitates moving the camera during a shot.

C Shoulder camera mounts are especially designed to keep the DSLR camera steady during longer takes.

5.17 POCKET CAMCORDER SUPPORTS

A This tiny tripod has flexible legs to support a pocket camcorder on various surfaces.

B The suction cup on this flexible cable can be attached to any smooth surface to support a pocket camcorder.

5.18 HANDHELD STABILIZER

This handheld stabilizer is built for small camcorders. If you're strong enough, you can carry it with one hand. The foldout monitor helps you get the right shots.

Body-mounted stabilizers A more elaborate but more comfortable way to operate a camera relatively wobble-free is by wearing a stabilizer harness. **SEE 5.19** For large camcorders, the operator wears a harness that is similar to the one for small camcorders except that the stabilizing system of gimbals and springs is built for the heavier camera. Despite the relative comfort of the vest, you will find that wearing such a device and operating the camcorder for even a relatively short period of time can be, at least initially, a challenge for even a strong person. **SEE 5.20**

5.19 BODY-MOUNTED STABILIZER FOR SMALL CAMCORDERS

Wearing a camera support vest facilitates camera operation and is certainly less tiring than using a handheld stabilizer. The harness has a spring-loaded mechanism that lets you walk and even run with the camera, using the foldout monitor as your primary viewfinder.

5.20 BODY-MOUNTED STABILIZER FOR LARGE CAMCORDERS

This sturdy harness is designed to support a large camcorder or an ENG/EFP camera. The mechanism of gimbals and springs allows you to walk, run, and jump, with the camera remaining steady. Part of the counterweight is a large monitor.

5.21 JIB ARM
This camera support operates like a big camera crane except that one person can operate both the jib and the camera. You can use it in the studio or in the field, and you can disassemble it for easy transport in a van to a remote location.

Jib arm   The *jib arm* operates just like a crane except that it is lighter, easier to operate, and less expensive. Jib arms are designed for shooting on-location and in studios. You can operate the jib arm and the attached camera or camcorder all by yourself. With the remote controls on the jib arm handles, you can lower the camera close to the ground or studio floor, elevate it to at least 10 feet, and pan, tilt, zoom, and focus the camera at the same time. Some long jib arms have an 18-foot reach but can be easily dismantled and transported in a small van. **SEE 5.21**

Studio Pedestal

Studio cameras, or ENG/EFP cameras converted for studio use, are usually mounted on studio pedestals. A *studio pedestal* is a relatively expensive camera mount that supports even the heaviest camera and additional equipment, such as a big zoom lens and a teleprompter. The studio pedestal lets you pan, tilt, truck, arc, and pedestal while the camera is on the air. By turning the steering ring, you can move the camera in any direction; by pulling it up or pushing it down, you can change the camera height. The telescoping center column is pneumatically counterbalanced so that the camera stays put at any height, even if you let go of the steering ring. If the camera begins to creep up or down by itself, the center column must be rebalanced. Instead of the three cable guards of the tripod dolly, the studio pedestal has a skirt, or housing, on the pedestal base to prevent the cable from getting caught in the casters. **SEE 5.22**

Parallel and tricycle steering   The studio pedestal has two different steering positions. In the parallel, or crab, position, the steering ring points all the casters in the same direction. **SEE 5.23A** Parallel steering is used for all normal camera moves. In the tricycle position, only one wheel is steerable. **SEE 5.23B** You use this steering position if you need to rotate the pedestal itself to move it closer to a piece of scenery or the studio wall.

Mounting head   Like the tripod, the center column of the studio pedestal has a camera mounting head attached to it. To accommodate the combined weight of the studio camera, its heavy lens, and the teleprompter, the customary tripod head has been replaced by a sturdier and more elaborate camera mount. Its operational controls are similar to those of the mounting heads for lightweight cameras: pan and tilt drags, locking devices, and panning handles. Some studio cameras have a wedge mount attached to the underside, which fits a receptacle on the top of the mounting

5.22 STUDIO PEDESTAL

The studio pedestal permits you to pan, tilt, truck, arc, and pedestal while the camera is on the air. If the pedestal is equipped with a telescoping column, you can move the camera from about 2 feet to about 5 feet above the studio floor.

5.23 PARALLEL AND TRICYCLE STEERING

A In the parallel steering position, the three casters point in the same direction.

B In the tricycle steering position, only one wheel is steerable.

5.24 STUDIO CAMERA MOUNTING HEAD

This mounting head is designed especially for heavy studio cameras. The counterbalance and tilt-and-drag systems allow extremely smooth tilts and pans. The wedge mount ensures proper camera balance each time the camera is put back on the pedestal.

head. Once the camera is balanced, the wedge mount ensures proper balance every time the camera is put back on the pedestal. **SEE 5.24**

The mounting head has two panning handles that allow you to pan and tilt smoothly while simultaneously operating the attached zoom and focus controls. Before operating the studio camera, always unlock the mounting head and adjust the pan and tilt drags. When leaving the camera unattended, even for a short time, you should lock the mounting head—but never use the drag controls to do it. You should also cap the lens by putting the metal or plastic cap over the front of it or, when operating a studio camera, by asking the video operator to close the iris electronically so that no light will go through the lens.

Vinten Radamec

5.25 ROBOTIC PEDESTAL

The robotic pedestal can pan, tilt, pedestal, dolly, truck, and zoom according to computer instructions instead of those of a camera operator. It is used mainly for news presentations.

Robotic pedestal   You have probably seen small robotic camera mounts for little cameras in lecture halls. They are usually mounted on the wall and aimed at the lectern. Similar robotic mounting heads can also be attached to simple tripods or pedestals for small camcorders. Robotic studio pedestals, however, are much larger because they must support heavy studio cameras. You can see them in news studios, where a single robotic-pedestal technician/camera operator/director runs two or three large studio cameras from the control room. In fact, if you are the floor manager in such a studio, watch out that you don't get run over by such a moving robot. Robotic pedestals can be preprogrammed to pan, tilt, dolly, truck, and zoom for specific camera shots, such as a two-shot of the anchors or a medium shot of the weather set. Much like in a sci-fi movie, they move silently from place to place. **SEE 5.25**

◼ OPERATIONAL FEATURES

Now that you know how to carry or move the camera, you need to learn about focusing, adjusting shutter speed, zooming, and white-balancing before composing your unforgettable shots with a camcorder or studio camera.

Focusing

Normally, we want all pictures on-screen to appear in focus (sharp and clear). You can achieve focus by manual or automatic controls.

Manual focus   To ensure sharp, clear pictures, you should focus manually rather than rely on the automatic focus. The manual focus control of all non-studio lenses is on a ring at the front of the lens that you can turn clockwise or counterclockwise. **SEE 5.26** **ZVL2** CAMERA→ Focusing→ focus ring | try it

When operating a studio camera, you stay in focus by turning a twist grip mounted on the left panning handle and connected to the zoom lens by a cable. **SEE 5.27**

Calibration, or presetting the zoom lens   Assume that you are to video-record a local high-school fund-raising event. The principal is auctioning off works of pottery made by students in the ceramic shop. She stands about 10 feet in front of the display tables along the back wall of the gym. During the video recording, you are asked to zoom from a medium shot of the principal to a fairly tight close-up of a ceramic pot, but during the zoom the shot gets progressively out of focus. When you reach the desired close-up, you can hardly make out the shape of the pot. What happened? You neglected to calibrate, or preset, the lens before zooming in for the close-up.

To *calibrate the zoom lens* means to adjust it so that it will maintain focus during the entire zoom. You must first zoom in to the desired close-up of the farthest target object—the pot—and bring it into focus by turning the focus ring at the front of the lens (or the twist grip on the studio panning handle). When you then zoom back to the medium shot of the principal, she will be in focus (although you may have to adjust the focus a little). When you zoom in again to another piece of pottery next to the previous pot, you will stay in

Focus ring   Zoom lever

Fujinon, Inc., Broadcast and Communications Products Division

5.26 MANUAL FOCUS ON CAMCORDERS AND ENG/EFP CAMERAS

The manual focus control on camcorders and ENG/EFP cameras is a ring at the front of the lens that can be turned by hand.

Focus control

Edward Aiona

5.27 MANUAL FOCUS CONTROL ON STUDIO CAMERAS

The focus control on a studio camera is a twist grip attached to the left panning handle. To focus you turn it either clockwise or counterclockwise.

focus and the close-up of the new pot will be sharp and clear. As soon as you reposition the camera, however, or if the principal moves toward or away from the display tables, you will need to recalibrate the lens. This means zooming in on the farthest pot again, focusing, zooming back to include the principal, and seeing whether you have to tweak the focus a little to keep her sharp and clear in subsequent zooms.

Now let's move into the studio, where your camera is assigned to cover a famous jazz pianist from the side so that you can zoom in from a medium shot to a tight close-up of the keyboard and the pianist's hands. How do you preset the zoom lens for this? You zoom in for a tight close-up of the keyboard and bring the lens into focus by turning the twist grip on the left panning handle. But exactly where on the keyboard should you focus? Probably the far end because you can then zoom in and out and stay in reasonably sharp focus regardless of whether the pianist displays his virtuosity at the near or far end of the keyboard.

Auto-focus   Most handheld camcorders and some large cameras are equipped with an automatic focusing system, called the auto-focus. Through some electronic wizardry (reading the angle of a little radar beam or measuring the contrast), the camera focuses on a scene all by itself. Most of the time, these systems work well, but there are times when the camera cannot accommodate very bright or low-contrast scenes, leaving you with a blurred image. Or it may not detect exactly which object in the picture to bring into focus. You may not want to focus on the obvious foreground object but instead on the middleground. Unable to infer your artistic intent, the auto-focus will focus on the most prominent object closest to the camera. To achieve such a selective focus (see Lenses and Depth of Field in chapter 6), you need to switch from auto-focus to manual. The auto-focus can also have trouble keeping up with fast zooms. **ZVL3** CAMERA→ Focusing→ auto-focus

When working with a high-definition video camera, you may have trouble focusing. Because everything looks so much sharper than with standard television, you may not see in the relatively small viewfinder when your shots are slightly out

> **KEY CONCEPT**
>
> To calibrate a zoom lens, zoom in as close as possible on the farthest target object and bring it into focus. All subsequent zooms will be in focus so long as the camera-to-subject distance remains the same.

Gary Palmatier

5.28 FOCUS-ASSIST
The focus-assist feature enlarges the center of the image. Once you bring this section into focus, the whole image will be in focus.

of focus. The increased sharpness of the high-definition image also lures you into perceiving a much greater depth of field than you actually have—foreground and background seem to be in focus. When watching your shots on a high-quality monitor or a flat-panel display, however, you may discover that not only is the background out of focus but the foreground is as well. Switching to manual focus and racking in and out of focus will help you determine where the optimal focus lies. If you have a choice, always focus by looking at the black-and-white viewfinder and not the foldout color monitor; usually, the black-and-white image has a higher resolution.

Focus-assist   The difficulty of focusing high-definition pictures, especially on a color viewfinder, led to the development of a focus-assist feature. In most applications the center of the viewfinder shows an enlarged section of the image that lets you readily see whether it is in focus. If this center section is in focus, the whole image is in focus. **SEE 5.28**

Adjusting Shutter Speed

Like on a still camera, the camcorder has a variable **shutter speed** control to avoid image blur when shooting a fast-moving object. Although the way the shutter speed is controlled in both types of cameras is quite different, the effect is the same. If, for example, a cyclist with a bright yellow jersey is racing from one side of the screen to the other, you need to set a higher shutter speed than if the cyclist were pedaling along casually. When setting a fairly high electronic shutter speed (such as $\frac{1}{2,000}$ second), you will notice that the yellow jersey looks considerably darker than with lower shutter speeds. All of this translates into a simple formula, which is similar to still photography: the higher the shutter speed, the more light you need.

> **KEY CONCEPT**
>
> The higher the shutter speed, the less blurring occurs but the more light you need.

Zooming

All camcorders have a rocker switch on the lens that activates the zoom mechanism. By pressing the front of the switch, usually labeled *T* for *telephoto* or *tight,* you trigger a motor that rearranges elements in the zoom lens for the zoom-in effect.

Zoom-out (W = *wide*)   Zoom-in (T = *telephoto* or *tight*)

Nikon, Inc.

Thumb zoom control

Camera panning handle

Edward Aiona

5.29 CAMCORDER ZOOM CONTROL
Camcorders have a rocker switch near the lens that controls the zoom-in and zoom-out motion.

5.30 STUDIO ZOOM CONTROL
The zoom control of the studio camera is a rocker switch on the right panning handle that is activated by the thumb of your right hand.

By pressing the back of the switch, labeled *W* for *wide,* you zoom out. This motorized servo-zoom mechanism, which is activated by the rocker switch, keeps the zooming smooth and steady. **SEE 5.29**

Some cameras offer a choice between a slow and a fast zoom speed. You may also find on some shoulder-mounted-camcorder lenses an additional manual zoom control that allows you to override the motorized mechanism by turning the zoom lever on the lens barrel for extremely fast zooms (see figure 5.26).

Studio cameras have a rocker switch mounted on the right panning handle. This thumb-operated switch is connected by cable to the servo-zoom mechanism of the studio lens. By pressing the *T* side of the switch, you zoom in; by pressing the *W* side, you zoom out. **SEE 5.30**

Because the servo-zoom mechanism makes zooming relatively easy, you may be tempted to zoom in and out unnecessarily. Keep zooming to a minimum; frequent and unmotivated zooming reveals the inexperience of the camera operator as readily as excessive camera movement. **ZVL4** CAMERA→ Zoom lens→ focal length | zoom control

> **KEY CONCEPT**
> Keep zooming to a minimum.

White-Balancing

To **white-balance** means to adjust the camera so that a sheet of white paper looks white on the television screen regardless of whether the light that illuminates the page is reddish, such as candlelight, or bluish, such as outdoor daylight. Most handheld camcorders do this automatically, although some have you set the white-balance switch to the proper setting, such as outdoors or indoors.

High-end handheld and shoulder-mounted camcorders, as well as all ENG/EFP cameras, have a semiautomatic white balance, which means that you have to activate a white-balance switch. (See chapter 8 for a more detailed explanation of white-balancing.) **ZVL5** LIGHTS→ Color temperature→ white balance

> **KEY CONCEPT**
> Unless the camera has a fully automatic white-balance system, you need to white-balance every time you enter a new lighting environment.

■ GENERAL GUIDELINES

Whether you are operating a small camcorder or a large studio camera, treat it with extreme care as with all electronic equipment. Always be mindful of safety—yours and others'. Do not risk your neck and the equipment to get an especially spectacular shot that merely embellishes, rather than tells, the story. Do not abandon standard operational procedures for the sake of expediency. Whatever you do, use common sense. Like bicycling, you learn to operate a camera only by doing it. The following guidelines can make learning easier and also serve as useful checklists.

CHECKLIST: CAMCORDERS AND ENG/EFP CAMERAS

☑ **Don't expose the camera to the elements** Never leave the camera unprotected in the sun or in a hot car. Also watch that the viewfinder is not pointed into the sun; the magnifying glass in the viewfinder can collect the sun's rays and melt the viewfinder housing and electronics. Use plastic camera covers, called "raincoats," or a large umbrella when shooting in the rain or extreme cold. In case of emergency, a plastic grocery bag will do.

☑ **Leave the camera with care** Lock the mounting head on the tripod whenever you leave the camera unattended. When putting the camera down, place it upright. Laying it on its side may damage the viewfinder or attached microphone.

☑ **Use the lens cap** Even if a camera can be "capped" internally to prevent light from reaching the imaging device, always put the plastic or metal cap over the front of the zoom lens. This lens cap protects the delicate surface of the expensive lens.

☑ **Use fully charged batteries** Always see to it that the battery is fully charged. Normally, batteries must first be "trained" to avoid memory. When first using a new battery, run it until it is totally discharged, then charge it again. From now on it should fully charge regardless of how much charge was left before the charging. Do not drop batteries or expose them to extreme heat.

☑ **Verify the recording media** Make sure that the recording media fits the camera model. Even though different makes of cassettes, memory cards, and optical discs look similar to the eye, they may not fit a particular camera.

☑ **Examine all connections** Check all connectors, regardless of what they connect, to see whether they fit their designated jacks (see figure 4.23). Use adapters only in an emergency; an adapter is by design a stopgap and, as such, a potential trouble spot. Small camcorders normally use RCA phono connectors; larger camcorders have three-pin (XLR) audio connectors. (See chapter 7 for further information about audio connectors.)

☑ **Test the camera** Even when in a hurry, always do a brief test recording to verify that the camcorder records video as well as audio. Bring headphones along to check the audio. Use the same power supply and connectors that you intend to use during the actual video recording. Check the full range of the zoom lens and the focus. In extremely cold or damp conditions, zoom lenses sometimes stick or give up altogether.

☑ **Set the switches** Have all the switches—such as auto-focus or manual focus, auto-iris, zoom speed, and shutter speed—in the desired positions. The faster the action in front of the camera, the higher the shutter speed must be to prevent the moving object from blurring. Remember that higher shutter speeds require higher light levels. This presetting of major functions is especially important when working in the field, where the sun can render the camcorder monitor useless.

☑ **Perform a white balance** White-balance the camera before beginning the video recording, unless the system is fully automatic. White-balance under the light that actually illuminates the event.

☑ **Always capture audio** Make it a habit to turn on the camera microphone and record ambient sound with the pictures. This sound will help you identify the event location and will aid shot continuity during postproduction editing.

☑ **Heed the warning signs** Take note of caution signals in the viewfinder display and try to address the problem immediately. You may be able to dismiss the "low light level" warning on the camera if you are not concerned with picture quality, but you cannot ignore a "low battery" warning.

CHECKLIST: STUDIO CAMERAS

☑ **Get in touch and in control** Put on your headset to establish contact with the control room and the video operator. Unlock the mounting head and adjust the pan and tilt drags. Pedestal up and down to get a feel for the pedestal range and motion. A properly balanced pedestal should prevent the camera from creeping up or down when left in a vertical position.

☑ **Tame the cables** Position the cable guards close enough to the floor to prevent the pedestal from rolling over the camera cable. Uncoil the cable and check its reach. To avoid the inevitable tug of the cable during a dolly, tie it to the pedestal but leave enough slack so that you can freely pan, tilt, and pedestal.

☑ **Test-zoom and focus** Ask the video operator to uncap the camera so that you can rack through the zoom and focus ranges and, if necessary, adjust the viewfinder. Practice calibrating the zoom lens so that the scene remains in focus during subsequent zooms.

☑ **Practice your moves** Use masking tape on the studio floor to mark the critical camera positions. Write down all on-air camera moves so that you can set the zoom lens in the wide-angle position before the required move.

☑ **Move carefully** Ask a floor person to help you steer the camera during an especially tricky move. If the cable gets tangled up during a dolly, don't drag the whole mess along. Signal the floor person to untangle it for you. When dollying or trucking, start slowly to overcome the inertia of the heavy pedestal and slow down just before the end of the dolly. When raising or lowering the camera, brake the pedestal column before it reaches its maximum or minimum height; otherwise the camera and the picture might receive a hefty jolt.

☑ **Don't jump the red light** Wait for the tally light (the red light inside the viewfinder and on top of the camera) to go out before moving the camera into a new position or presetting the zoom lens. The tally light tells the camera operator, talent, and studio production crew which camera is hot. During special effects the tally light may remain on even if you think your shot is finished. Normally, the ENG/EFP camera or camcorder has only a viewfinder tally light, which tells only the camera operator when the camera is operating.

☑ **Avoid nervous camera movements** Keep your eyes on the viewfinder and correct slowly for minor compositional defects. If a subject bounces back and forth on a close-up, don't try to keep it in the frame at all costs. It is better to let it move out of the frame from time to time than to play catch-up by rapid panning.

☑ **Let the director direct** Always follow the director's instructions even if you think he or she is wrong. Do not try to outdirect the director from your position— but do alert the director if you are asked to do such impossible things as dollying or trucking on the air with your lens in the narrow-angle (zoomed-in) position.

☑ **Be observant and attentive** Be aware of the activity around you. Pay particular attention to where the other cameras are and where they are asked to move. By listening to the director's instructions, you will be able to stay out of the way of the other cameras. When moving a camera, especially backward, watch for obstacles that may be in your path. Ask a floor person to guide you. Avoid unnecessary chatter on the intercom.

☑ **Anticipate your next shot** Try to line up the next shot before the director calls for it, even if you work without a shot sheet that lists the nature and the sequence of your shots. For example, if you hear on the intercom that the other camera is on the air with a close-up, pull out to a medium shot or get a different angle to provide the director with another field of view. Do not duplicate the shot of another camera.

☑ **Put all tools away properly** At the end of the show, wait for the "all clear" signal before preparing your camera for shutdown. Ask the video operator to cap the camera. As soon as the viewfinder goes dark, release the pan and tilt drags, lock the mounting head, and cap the lens. Park the camera in its usual place and coil the cable in the customary figure-eight loops. If your dolly has a parking brake, activate it.

M A I N   P O I N T S

▶ **Camera Movements**

The movements include pan, tilt, cant, pedestal, dolly, truck or track, arc, crane or boom, and tongue. The zoom is also included, although the camera does not move.

▶ **Camera Mounts**

There is a wide variety of basic tripods and mounts for handheld camcorders, DSLR cameras, and pocket camcorders. Larger field productions require special mounts such as the jib arm and the Steadicam. Studio productions require studio pedestals. Whenever possible, put the camcorder or ENG/EFP camera on a tripod. Keep the handheld or shoulder-mounted camera as steady as possible and zoomed out when moving.

▶ **Camera Mounting Head**

This mechanism connects the camera to the tripod or the studio pedestal. It facilitates pans and tilts. Always lock the mounting head when leaving the camera unattended.

▶ **Focus and Shutter Speed**

Normally, we want all pictures on-screen sharp and clear. You can achieve focus by manual or automatic controls. A high shutter speed reduces the blurring of bright, fast-moving objects. The higher the shutter speed, the less blurring occurs but the more light is needed.

▶ **Calibrating the Zoom Lens**

To preset a zoom, the lens must be zoomed in on the farthest target object and brought into focus. All subsequent wide-angle zoom positions will be in focus so long as the camera-to-subject distance remains the same.

▶ **White-Balancing**

This procedure ensures that white and all other colors look the same under different lights. It needs to be done every time the camera operates under new lighting conditions, unless the camera has a fully automatic white-balance mechanism.

Z E T T L ' S   V I D E O L A B

For your reference or to track your work, the *Zettl's VideoLab* program cues in this chapter are listed here with their corresponding page numbers.

KEY TERMS

aspect ratio The ratio of the width of the television screen to its height. In STV (standard television), it is 4 × 3 (4 units wide by 3 units high); for HDTV (high-definition television), it is 16 × 9 (16 units wide by 9 units high). Mobile media devices have various aspect ratios, including vertical ones.

close-up (CU) Object or any part of it seen at close range and framed tightly. The close-up can be extreme (extreme or big close-up) or rather loose (medium close-up).

cross-shot (X/S) Similar to the over-the-shoulder shot except that the camera-near person is completely out of the shot.

depth of field The area in which all objects, located at different distances from the camera, appear in focus. Depends primarily on the focal length of the lens, its *f*-stop, and the distance from the camera to the object.

field of view The portion of a scene visible through a particular lens; its vista. Expressed in symbols, such as CU for close-up.

headroom The space between the top of the head and the upper screen edge.

leadroom The space in front of a laterally moving object or person.

long shot (LS) Object seen from far away or framed very loosely. The extreme long shot shows the object from a great distance. Also called *establishing shot*.

medium shot (MS) Object seen from a medium distance. Covers any framing between a long shot and a close-up.

noseroom The space in front of a person looking or pointing toward the edge of the screen.

over-the-shoulder shot (O/S) Camera looks over the camera-near person's shoulder (shoulder and back of head included in shot) at the other person.

point of convergence (POC) The point where z-axis vectors of the right and left 3D lenses meet, resulting in a perfect overlap of the right-eye and left-eye images.

psychological closure Mentally filling in missing visual information that will lead to a complete and stable configuration. Also called *closure*.

vector A directional screen force. There are graphic, index, and motion vectors.

z-axis Indicates screen depth. In standard two-dimensional video space, it extends from the screen (camera lens) to the background (horizon). In three-dimensional video space, it also extends from the screen to the viewer.

Looking through the Viewfinder

Effective camera operation depends not only on how to use certain buttons and levers but especially on how to frame impressive shots. In fact, good camera operation requires first and foremost a keen and sensitive eye and a basic knowledge of picture *aesthetics*—what makes one shot composition superior to another. Despite all the automated features, the camera cannot make aesthetic decisions for you. You must therefore also learn the basic compositional principles so that you can produce pictures that have impact and convey meaning.

Framing a good shot has lately become more difficult because you must account for different aspect ratios (shapes of a frame), various screens sizes, and 3D (three-dimensional) video. For example, the large home theater–type display and digital movie screens can show small details quite well even without close-ups. For the tiny cell-phone display, however, close-ups are essential; the relatively small screen and the limited presentation time make it impractical to introduce a scene by moving from an overall view to a close-up. Rather, you need to select only the most significant event details and show them as a series of close points of view. In this way you not only reveal the features necessary to tell the story but also establish the energy of an event that might otherwise get lost on the small screen.

Because video viewing is done mostly at home, however, such a close-up technique is also effective when composing shots for the large high-definition television (HDTV) screen. Even motion pictures intended for theater viewing have finally learned from television the high-energy impact of telling a story primarily in a series of close-ups. When dealing with 3D, however, the close-up is generally considered a problem. Having the nose stick out of the frame, with the ears relegated to the background does not make for a pleasing portrait.

This chapter takes a closer look at the aesthetics of picture composition. Note that in video you are working mostly with moving images, so some of the traditional compositional principles for still photography must be modified to fit a shot series rather than a single picture. Such considerations are especially important when editing the various shots—called clips—to tell a story. (We discuss such principles in chapter 13.)

▶ **FRAMING A SHOT**
  Aspect ratio, field of view, vectors, composition, and psychological closure

▶ **MANIPULATING PICTURE DEPTH**
  Defining the z-axis and the 3D z-axes, 3D lens separation and convergence, lenses and perceived z-axis length, lenses and depth of field, and lenses and perceived z-axis speed

▶ **CONTROLLING CAMERA AND OBJECT MOTION**
  Camera movement and zooms, and shooting moving objects

■ FRAMING A SHOT

The most basic considerations in framing a shot are how much territory you include in the shot, how close an object appears to the viewer, where to place the object relative to the screen edges, and how to make viewers perceive a complete object when only parts of it are visible on-screen. In the terminology of photographic arts, including video, these factors are known as aspect ratio, field of view, vectors and composition, and psychological closure.

Aspect Ratio

Your framing of a shot depends to a great extent on the kind of frame you have available—the relationship of the width of the screen to its height, or **_aspect ratio_**. In video you will most often work with two aspect ratios: the 4 × 3 aspect ratio of standard television (STV) and the 16 × 9 aspect ratio of high-definition television. A 4 × 3 aspect ratio means that the screen is 4 units wide by 3 units high; a 16 × 9 screen is 16 units wide by 9 units high. When working in digital television (DTV), many cameras allow you to switch between the standard 4 × 3 ratio and the wide-screen 16 × 9 ratio of HDTV.

You will find that on the small screen your compositions will not differ significantly between the two aspect ratios. **SEE 6.1 AND 6.2**

6.1 4 × 3 ASPECT RATIO
The aspect ratio of STV is 4 units wide by 3 units high.

6.2 16 × 9 ASPECT RATIO
The HDTV aspect ratio is 16 units wide by 9 units high. Most DTV cameras permit switching between the standard 4 × 3 ratio and the wide-screen 16 × 9 ratio.

On a large video display or when video is projected onto a movie screen, however, the difference between the two aspect ratios is prominent. A close-up of a face is much simpler to compose in the 4 × 3 ratio than on the HDTV screen. On the other hand, the 16 × 9 ratio allows you to frame wide vistas without losing too much event impact. The wider aspect ratio not only preserves but emphasizes the landscape character of a horizontal vista. **SEE 6.3** It also makes it easier to frame a profile shot of two people talking to each other.

Letterbox and pillarbox　When using an STV screen or monitor with a 4 × 3 aspect ratio, you may have to show a movie or HDTV program that was originally shot in a 16 × 9 or slightly wider aspect ratio. Making the entire frame of a wide-screen movie fit into the 4 × 3 aspect ratio of STV results in empty (black) space at the top and the bottom of the screen. The resulting horizontal aspect ratio is called a letterbox. **SEE 6.4** When showing a standard 4 × 3 television image on the 16 × 9 screen, there are empty dead zones, or side bars, on both sides of the screen. The resulting vertical aspect ratio is called a pillarbox. **SEE 6.5** Because of such manipulations of aspect ratios, good directors try to restrict the major action as much as possible to the center of the screen.

Herbert Zettl

6.3　WIDE VISTA EMPHASIZED
The wide 16 × 9 aspect ratio accentuates the horizontal stretch of this airfield.

© Cengage Learning 2011

© Cengage Learning 2011

6.4　LETTERBOX
Making the entire frame of a 16 × 9 or movie aspect ratio fit into a 4 × 3 frame will leave empty space at the top and the bottom of the screen. The resulting horizontal aspect ratio is called a letterbox.

6.5　PILLARBOX
Using the total height of a 16 × 9 frame for showing a 4 × 3 aspect ratio will leave dead zones on both sides of the screen. The resulting vertical aspect ratio is called a pillarbox.

Effects   You will find that on a large screen, the 16 × 9 aspect ratio can make certain special effects much more obvious if not overbearing. The reverse happens on the small mobile media display: most special effects lose their impact. To help you get used to framing for the wider screen, in this book we display all the camera framings in the 16 × 9 aspect ratio. ZVL1 ▶ CAMERA→ Screen forces→ aspect ratio

Field of View

Field of view refers to how close the object seems to the viewer, or how much of the "field," or scenery, in front of you is in the shot. When organized by how close we see the object, there are five field-of-view designations: extreme long shot (ELS or XLS), **long shot (LS)**, **medium shot (MS)**, **close-up (CU)**, and extreme close-up (ECU or XCU). **SEE 6.6**

When categorized by how much of a person we see, the shots are called: bust shot, which frames the upper part of a person; knee shot, which shows the person approximately from the knees up; two-shot, which shows two people or objects in the frame; three-shot, which shows three people or objects in the frame; **over-the-shoulder shot (O/S)**, which shows the camera looking at someone over the shoulder of another person closer to the camera; and **cross-shot (X/S)**, which looks alternately at one or the other person, with the camera-near person completely out of the shot. **SEE 6.7**

The field of view is relative, which means that what you consider a close-up someone else may think of as a medium shot. As mentioned, the relatively small size of the standard video screen made the close-up the most frequently used field of view in video production. These field-of-view designations hold true regardless of whether you shoot for a small screen or a large screen or for a 4 × 3 or a 16 × 9 aspect ratio.

You can change the field of view either by moving the camera closer to the event or farther away from it or by changing the focal length of the lens by zooming in or out. As you learned in chapter 4, zooming in puts the lens in the narrow-angle (telephoto) position and brings the subject closer to the camera for a close-up view. When you zoom out, the lens gradually assumes a wide-angle position and shows

6.6 FIELD-OF-VIEW DISTANCE STEPS
The field-of-view distance steps are relative and depend on how a long shot or close-up is visualized.

Extreme long shot (ELS), or establishing shot

Long shot (LS), or full shot

Medium shot (MS), or waist shot

Close-up (CU)

Extreme close-up (ECU)

Edward Aiona

Bust shot

Knee shot

Two-shot (two persons or objects in frame)

Three-shot (three persons or objects in frame)

Over-the-shoulder shot (O/S)

Cross-shot (X/S)

Edward Aiona

6.7 OTHER SHOT DESIGNATIONS

Other shot designations tell where the subject is cut off by the upper or lower part of the frame, how many subjects are in the frame, or how they are arranged.

more territory farther away. There are important visual differences between moving the camera closer or farther away from the subject and zooming in and out. (We discuss these differences in the context of controlling camera and object motion later in this chapter.) **ZVL2** CAMERA→ Composition→ field of view

Vectors

A *vector* is a directional screen force with varying strengths. This concept will help you understand and control the specific screen forces generated by someone looking, pointing, or moving in a particular direction or even by the horizontal and vertical lines of a room, desk, or door. A thorough understanding of vectors will aid you in blocking—designing effective positions and movements of talent and cameras.

Graphic vectors These vectors are created by lines or an arrangement of stationary objects that lead the eye in a general direction. Look around you. You are surrounded by graphic vectors, such as the horizontal and vertical lines that are formed by this book, the window and door frames in the room, or the line where the walls meet the ceiling. The lines of a skyscraper form a series of graphic vectors. **SEE 6.8**

Edward Aiona

6.8 GRAPHIC VECTORS

Graphic vectors are created by lines or an arrangement of stationary objects that leads the eye in a certain direction.

6.9 INDEX VECTORS
Index vectors are created by someone or something that points unquestionably in a particular direction.

Index vectors   These are created by something that points unquestionably in a specific direction, such as an arrow, a one-way-street sign, or somebody looking or pointing. **SEE 6.9** The difference between graphic and index vectors is that index vectors are much more definite as to direction. Going against the index vector of a one-way sign may jolt your sense of good composition as well as your body.

> **KEY CONCEPT**
>
> There are three basic vectors: graphic vectors, index vectors, and motion vectors.

Motion vectors   A motion vector is created by an object that is actually moving, or is perceived to be moving, on-screen. People walking, a car speeding along the highway, a bird in flight—all form motion vectors. For an illustration of motion vectors, look around you where things are moving or turn on your TV set (motion vectors obviously cannot be illustrated by a still picture). **ZVL3** CAMERA→ Screen forces→ vectors

Composition

Our perceptual faculties are always striving to stabilize the chaotic world around us. Good picture composition helps us in this task. In fact, professional videographers apply effective compositional principles even when shooting under extreme pressure, such as while covering a storm or a war. Some of the most basic compositional factors involve subject placement, headroom and leadroom, and the horizon line.

> **KEY CONCEPT**
>
> The most stable picture area is screen-center.

Subject placement   The most stable and prominent picture area is screen-center. If you want to draw attention to a single subject, place it there. **SEE 6.10** The same goes for framing a person who is addressing viewers directly, such as a newscaster or a company president. **SEE 6.11**

If the newscaster has to share screen space with a visual, such as the secondary frame—the box—over her shoulder, you obviously need to move her to one side, not only to make room for the visual but also to balance the two picture elements within the frame. **SEE 6.12**

Sometimes when you frame large vistas that contain a distinct single vertical element, such as a telephone pole, tree, or skyscraper, you can place the single vertical element off-center, at about the one-third or two-thirds mark of screen width. Such nonsymmetrical framing in which the two unequal parts of the screen con-

6.10 SCREEN-CENTER PLACEMENT
The most stable screen position is screen-center. All screen forces are neutralized at this point.

6.11 SCREEN-CENTER PLACEMENT OF NEWSCASTER
A single newscaster should be placed screen-center. This position draws undivided attention to the newscaster and what she is saying.

tain different visual elements is often called the rule of thirds. You may have heard of framing according to the golden section. In this case, the horizontal division is placed at the two-fifths or three-fifths mark. Either division makes the picture look more dynamic and the horizon less divided than if you placed the vertical object at exactly midpoint. **SEE 6.13**

The rule of thirds also applies to placing objects within the frame, such as having a person stand at the one-third mark of the screen width. Some directors and DPs (directors of photography) use the rule of thirds as a guide for close-ups, placing the eyes of a person in the upper third of the screen. Such a placement, however, depends on how big the close-up is, whether the subject wears a hat, and whether you need adequate headroom. If, for example, you would tilt down a bit to place the eyes of the man in figure 6.15 in the upper third of the frame, you would severely cramp the necessary headroom. But why do we need headroom anyway?

6.12 PICTURE BALANCE
When the newscaster has to share the screen space with other visuals, the elements must be placed in opposite screen halves so that they balance each other.

6.13 NONSYMMETRICAL FRAMING
A prominent horizontal line can best be divided by a vertical object located at about two-fifths (for the STV aspect ratio) or one-third (for the HDTV aspect ratio) the distance from either the left or the right screen edge. In this way the screen is not divided visually into two equal halves, which makes for a more dynamic and interesting composition.

6.14 NO HEADROOM
Without headroom the person seems glued to the top edge of the screen.

6.15 PROPER HEADROOM
Correct headroom neutralizes the magnetic pull of the upper edge and makes the person look comfortable within the frame.

6.16 TOO MUCH HEADROOM
Too much headroom tends to dwarf the person and push the image against the lower half of the screen.

Headroom, noseroom, and leadroom   Somehow the edges of the video screen seem to act like magnets and attract objects close to them. This pull is especially strong at the top and bottom edges of the screen. For example, if you frame a man so that his head touches the upper screen edge, his head seems to be pulled up, or even attached, to the frame. **SEE 6.14** To counteract this pull, you must leave adequate space, called *headroom*. **SEE 6.15**

If you leave too much headroom, however, the bottom edge exerts its force and seems to pull the man downward. **SEE 6.16** Because you may lose some picture space when transmitting via cable or an on-the-air channel or because of a slightly misaligned TV receiver, you should leave just a little more headroom than what seems appropriate; this way the viewer will see framing with exactly the right headroom. **SEE 6.17** **ZVL4** CAMERA→ Composition→ headroom

The sides of the frame are similar graphical "magnets" that seem to pull persons or objects toward them, especially when they are oriented toward one or the other side of the screen. Take a look at the next figure. **SEE 6.18** Do you feel that this is a good composition? Of course not. The person seems to push his nose into the right screen edge. Correct framing requires some breathing room to reduce the force of his glance—his screen-right index vector—and the pull of the frame, which is why

Picture loss

6.17 HEADROOM FOR TRANSMISSION
The framing on the left is correct for the viewfinder display, but the inevitable picture loss during transmission or video recording requires more initial headroom. The framing on the right is therefore more appropriate.

6.18 NO NOSEROOM
Without any space between the nose and the screen edge, the person seems to be glued to the frame or crashing into it.

6.19 PROPER NOSEROOM
This noseroom is sufficient to counter the pull of the screen edge and the force of the glance.

this type of framing is called **noseroom**. **SEE 6.19** Note that the rule of thirds also applies to noseroom: as you can see, the center of the person's head is approximately in the left third of the frame.

The same "breathing room" principle applies when you frame someone moving laterally. **SEE 6.20** You must leave some room in the direction of movement to show where the person is going and to absorb some of the directional energy of the motion vector. Because the camera must be somewhat ahead of the subject's motion and should lead the action rather than follow it, this is called **leadroom**. It is not always easy to keep proper leadroom for a moving person or object, especially if the subject moves quickly. **SEE 6.21** **ZVL5** CAMERA→ Composition→ leadroom

Now that you have learned all about the rule of thirds, a word of caution is in order: if you always apply this rule in a mathematical fashion, your pictures will look mechanical, as though you consistently edited them to a musical beat. In certain circumstances you need to break this rule and frame the subject unconventionally to give your pictures an additional edge. For example, if you want to emphasize the beautiful colors of the evening sky, you should ignore the rule of thirds and tilt the

6.20 NO LEADROOM
Without proper leadroom the laterally moving subject or object seems oddly impeded by the screen edge.

6.21 PROPER LEADROOM
With proper leadroom the laterally moving subject or object seems able to move freely in the given direction.

6.22 **LEVEL HORIZON LINE**
When framing a person standing in front of a prominent horizon line, make sure that it is level.

6.23 **TILTING THE HORIZON LINE**
A tilted horizon line increases the dynamic tension of the event.

camera up to lower the horizon line as much as possible. Or you may want to place a person right next to the screen edge to intensify his claustrophobia. As you can see, you can—and should—bend the compositional rules if it intensifies the message. But before you can bend a rule, you must understand it.

Horizon line   Normally, we expect buildings and people to stand upright on level ground. This principle is especially important when you shoot outdoors and where there are distinct vertical and horizontal graphic vectors. For instance, when video recording a weathercaster reporting from the shores of a lake, make sure that the background lines (graphic vectors) of the lake are parallel to the upper and lower screen edges. **SEE 6.22** A slight tilt of the handheld camcorder may not readily show up on the weathercaster in the foreground but is easily detectable by the tilted horizon line in the background.

If you intend to upset a stable environment by deliberately canting the camera, however, a tilted horizon line can make the picture more dynamic and increase its aesthetic energy. Of course, the subject matter must lend itself to such aesthetic manipulation. **SEE 6.23** Canting the camera on a dull speaker will not improve his speech; it will simply alert the viewer to sloppy camera work.

Psychological Closure

Our minds try to make sense of the bombardment of impressions we receive every second and to stabilize the world around us as much as possible. Our perceptual

6.24 **PSYCHOLOGICAL CLOSURE**
We perceive these three angle brackets as a triangle by mentally filling in the missing parts.

6.25 FRAMING A CLOSE-UP
A properly framed close-up leads our eyes into off-screen space to complete the figure.

mechanism does this by ignoring most sense impressions that are not immediately relevant and by combining visual cues or filling in missing visual information to arrive at complete and stable configurations. This process is called *psychological closure*, or closure for short.

Take a look at the arrangement of angle brackets on the facing page. **SEE 6.24** Although we actually see three separate brackets, we perceive a single triangle. Through psychological closure we automatically fill in the missing lines. In fact, you will probably have a hard time seeing them as three isolated angles without covering two of the three.

Now look at the close-up above. **SEE 6.25** Again you mentally fill in the rest of the subject's body although you actually see only her head and shoulders on-screen.

The graphic vectors of the shoulders that led your eye outside the frame helped you to apply closure to fill in the missing parts. One of the most important principles in framing a close-up in which only part of the subject is shown is to provide sufficient visual clues (in this case, graphic vectors) that enable the viewer to mentally complete the figure in off-screen space. Below are two different ECUs of the same person. Which one do you prefer? **SEE 6.26**

6.26 CHOOSING THE PROPER FRAMING
Here are two extreme close-ups. Which one looks better to you?

6.27 IMPROPER AND PROPER FRAMING
A This extreme close-up is improperly framed because it invites us to apply closure within the frame (an oval) without extending into off-screen space.

B This framing properly extends into off-screen space and allows us to apply closure to the whole figure.

KEY CONCEPT

Close-ups that show only part of the object must provide sufficient visual clues for closure in off-screen space.

Most likely, you chose the photo on the right (figure 6.26b) as the better ECU. But why? Because, as you can see in figure 6.27b, the close-up on the right has sufficient clues (graphic vectors) to tell us that the subject is continuing in off-screen space. In contrast, the framing on the left gives practically no visual clues that would lead us into off-screen space (see 6.27a). In fact, our perceptual mechanism is happy with having found a stable configuration within the frame: the head forms an oval. **SEE 6.27**

The disagreement between our experience, which tells us that there must be a body attached to the head, and our automated perception, which is perfectly happy with the circlelike configuration, is the principal reason why we feel uncomfortable with such a composition. **ZVL6** CAMERA→ Composition→ close-ups | try it

The need for psychological closure can also produce visual paradoxes and bad compositions by combining parts of the foreground and the background into a single configuration. Examples are the rubber plant on the set that seems to grow out of the guest's head as well as the tree or street sign that extends out of the person standing in front of it. **SEE 6.28** Although we know that such elements are in the background, our perceptual need for stable figures makes us perceive such visual paradoxes as a single unit.

6.28 UNDESIRABLE CLOSURE
Because of our tendency to stabilize the environment, we perceive this background object as part of the main figure.

When looking through the viewfinder, you must learn to see not only the foreground (target) object but also what is *behind* it. By looking behind the target object or scene, you will readily discover potential closure problems, such as the street sign that the reporter seems to balance on his head. Looking behind may also reveal other visual hazards, such as billboards that compete with your sponsor, or garbage cans, camera or mic cables, or light stands in the shot. **ZVL7** CAMERA→ Composition→ background

■ MANIPULATING PICTURE DEPTH

So far we have been concerned mainly with organizing the two-dimensional area of the video screen.[1] This section explores the depth dimension. Whereas the width and the height of the video screen have definite limits, the depth dimension extends from the camera lens to the horizon. Although illusory, the screen depth, or z-axis (a term borrowed from geometry), is the most flexible screen dimension. The *z-axis* is an imaginary line that stretches from camera lens to horizon, regardless of where the lens is pointing. You can place many more objects along this depth axis than across the width of the screen. You can also have objects move toward and away from the camera at any speed without having to worry about losing them in the viewfinder or providing adequate leadroom. **ZVL8** CAMERA→ Picture depth→ z-axis

Defining the Z-Axis

If you point a camera at the cloudless sky, you have just about as long a z-axis as you can get—but it does not show its depth. To show screen depth, you need to define the z-axis by placing objects or people along it. The traditional way of creating the illusion of depth is to place objects in a distinct foreground, middleground, and background. **SEE 6.29** Even on a relatively small set, a prominent foreground piece or person will help define the z-axis and suggest screen depth. **SEE 6.30**

---

1. For more information about picture composition, see Herbert Zettl, *Sight Sound Motion: Applied Media Aesthetics*, 6th ed. (Boston: Wadsworth, 2011), pp. 103–14.

6.29 FOREGROUND, MIDDLEGROUND, AND BACKGROUND
A distinct division of the z-axis into foreground (trees and benches), middleground (river), and background (skyline) creates the illusion of depth.

6.30 FOREGROUND PERSON TO CREATE DEPTH
The person standing in the foreground increases the illusion of screen depth.

6.31 **2D Z-AXIS VECTOR**

In a two-dimensional monocular projection, the z-axis stretches from the screen (camera lens) to the background (horizon).

6.32 **3D Z-AXIS VECTORS**

In a three-dimensional projection, the z-axis extends from the screen to the horizon but also through the screen to the viewer. In effect, you have a z-axis in front of the screen that extends to the viewer and another one in back of the screen that extends to the horizon.

Defining the 3D Z-Axes

In 2D projection the z-axis goes from the screen to horizon. In 3D projection the z-axis goes from the screen to the horizon and also through the screen toward the viewer.

The crucial perceptual difference between a two-dimensional and a three-dimensional stereo projection is that in the standard 2D projection the z-axis extends only from the screen (camera lens) to the background (horizon). In 3D stereo projection, however, you have two z-axes: one goes from the screen to the background, and the other goes from the screen to the viewer. Depending on the projected motion, the z-axis can go from the background *through* the screen toward the viewer. **SEE 6.31 AND 6.32** This screen penetration by the z-axis that extends toward the viewer is one of the unique perceptual components of z-axis projection.

3D Lens Separation and Convergence

As you recall from chapter 4, your left eye sees an object from a slightly different angle than your right eye, but your brain fuses the two images, giving you an added and fairly accurate binocular clue of how far the object is from you. When duplicating this sensation in photography, including video and film, we use two cameras whose lenses substitute for our eyes.

Lens separation   Contrary to our eyes, which are at a fixed distance of about 2.5 inches (6.35 centimeters) from each other, the 3D camera rig or 3D software allows you to adjust the spread between the two lenses.[2] **SEE 6.33** The farther the lens-eyes are apart, the greater the difference of how each lens sees the same object or scene and therefore the more exaggerated the stereo effect becomes. The stereo image

---

2. The distance between the eyes is technically called the interocular distance. The interocular distance between lenses can be adjusted by either physically moving the cameras or through a mirror/prism system.

6.33 LENS SEPARATION AND STEREO EFFECT

A When the lenses of both the left-eye camera and the right-eye camera are parallel, the resulting stereo effect shows objects positioned on their z-axis (1 and 2) on the z-axis from screen to viewer. The objects seem to float in front of the screen.

B When you increase the distance between the cameras, the z-axis in front of the screen stretches. It also increases the perceived distance between objects 1 and 2, with object 1 now appearing to be much closer to the viewer.

produces a highly exaggerated z-axis that stretches from the screen to the viewer. Perceptually, the objects closest to the lenses seem to float right in front of your nose.

This is a great special effect if you want to invade the viewer's personal space or make something shoot out of the screen, causing the audience to duck from the oncoming object. But such maneuvers are also likely to give the viewer a severe headache because the brain is working overtime to fuse the two disparate images into a single stereo one.

Convergence   The lenses can either sit side-by-side pointing straight ahead to create parallel z-axes from cameras to the horizon or be swiveled toward each other to a certain degree. By having the lenses not only closer or farther away from each other but also slightly pigeon-toed to various degrees, their z-axes intersect at a predetermined point. This intersection is the ***point of convergence (POC)***, or convergence

6.34 3D POINT OF CONVERGENCE

When the point of convergence lies behind object 1, but in front of object 2, object 1 appears to be in front of the screen and object 2 in the screen background.

point: the location at which the pictures of the left-eye camera and the right-eye camera overlap perfectly, nullifying any stereo effect.

In stereo video or film, the POC generally marks the screen position—the reference plane of what is perceived to be behind and in front of the screen. Whatever is positioned in front of the POC appears to float in front of the screen, and whatever is behind the POC appears to lie behind the screen. **SEE 6.34**

But what if both lenses are fixed in a parallel position, preventing their z-axes from converging? Everything they see appears to float in front of the screen. In this case, the point of convergence must then be set in postproduction. You should realize that good 3D is not just having something pop out of the screen (along the z-axis from screen to viewer) but also, if not especially, giving more air between objects behind the screen (along the z-axis from screen to horizon). In fact, a good 3D director tries to keep most of the action behind the screen and away from the screen edges; otherwise you may end up with partial close-ups bleeding out of the side of the screen, a problem known as a window violation.

Going any further with explaining the pitfalls of 3D video and film would prove counterproductive at this point because many of the standard 2D production aspects yet to be learned differ considerably from what is currently being explored in 3D video. So, for now, we'll return to the 2D world.

6.35 WIDE-ANGLE Z-AXIS
The wide-angle lens stretches the z-axis and increases the perceived distance between objects (palm trees).

6.36 NARROW-ANGLE Z-AXIS
The narrow-angle (telephoto) lens shrinks the z-axis, compresses the distance between objects (palm trees), and enlarges the background (building).

Lenses and 2D Z-Axis Length

In standard two-dimensional video, the focal length of a lens has a great influence on our perception of z-axis length and the distance between objects placed along the z-axis.

Wide-angle position   When zoomed all the way out (wide-angle position), the z-axis appears elongated and the objects placed along it seem to be farther apart than they really are. **SEE 6.35**

Narrow-angle position   When zoomed all the way in (narrow-angle, or telephoto, position), the z-axis seems to be shorter than it really is and the distance between the objects placed along it seems reduced. The z-axis and its objects seem compressed. **SEE 6.36**

Lenses and Depth of Field

You have probably noticed when zoomed all the way in (with the lens in the telephoto position) that you have more trouble keeping in focus an object traveling along the z-axis than when zoomed all the way out to a wide-angle position. When zoomed in, the z-axis area that is in focus is considerably shallower than when zoomed out. We call this area in which objects are in focus ***depth of field***. **SEE 6.37**

6.37 DEPTH OF FIELD
The area along the z-axis in which objects appear in focus is called depth of field.

6.38 SHALLOW DEPTH OF FIELD
Narrow-angle (telephoto) lenses have a shallow depth of field. When zoomed in, the depth of field is shallow.

6.39 GREAT DEPTH OF FIELD
Wide-angle lenses have a great depth of field. When zoomed out, the depth of field is great.

In the narrow-angle position, lenses have a shallow depth of field. This means that if you are focused on a foreground object, objects in the middleground and the background are out of focus. If you shift your focus to an object in the middleground, the foreground and background objects are out of focus. If you focus on the background, the middleground and foreground objects are out of focus. Note that with a shallow depth of field, an object can move only a short distance along the z-axis before it goes out of focus. **SEE 6.38** `ZVL9` CAMERA→ Focusing→ depth of field | shallow

A wide-angle position creates a great depth of field: objects that are widely scattered along the z-axis are all in focus. For example, when you focus on the foreground object in a large depth of field, the middleground and background objects remain in focus as well, and an object can travel a great distance along the z-axis and still be in focus. **SEE 6.39**

In practice this means that when zoomed out to a wide-angle position, you don't have to worry much about staying in focus. But when zoomed in to a narrow-angle position, you need to adjust the focus constantly whenever the camera or the object moves along the z-axis.

Depth of field is also influenced by object-to-camera distance and the size of the lens aperture. The closer the camera is to the object, the shallower the depth of field becomes; the farther away you are, the greater the depth of field. A large aperture reduces the depth of field; a small one increases it. (See chapter 4 for a discussion of lens apertures.) `ZVL10` CAMERA→ Focusing→ depth of field | great depth

You will find that a great depth of field is desirable for most routine productions. Especially when running after a news story, you want to show as much of the event as clearly as possible without having to worry about keeping the picture in focus. This is why you should zoom out and keep the lens in the wide-angle position. When you need a closer shot, you simply move the camera closer to the event. With the wide-angle lens position, the depth of field remains great enough to stay in focus even when you or the object moves.

For a more deliberate production, there are many instances in which a shallow depth of field is preferred. By focusing on the target object while keeping everything

> **KEY CONCEPT**
>
> With the zoom lens in a narrow-angle position (zoomed all the way in), depth of field is shallow and keeping focus is difficult. With the zoom lens in a wide-angle position (zoomed all the way out), depth of field is great and keeping focus is relatively easy.

> **KEY CONCEPT**
>
> Depth of field is dependent on the focal length of the lens, the distance from camera to object, and the lens aperture.

Edward Aiona

6.40 SHALLOW DEPTH OF FIELD IN CLOSE-UPS
Regardless of the focal length of the lens, close-ups have a shallower depth of field than long shots. The clue is the out-of-focus background.

else out of focus, you can emphasize the target without eliminating the environment. Another favorite technique is to shift emphasis from person to person by alternately focusing on one person, with the other person out of focus, and then switching. Realize, however, that this rack-focus effect is so popular that it has become a cliché.

If you move the camera extremely close to the object, the depth of field will shrink even if the lens is zoomed out to the wide-angle position. Because the camera-to-object distance influences the depth of field, as does the focal length of the lens, we can say that, in general, tight close-ups have a shallow depth of field. SEE 6.40 `ZVL11` CAMERA→ Focusing→ depth of field

Lenses and Z-axis Speed

Because a narrow-angle lens position compresses the z-axis, the movement of objects along the z-axis is equally compressed. When the lens is zoomed all the way in, cars seem to be much more crowded and moving more slowly than they actually are. With the lens zoomed all the way out, they seem to be farther apart and moving much faster than they actually are. By simply putting the zoom lens in a narrow-angle or wide-angle position, you can manipulate the viewer's perception of the distance between objects and how fast they move along the z-axis. `ZVL12` CAMERA→ Picture depth→ lens choice | perspective and distortion `ZVL13` CAMERA→ Screen motion→ z-axis

> **KEY CONCEPT**
>
> A narrow-angle lens position compresses the z-axis and slows down z-axis motion. A wide-angle lens position stretches the z-axis and speeds up z-axis motion.

■ CONTROLLING CAMERA AND OBJECT MOTION

Here we cover a few of the main aesthetic principles of camera and object motion. These include the most obvious do's and don'ts of moving the camera, zooming, and blocking object movement. (Additional information about controlling camera and object motion is presented in subsequent chapters.)

Controlling Camera Movement and Zooms

If there is a single indication of an inexperienced camera operator, it is excessive camera movement and zooms. The wildly roaming camera reminds us more of a firefighter's nozzle than photographic artistry, and the fast out-of-focus zooms produce more eyestrain than dramatic impact.

Moving camera   For some reason most beginners think that it is the camera that has to do the moving rather than the object in front of it, especially when there is not much object motion. If nothing moves, so be it. Aesthetic energy does not come from unmotivated camera movement but from the event itself, regardless of whether it is in motion. If there are any hard-and-fast aesthetic rules in camera operation, this is one of them: always try to keep the camera as steady as possible and have the people and the objects in front of the camera do the moving. The problem with an incessantly moving camera is that it draws too much attention to itself. It is, after all, the event you want to show, not your virtuosity of zooming and camera handling.

For variety and to provide viewers with different points of view, you can shift camera angles or change the camera-to-object distance. Even if there is absolutely no movement in the event, different angles and fields of view will provide enough change to hold viewers' interest and give them more information about the event. To keep camera movement to a minimum, use a tripod or other camera mount whenever possible, even if the camera is small.

Fast zooms   Fast, unmotivated zooms are as annoying as a needlessly roving camera. The major problem is that the zoom—even more than camera motion—is a highly visible technique that draws attention to itself. One of the worst things you can do is follow a fast zoom-in or zoom-out with an equally fast zoom in the opposite direction. Rest on the target object for a while before switching to another angle and point of view. Constant zooming in and out makes viewers feel cheated: you bring the event to them through zooming in only to take it away by immediately zooming out. In the worst case, it may make viewers slightly nauseated. Unless you are planning a highly dramatic effect, a zoom should remain largely unnoticed by the viewer. If you must zoom, do it slowly.

In general, zooming in to a close-up increases tension; zooming out releases it. You will find that it is easier to start with a close-up view of an object and then zoom out than the other way around. When zooming out from a close-up, it is also easier to stay in focus than when zooming in, especially if you have not had time to calibrate the zoom lens (see chapter 5). Even with an automatic focus, fast zooms cause problems because the auto-focus mechanism may not be able to keep up with the speed of the image change. Consequently, the picture will pop in and out of focus during the zoom.

Zoom versus dolly   There is an important aesthetic difference between a zoom and a dolly. When you zoom in or out, the event seems to move toward or away from the viewer; when you dolly in or out, the viewer seems to move toward or away from the event.

If, for example, you want to show that the ringing telephone bears an important message, you zoom in on the phone rather than dolly in. The fast zoom virtually catapults the phone toward the screen and the viewer. But when you want to have the viewer identify with a student who is late for class, you dolly the camera toward the only empty chair rather than zoom in on it. The dolly will accompany the student— and the viewer—to the empty chair. A zoom would bring the chair to the student (and the viewer), and that rarely happens, even in a friendly classroom atmosphere. The reason for this aesthetic difference is that the camera remains stationary during the zoom, whereas during a dolly it actually moves into the scene. **ZVL14** CAMERA→ Camera moves→ dolly | zoom

Controlling Object Motion

Despite all the theory about providing leadroom for an object moving laterally from one screen edge to the other, it is hard to keep it properly framed on the traditional 4 × 3 STV screen. Sometimes even experienced camera operators have trouble following an object that moves laterally in a tight shot. Just try following somebody moving sideways fairly close to the camera—you will be glad just to keep the person in the viewfinder! Framing lateral motion—that is, motion along the x-axis—is somewhat easier with a wide-angle lens position or when shooting for the 16 × 9 aspect ratio. In any case, when the subject moves in a straight line along the z-axis—toward or away from the camera—you will have much less trouble keeping the person in the shot and properly framed, even if he or she walks briskly. Blocking people along the z-axis rather than the x-axis not only is easier on the camera operator but also produces shots with greater impact.

Z-axis blocking refers to placing people behind rather than next to one another. **SEE 6.41** This arrangement makes it relatively easy to keep several people in a single shot and to capture their movements without excess camera motion. With the lens in the wide-angle position, z-axis movement can look dramatic and spectacular. Also, as you have just learned, the wide-angle lens provides a large enough depth of field so that you need to do little, if any, focusing.

Even when you have no control over the event and cannot influence the blocking, as is the case in most electronic news gathering, you can still conform the object motion to the aesthetic requirements of the small screen and the stable camera: simply position the camera in such a way that most of the object movement occurs along the z-axis. For example, if you cover a parade, don't stand on the sidewalk and try to capture the various bands and floats as they move past you; instead step onto the street and shoot against the oncoming parade traffic. With a zoom lens in the wide-angle position, you will have little trouble covering the event in long shots and close-ups while staying in focus. **ZVL15** CAMERA→ Picture depth→ z-axis

Edward Aiona

© Cengage Learning 2011

6.41 Z-AXIS BLOCKING
Blocking along the z-axis suits the small video screen.

KEY CONCEPT

Z-axis blocking looks dramatic and requires little camera movement. It is essential for framing several people and capturing motion on the small mobile media display.

M A I N   P O I N T S

▶ **Aspect Ratio**

The standard television (STV) aspect ratio is 4×3. The high-definition television (HDTV) aspect ratio is 16×9.

▶ **Field of View**

The field of view is usually expressed in five shots, ranging from extreme long shot (ELS or XLS) to extreme close-up (ECU or XCU). Other shot designations refer to how much of a person we see (such as bust shot or knee shot) or how many people we see (two-shot or three-shot). In an over-the-shoulder shot (O/S), we see the shoulder and the back of the head of the camera-near person while looking at the camera-far person. A cross-shot (X/S) is closer, with the camera-near person out of the shot.

▶ **Close-Up Medium**

Video is a close-up medium. Select those event details that tell the real story with clarity and impact.

▶ **Vectors**

Vectors are directional screen forces of varying strengths that influence composition and the blocking of talent and cameras. There are graphic vectors, which suggest a direction through lines or objects that form a line; index vectors, which point unquestionably in a specific direction; and motion vectors, which show the actual event or its screen image in motion.

▶ **Screen Forces**

The most stable picture area is screen-center. Headroom neutralizes the pull of the upper screen edge. Noseroom and leadroom neutralize the index and motion vector forces, respectively, and the pull of the frame.

▶ **Psychological Closure**

Through psychological closure we are able to perceive a complete figure even if it is shown only partially in a close-up. Close-ups that show only part of the object must provide sufficient visual clues for closure in off-screen space.

▶ **Picture Depth**

The standard 2D depth dimension depends on defining the z-axis into foreground, middleground, and background. Wide-angle zoom lens positions (zoomed out) make the z-axis look longer; objects seem farther apart, and their z-axis movement appears faster than it actually is. Narrow-angle zoom lens positions (zoomed in) make the z-axis look shorter; objects seem more compressed, and their z-axis movement appears slower. Wide-angle lens positions show a great depth of field; narrow-angle lens positions show a shallow one. In 2D video space, the z-axis extends from the screen (camera lens) to the background (horizon). In 3D video space, it also extends from screen to viewer.

▶ **Motion**

Whenever possible, keep the camera still and let the event do the moving. A zoom-in brings the object to the viewer; a dolly-in takes the viewer to the object. Z-axis movement is well suited to the relatively small TV screen of both aspect ratios. It is essential for the mobile media display.

ZETTL'S VIDEOLAB

For your reference or to track your work, the *Zettl's VideoLab* program cues in this chapter are listed here with their corresponding page numbers.

Image Creation: Sound, Light, Graphics, and Effects

When you review your latest video recordings a little more critically, you can see that your composition has improved considerably. You left proper headroom and leadroom, and your horizon lines are level. But now you are discovering other problems that went unnoticed before. What is most annoying are the hollow sounds you got when you interviewed people in their living room and the crackling of wind and traffic noise when the interview took place on a street corner. Apparently, you forgot to listen to the environment while composing your impressive shots. Despite the good composition, some shots looks grossly overexposed; others hide all the detail in dense shadows. Some of the indoor shots have a strange green tint, and the white wedding gown of your friend's bride looks light blue in your outdoor shots.

Part III introduces you to basic audio and lighting techniques that will help you avoid such problems—and also gives you some pointers on effective graphics and visual effects.

KEY TERMS

cardioid Heart-shaped pickup pattern of a unidirectional microphone.

condenser microphone A high-quality, sensitive microphone for critical sound pickup.

dynamic microphone A relatively rugged microphone. Good for outdoor use.

fader A volume control that works by sliding a button horizontally along a scale. Identical in function to a pot. Also called *slide fader*.

hypercardioid Very narrow unidirectional pickup pattern with a long reach. The mic is also sensitive to sounds coming directly from the back.

jack A socket or receptacle for a connector.

lavalier A small microphone that is clipped to clothing. Also called *lav*.

mini plug Small audio connector.

omnidirectional Pickup pattern of a microphone that can hear equally well from all directions.

pickup pattern The territory around the microphone within which the mic can hear well.

polar pattern The two-dimensional representation of the microphone pickup pattern.

pop filter A wire-mesh screen attached to the front of a mic that reduces breath pops and sudden air blasts.

RCA phono plug Connector for video and audio equipment.

ribbon microphone A high-quality, highly sensitive microphone for critical sound pickup in the studio, usually for recording string instruments.

sweetening The postproduction manipulation of recorded sound.

unidirectional Pickup pattern of a microphone that can hear best from the front.

volume-unit (VU) meter Measures volume units, the relative loudness of amplified sound.

waveform Graphic representation of a sound that occurs over a period of time.

windscreen Acoustic foam rubber that is put over the entire microphone to cut down wind noise.

windsock A moplike cloth cover that is put over the windscreen to further reduce wind noise in outdoor use. Also called *wind jammer*.

XLR connector Professional three-wire connector for audio cables.

Audio and Sound Control

Television is primarily a visual medium, right? Wrong. Video programs rely on the sound portion even more than films do. The audio portion not only conveys information but adds aesthetic energy and structure to the video sequences. You have also no doubt heard that the worst sin you can commit in video production is showing "talking heads"—a criticism that is a total misconception. You will find that there is nothing wrong with talking heads so long as they talk well.

In fact, much of the information in video programs is conveyed by somebody talking. You can do a simple experiment to prove this point: Turn off the video portion of the program and try to follow what is going on; then turn on the video again but turn off the audio. You will probably have little trouble following the story by only hearing the sound track, but in most cases you will have difficulty knowing what is going on by only seeing the pictures. Even if you can follow the story by watching the pictures, the lack of sound leaves the message strangely incomplete. Just turn off the sound for a moment while watching a football game. Without the crowd noise, the play seems to have lost most of its excitement.

Much amateur video is characterized not just by the madly moving camera and the fast zooms but also by the bad audio. Even professional video productions tend to suffer more from poor sound than bad pictures. Why? At first glance the production of sound seems much easier to achieve than the corresponding video. When working a camcorder, you are probably concentrating so hard on getting good pictures that you don't pay much attention to the sounds and assume that the built-in microphone will do the job when set to the automatic volume control. Many times this may be sufficient. For good sound, however, simply turning on the camera mic, or sticking a mic into a scene at the last minute, is not the way to go.

Not all microphones sound the same, nor do they sound the same in different environments. When outdoors there is the additional hazard of wind noise and other unwanted environmental sounds. Unless you do a routine show, you need to consider the audio requirements as an essential part of the production process. The better the original audio pickup, the more time you will save in postproduction. **ZVL1** AUDIO→
Audio introduction

This chapter examines the various tools and techniques of producing good audio for video.

▶ **SOUND PICKUP PRINCIPLE**

How microphones change sound waves into sound signals

▶ **MICROPHONES**

How well they hear, how they are made, and how they are used

▶ **SOUND CONTROL**

Working the audio mixer and the audio console

▶ **SOUND RECORDING**

Digital recording equipment and other audio-recording devices

▶ **AUDIO POSTPRODUCTION**

Audio postproduction room, sound waveform, and automated dialogue replacement

▶ **SYNTHESIZED SOUND**

Computer-generated sounds

▶ **SOUND AESTHETICS**

Context, figure/ground, sound perspective, continuity, and energy and mood

◼ SOUND PICKUP PRINCIPLE

Like the translation process in video, in which the lens image of the object is converted into the video signal, in audio the sounds the microphone hears are *transduced* (transformed) into electric energy—the audio signal. This signal is made audible again through the loudspeaker. The basic sound pickup tool is the microphone, or mic (pronounced "mike").

You can also create sounds synthetically, by electronically generating and recording certain frequencies, a process similar to creating computer-generated video images. We focus first on microphone-generated sounds, then turn briefly to synthesized sounds

> **KEY CONCEPT**
>
> Microphones transduce sound waves into electric energy—the audio signal.

◼ MICROPHONES

Although all microphones fulfill the same basic function of transducing sounds into audio signals, they do so in different ways and for different purposes. Good audio requires that you know how to choose the right mic for a specific sound pickup—not an easy task when faced with the myriad mics available. Despite all the brand names and numbers, you can make sense of the different microphones by classifying them by how well they hear, how they are made, and how they are generally used.

How Well Mics Hear: Sound Pickup

Not all microphones hear sounds in the same way. Some are built to hear sounds from all directions equally well; others favor sounds that come from a specific direction. The directional characteristic—the zone within which a microphone can hear well—is specified by its *pickup pattern*. Its two-dimensional representation is called the *polar pattern*.

In general, you will find that most microphones used in video production are omnidirectional or unidirectional. The *omnidirectional* mic hears equally well from all directions. Visualize the omnidirectional mic at the center of a sphere. The sphere itself represents the pickup pattern. **SEE 7.1**

The *unidirectional* mic is designed to hear especially well from one direction—the front. Because the pickup pattern of a unidirectional mic is roughly heart-shaped, it is also called *cardioid*. **SEE 7.2**

Pickup pattern

Polar pattern

© Cengage Learning 2011

7.1 OMNIDIRECTIONAL MICROPHONE PATTERNS
The omnidirectional microphone hears equally well from all directions.

Pickup pattern

Polar pattern

© Cengage Learning 2011

7.2 CARDIOID MICROPHONE PATTERNS
The unidirectional microphone favors sounds that are in front of it. Its pickup pattern is heart-shaped, hence the term *cardioid*.

7.3 HYPERCARDIOID MICROPHONE PATTERNS

The hypercardioid pickup pattern is narrower than the cardioid and has a longer reach. Hypercardioid mics can also hear sounds coming from behind the mic.

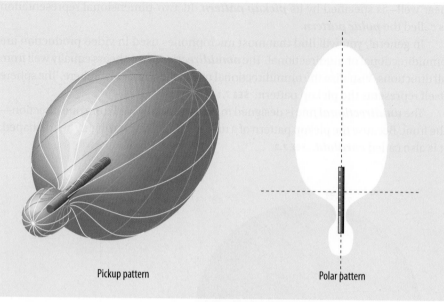

Pickup pattern   Polar pattern

When this pickup pattern gets progressively narrower, the mics are supercardioid, hypercardioid, or ultracardioid. The "heart" of the cardioid pickup pattern has now been stretched to the shape of a thin watermelon. **SEE 7.3** The ***hypercardioid*** and ultracardioid mics have a long reach, which means you can produce sounds that seem to come from fairly close by although they may actually be quite far away. Hyper- and supercardioid mics are also somewhat sensitive to sounds that come directly from behind. Because these microphones are usually fairly long and are aimed in the direction of the sound source, they are commonly called shotgun mics. **ZVL2** AUDIO→ Microphones→ pickup patterns

How Mics Are Made

When selecting a mic for a particular audio task, you need to consider both its specific pickup pattern and its basic mechanics—its sound-generating element. When classifying microphones by how they are made, there are three types used in video production: dynamic, condenser, and ribbon.

The dynamic mic uses a small coil that moves within a magnetic field when activated by sound. The movement of the coil produces the sound signal. The condenser mic has a movable plate—a diaphragm—that oscillates against a fixed plate to produce the sound signal. The ribbon mic has a tiny ribbon, rather than a coil, that moves in a magnetic field. But don't worry too much about exactly how these sound elements work; it is more important to know how these mics differ in their use.

Dynamic   The ***dynamic microphone*** is the most rugged. You can take it outside in all kinds of weather, and it can even withstand occasional rough handling. You can work with the mic close to extremely loud sounds without damaging it or distorting the sound too much. Many dynamic microphones have a built-in ***pop filter***, which

Shure, Inc.

7.4 DYNAMIC MICROPHONE WITH POP FILTER
Dynamic microphones are the most rugged. They can withstand rough handling and extreme temperatures. The built-in pop filter reduces breath pops. This omnidirectional mic is ideally suited for field interviews.

eliminates the breath pops that occur when someone speaks into the mic at very close range. **SEE 7.4** `ZVL3` AUDIO→ Microphones→ transducer→ dynamic mic

Condenser   These microphones are much more sensitive to physical shock and temperature than are dynamic mics, but they produce higher-quality sounds. ***Condenser microphones*** are generally used for critical sound pickup indoors, but they are also used in the field. They are especially prominent in music recording. Unlike dynamic mics, condenser microphones need a power supply to activate the sound-generating device inside the mic and to amplify the electrical signal before it leaves the mic. Some have a battery in the microphone housing. **SEE 7.5** Others get their power supply through the cable from the audio console, mixer, or camcorder (usually called phantom power). If you use a battery, see to it that it is inserted properly (with the + and – poles as indicated in the housing) and that the battery is not run-down. Always have a spare battery handy when using a condenser mic. `ZVL4` AUDIO→ Microphones→ transducer→ condenser mic

When using a condenser shotgun mic (or any shotgun mic) outdoors, you need to protect the entire microphone from wind noise by covering it with a ***windscreen***. **SEE 7.6** Windscreens are made of acoustic foam rubber or other synthetic material, which lets normal sound frequencies enter the mic but keeps most of the lower wind rumbles out. For ENG/EFP (electronic news gathering/electronic field production)

Edward Aiona

7.5 BATTERY POWER SUPPLY FOR CONDENSER MIC
Most condenser mics use a battery to charge the condenser plates. When fed to the microphone from the audio console, the power is called phantom power.

AKG Acoustics, Inc.

7.6 WINDSCREEN ON SHOTGUN MICROPHONE
The windscreen, made of porous material, protects the mic from excessive wind noise.

Edward Aiona

Royer Labs

7.7 WINDSOCK PULLED OVER WINDSCREEN
The windsock is used on top of the windscreen to further reduce wind noise.

7.8 RIBBON MICROPHONE FOR HIGH-QUALITY SOUND PICKUP
This ribbon mic is amazingly rugged without sacrificing its warm sound quality. It is an ideal microphone for recording voice-over narration, piano, and a variety of brass, woodwind, and string instruments.

microphones that are used primarily outdoors, you may want to add a ***windsock***, also called a wind jammer—a fuzzy cloth resembling a mop that can be pulled over the windscreen. **SEE 7.7**

Ribbon   You may still find ***ribbon microphones*** in some audio-recording studios or for critical music pickup for television. These highly sensitive mics are normally used for recording acoustic string instruments. **SEE 7.8** For normal video work, however, ribbon mics are just too sensitive. A loud sound burst close to the mic can put it out of commission. **ZVL5** AUDIO→ Microphones→ transducer→ ribbon mic

How Mics Are Used

Now that you know the basic types of microphones, you need to learn how to use them effectively. A good way to start mic placement is to get the mic as close to the sound source as possible and listen to how the pickup sounds. Even the most sophisticated and expensive mic will not guarantee good sound unless it is placed in an optimal pickup position. In fact, the proper positioning of the mic relative to the sound source is often more important than its sound-generating element. In video production, microphones are therefore identified by the way they are used rather than how they are made: lavalier microphones; hand microphones; boom microphones; desk and stand microphones; headset microphones; and wireless, or radio, microphones.

Lavalier microphones   The ***lavalier*** mic, or lav for short, is a very small, rugged, usually omnidirectional microphone (dynamic or condenser) that is used principally for voice pickup. The quality of even the smallest lav, which is about the size of a fingernail, is amazingly good. The combination of small size, ruggedness, and high quality has made the lavalier indispensable in video production. It is usually clipped to clothing, such as the lapel of a jacket or the front of a shirt, 6 to 8 inches below the chin. **SEE 7.9**

Although it is primarily intended for voice pickup, you can also use the lavalier for music. Sound technicians have used the lav successfully taped to violins and string basses. Don't be overly influenced by the normal use of such mics: try them out in a variety of ways and listen to the sound they deliver. If it sounds good to you, you've got the right mic.

The obvious advantage of the lavalier is that the talent has both hands free when wearing it, but there are numerous other advantages to using a lavalier mic, as well:

Edward Aiona

7.9 LAVALIER MICROPHONE
The small lavalier mic is usually clipped to the performer's clothing. It is used primarily for voice pickup.

- Because the distance from mic to sound source does not change once the mic is properly attached, you do not have to ride gain (adjust the volume) once you adjust the volume at the beginning of the shoot.

- Unlike lighting for the boom mic, which must be done in such a way that the boom shadows are hidden from camera view, the lavalier needs no special lighting considerations.

- Although the talent's action radius is somewhat limited by the mic cable, the lavalier lets him or her move more quickly than with a boom mic or even a hand mic. For greater mobility you can plug the talent's lavalier into a small body-pack transmitter and use it as a wireless mic.

There are also some disadvantages to using a lavalier mic:

- If the environment is very noisy, you cannot move the mic closer to the talent's mouth. Consequently, the surrounding (ambient) noise is easily picked up.

- You need a separate mic for each sound source. In a two-person interview, for example, you need separate lavaliers for the host and the guest. In a five-person panel show, you obviously need five lavs.

- Because it is attached to clothing, the lavalier may pick up rubbing noises, especially if the talent moves around a great deal. You may also get occasional popping noises from static electricity.

- If the mic must be concealed under clothing, the sound often takes on a muffled character and the danger of rubbing noises is greatly increased.

- One of the advantages we listed can also be a disadvantage: because the distance from the mic to the mouth does not change, the sounds do not seem to come from a closer distance on a close-up or from farther away on a long shot. Therefore you cannot achieve a desirable sound perspective. (We discuss sound perspective later in this chapter.)

Here are some points to consider when using a lavalier microphone:

- Once the mic is attached to the mic cable but not yet to the talent, watch that you do not pull the mic off a table or chair and drop it on the floor. Although the lavalier is fairly rugged, it does not tolerate mistreatment. If you accidentally drop the mic during the setup or strike (the clearing of the production space), test it immediately to check that it still functions properly. Ask the talent to avoid hitting it with his or her hand or some object that might be demonstrated on-camera.

- Be sure to put the mic on. As obvious as this sounds, on the opening cue many a performer has been found sitting on the mic rather than wearing it.

- To put on the microphone, bring it up underneath the talent's shirt or jacket and attach it securely on the outside. Do not put the mic next to jewelry or buttons. If you have to conceal the mic, don't bury it under layers of clothing; try to keep the top of the mic as exposed as possible. Tuck the cable into the talent's belt or clothing so that it cannot pull the mic sideways or, worse, completely off. To further avoid pops and rumbles, put a small loop in the cable just below the mic clip, or try putting a loose knot in the mic cable where it leaves the mic. Wedging a small piece of foam rubber between mic and clothing will further reduce rubbing noises.

- When outdoors, attach the little windscreen that slips over the top of the mic.

- When using a wireless lav, tell the talent to switch the body-pack transmitter to the *off* position during each break. This keeps the battery from running down prematurely and also prevents the transmission of sounds that might be embarrassing to the talent.

- After the show watch that the talent does not get up and walk off the set without first removing the microphone. **ZVL6** ▶ AUDIO→ Microphones→ mic types→ lav mic

Hand microphones   As the name implies, hand microphones are handled by the talent. You select a hand mic for situations in which the talent needs to exercise some control over the sound pickup.

A reporter can move a hand mic closer to his or her mouth when working in noisy surroundings, thereby eliminating much distracting ambience; the reporter can also point it toward the person he or she is interviewing. Because the talent can point the mic toward whoever is doing the talking, you need only a single microphone for an interview with one or even several guests. Performers who do audience participation shows like the hand mic because it allows them to approach people and talk to them spontaneously without an elaborate multiple-microphone setup.

A singer can control the intimacy of the sound (its presence) by holding the unidirectional hand mic very close to his or her mouth during an especially soft passage and pulling it farther away when the song gets louder and more external. Experienced singers use the hand mic as an important visual element; they work the mic during a song by switching it from one hand to the other to signal—visually—a transition or change of pace or simply to supply additional visual interest. **SEE 7.10**

7.10 USE OF DIRECTIONAL MICROPHONE BY SINGER
To emphasize the richness of his voice, the singer holds the directional hand mic close to his mouth.

Edward Aiona

When the hand mic is used outdoors for numerous production tasks and under a great variety of weather conditions, you need a rugged mic that tolerates rough handling and extreme conditions. Dynamic hand mics with built-in pop filters are popular for such productions. Singers, on the other hand, often demand more sound quality than a field reporter and prefer high-quality condenser hand mics.

The control of the mic by the talent can also be a disadvantage. Inexperienced talent often block their own and their guests' faces; this no-no becomes especially apparent when the mic has a large, colored pop filter attached to it. Also, in the excitement of the interview, an inexperienced reporter may aim the microphone toward the guest when asking the question and toward himself or herself when listening to the answer. As humorous as this unintentional comedy routine may seem to the viewer, it is not funny to the production people who see their professional efforts undermined by such a mistake.

Other disadvantages of using a hand mic are that the talent's hands are not free to do other things, such as demonstrate a product. And, unless it is a wireless hand mic, pulling the cable while working a hand mic is not always easy to do.

Here are some hints for working with a hand microphone:

- During rehearsal, check the action radius of the mic cable. Also see that the cable has free travel and will not catch on furniture or scenery. Checking the reach of the cable is especially important when the mic is connected to a camcorder.

- Test the microphone before the video recording or live transmission. Say a few of the opening lines so that the audio engineer or camcorder operator can adjust the volume of the audio signal. When there are several mics in the immediate vicinity and you need to find out which one is turned on, do not blow or whistle into it—or, worse, whack it; rather, lightly scratch the pop filter. This scratching noise will enable the audio technician to identify your microphone and separate it from the others.

- When using a hand mic in the field under normal conditions (the environment is not excessively loud, and there is little or no wind), hold the microphone at chest level and speak *across* rather than into it. **SEE 7.11** In noisy and windy conditions, hold the mic closer to your mouth. **SEE 7.12**

7.11 NORMAL POSITION OF HAND MICROPHONE
In a fairly quiet environment, the hand mic should be held at chest height. The performer speaks across the mic rather than into it.

7.12 POSITION OF HAND MICROPHONE IN NOISY SURROUNDINGS
In environments with a lot of ambient noise, the performer holds the mic closer to the mouth and speaks into the mic rather than across it.

■ When using a directional hand microphone, hold it close to your mouth and speak or sing directly into it, as shown in figure 7.10.

■ When using a hand mic to interview a child, do not remain standing; squat down so that you are at the child's level. In this way you establish personal contact with the child, and the camera can get a good two-shot. SEE 7.13

■ If the mic cable gets tangled during a take, do not panic and yank on it. Stop where you are and continue your performance while trying to get the attention of the floor manager or somebody else who can untangle it for you.

■ If you need to use both hands while holding a hand mic, tuck it temporarily under your arm so that it can still pick up your voice.

■ When the hand mic is connected directly to a camcorder, the camera operator should also turn on the camera mic (built-in or attached). The camera mic will supply a second audio track with the ambient sounds without interfering with the hand mic, which is supplying the primary audio. In fact, you should always turn on the camera mic, even if you don't intend to use the ambience. Most likely, these sounds will come in handy during postproduction editing. **ZVL7** AUDIO→ Microphones→ mic types→ camera mic

KEY CONCEPT

Always test the hand mic before using it in a production.

7.13 INTERVIEWING A CHILD
When interviewing a child, squat down and hold the mic toward the child. The child is now more aware of you than the mic, and the camera operator can include both faces in the shot.

Boom microphones   Whenever the microphone is to be kept out of the picture, it is usually suspended from a fishpole or big boom. Whatever microphone is suspended from such a device is called a boom mic, regardless of its pickup pattern or sound-generating element. But because the boom mic is usually farther away from its sound source than a lavalier or hand mic, hypercardioid or supercardioid shotgun mics are used. As you recall, such highly directional microphones can pick up sounds over a fairly great distance and make them seem to come from close by. You can aim the mic toward the principal sound source while eliminating or greatly reducing all other sounds that lie outside its narrow pickup pattern. Note, however, that it is equally efficient at picking up extraneous noise that lies in its pickup path.

Fishpole   A fishpole is a sturdy, lightweight metal pole that can be extended. The shotgun mic is attached to the pole with a shock mount, which absorbs the vibrations of the pole and the rubbing noises of the mic cable. Always test the microphone before each take to see if the shock mount is transferring the handling noise or pole vibrations. Even the best shotgun mic is rendered useless by a noisy pole or shock mount.

If a scene is shot fairly tightly (with tight medium shots and close-ups), you can use a short fishpole, which is much easier to handle than a long one. You can position it to pick up the sound from either above or below the source. If the sound pickup is from above, hold the boom in your outstretched arms and dip it into the scene as needed. **SEE 7.14** If the sound pickup is from below the source, turn the pole so that the mic is pointing up toward the person speaking. **SEE 7.15**

When the shots are wider and you need to be farther away from the scene, you must use a long fishpole. Because the long fishpole is heavier and more difficult to handle, you should anchor it in a belt and raise and lower it as you would an actual fishing pole. The long fishpole is usually held above the sound source. **SEE 7.16**

Pencil microphone   When picking up dialogue in the studio, some audio engineers prefer to use a pencil mic on a short fishpole. This is a short condenser mic with a cardioid pickup pattern that is often also used for music pickup. The advantage of a pencil mic is that it is very

7.14 SHORT FISHPOLE USED FROM ABOVE
The short fishpole is normally held high and dipped into the scene as needed.

7.15 SHORT FISHPOLE USED FROM BELOW
The short fishpole can also be held low with the mic pointed up for good sound pickup.

7.16 LONG FISHPOLE
The long fishpole can be anchored in a belt and raised and lowered much like an actual fishing pole. It is usually held above the sound source.

lightweight and has a wider pickup pattern than a shotgun. But isn't a shotgun the ideal mic for a boom because it is highly directional and can pick up sounds over a considerable distance? Yes, it is, especially if you are relatively far from the sound source or in a fairly noisy environment. But if you are to studio-record dialogue between two or more people in a scene that permits you to get close with the fishpole, the pencil mic's slightly wider pickup pattern is an advantage. Because the pickup pattern is a little wider than a shotgun's, you do not always have to point the mic from one person to the other during an exchange of dialogue but can often find an optimal pickup spot between the two speakers. As a side benefit, the lighter mic makes the fishpole operation considerably less tiring.

Here are some additional hints for operating a shotgun mic or pencil mic mounted on a fishpole:

- Always wear headphones so that you can hear what the mic is picking up (including unwanted sounds, such as the drone of an airplane during a Civil War scene). Listen especially for the low rumble of wind, which is easy to miss when concentrating on dialogue.

- With a fishpole it is especially important that you check the reach of the mic cable. Because you must concentrate on the position of the mic during the pickup, you will not be able to monitor the cable.

- Check that the cable is properly fastened to the pole and that it does not tug on the microphone.

- If the performers walk while speaking, you need to walk with them, holding the mic in front of them. If the camera shoots straight on (along the z-axis), you need to walk slightly ahead and to the side of the talent, holding the mic in front of them. If the blocking is lateral (along the x-axis), you need to stay in front, walking backward, while keeping your eyes on the talent and the mic; be careful not to bump into obstacles. Rehearse the walk a few times before the actual take. If possible, have a floor person guide you during the take.

- Watch for shadows that the boom may cast on persons or objects in camera range. **ZVL8** AUDIO→ Microphones→ mic types→ boom mic

Handholding a shotgun mic is as simple as it is effective. You become the boom—and a very flexible one at that. The advantage of holding the shotgun mic is that you can walk up to the scene as close as the camera allows, aiming the mic quickly and easily in various directions. **SEE 7.17**

Some audio people insist on covering the handheld shotgun with a windsock even when shooting indoors, but it is a must when shooting outdoors. As you have learned, the windsock reduces and often eliminates wind noise. Hold the microphone only by its shock mount—never directly. This minimizes handling noise and also prevents covering up the microphone ports—the openings in the mic barrel that make the mic directional.

Edward Aiona

7.17 **HANDHELD SHOTGUN MICROPHONE**
Hold the shotgun mic only by its shock mount. When it's used outdoors, the windscreen and windsock are a must.

Big boom   When used for an elaborate studio production, such as the video recording of a soap opera or sitcom, shotgun mics are suspended from a big boom, more accurately called a studio boom or perambulator boom. A boom operator, who stands or sits on the boom platform, can extend or retract the boom, tilt it up and down, pan it sideways, rotate the mic toward the sound source, and even have the whole boom assembly moved. This is all to have the microphone as close to the sound source as possible while keeping it out of the camera's view.

A studio boom is quite large and takes up a lot of operating space. In some cases it takes two operators: one to work the microphone boom and the other to reposition the boom during an especially tricky scene. You will discover that operating a boom is at least as difficult as running a camera.

Desk and stand microphones   Desk microphones are hand mics mounted on a tabletop stand. You use them for panel shows, public hearings, speeches, and news conferences. Because the people using them are usually more concerned with what they are saying than with the quality of the audio, they frequently (albeit unintentionally) bang on the table or kick it while moving in their chairs, and sometimes even turn away from the microphone while speaking. Considering all these hazards, which microphones would you suggest for a desk mic? If you recommend an omnidirectional dynamic mic, you are right. This type of microphone is best suited to abuse. If you need even more precise sound separation, use a unidirectional dynamic mic.

When placing the microphones, you can use a single mic for each speaker or to serve two people simultaneously. Because microphones can cancel each other's frequencies when positioned too closely together—known as multiple-microphone interference—you should place the individual mics at least three times as far apart as any mic is from its user. **SEE 7.18**

Despite your careful placement of the multiple desk mics, inexperienced—and even experienced—users are sometimes compelled to grab the mic and pull it toward them as soon as they are seated. To save your nerves and optimize sound pickup, simply tape the mic stands to the table.

7.18 SETUP FOR MULTIPLE DESK MICROPHONES

To avoid multiple-microphone interference when using several desk mics for a panel show, place them at least three times as far apart as any mic is from its user.

Stand mics are hand microphones that are clipped to a sturdy floor stand. They are used for singers, speakers, musical instruments, and any other sound source that has a fixed position. The quality of mics used on stands ranges from rugged dynamic mics for news conferences to high-quality condenser mics for singers and instrumental pickups.

For some performers, such as rock singers, the microphone stand is an important prop. They tilt it back and forth, hold themselves up by it, and even swing it through the air like a sword (not recommended, by the way, especially if the microphone is still attached).

Headset microphones   Sportscasters and other performers who are announcing an event often use a headset microphone. **SEE 7.19** This type of mic combines an

7.19 HEADSET MICROPHONE

The headset mic comprises a good-quality microphone and earphones that carry a split audio feed: one carries the program sound and the other carries instructions from the production team.

Mic

earphone headset with a good-quality microphone. The earphones can carry a split audio feed, which means that the talent can hear the program sound (including his or her own voice) in one ear and instructions from production people in the other. Use headset microphones for sportscasters and talent who announce live events in the field. They have their hands free to handle scripts or event lists, can listen to the program audio and the producer's or director's instructions, and speak into a high-quality microphone.

Wireless, or radio, microphones Wireless microphones are also called radio mics because they broadcast the audio signal from a microphone transmitter to a receiver, which in turn is connected to the camcorder, mixer, or audio console.

The most popular wireless microphones are hand mics used by singers. These high-quality mics have a transmitter and an antenna built into their housing. The performer is totally unrestricted and can move about unimpeded by a mic cable. The receiver is connected by cable to the audio console for sound control and mixing. Because each wireless mic has its own frequency, you can use several simultaneously without signal interference.

Another popular radio mic is the wireless lavalier, which is often used in news and interviews, in electronic field production, and occasionally in sports. If, for example, you are asked to pick up the breathing of a bicyclist during a race or of a climber on a summit bid, a wireless lav is the obvious choice. They are sometimes used for dramatic studio productions instead of boom mics.

The wireless lavalier is plugged into a small transmitter that is worn by the talent. You put the transmitter in the performer's pocket or tape it to the body and string the short antenna wire along the pants, skirt, or shirtsleeve or around the waist. The receiver is similar to that used with wireless hand mics. **SEE 7.20**

Unfortunately, using wireless mics is not without drawbacks. The signal pickup depends on where the talent is relative to the receiver. If the talent walks beyond the transmitter's range, the signal will first become intermittent and then be lost

Belt-pack transmitter

Lavalier mic with windscreen

Wireless mic receiver

Azden Corporation

7.20 WIRELESS LAVALIER MICROPHONE AND RECEIVER

Wireless lavaliers are connected to a small transmitter worn by the talent. The receiver picks up the signal and sends it by cable to the audio console.

altogether. For example, if the talent moves behind a tall building or near high-voltage lines or somebody using a cell phone, the audio may become distorted or totally overpowered by the extraneous signals. Concrete walls, X-ray machines, and even the talent's perspiration can affect the transmission and reduce or distort the signal strength. Although wireless equipment has an assigned frequency that is purposely different from police and fire transmissions, you may occasionally pick up a first-responder call instead of the talent's comments. **ZVL9** AUDIO→ Microphones→ mic types→ wireless mic

The table on the facing page gives an overview of some of the more popular microphones. Realize, however, that new mics are developed all the time and that model numbers change accordingly. **SEE 7.21**

■ SOUND CONTROL

When using a small camcorder to record a friend's birthday party, you are probably unconcerned about the various steps of audio control. All you need to do is put a tape or memory card in the camcorder and check that the built-in mic is turned on and in the AGC mode. *AGC* stands for *automatic gain control*—it automatically adjusts the volume of the various sounds to optimal levels, eliminating the need for manual volume control. But because the AGC cannot distinguish between desirable sounds and noise, it amplifies both indiscriminately.

If the audio requirement is more demanding, such as controlling the volume during an outdoor interview or when somebody is playing a musical instrument, you need to switch from AGC to manual control.

Manual Volume Control

As mentioned previously, the better (and more expensive) camcorders have two XLR (balanced) microphone inputs and allow you to switch from AGC to manual volume control for both inputs by using small pots (rotary controls) or the menu on the foldout monitor. Try to do this switchover before you are in the field; the commands are often buried in submenus and are not always easy to activate when you are in a hurry. Also, you will quickly learn that even the best foldout monitors wash out in bright sunlight, making the menus hard if not impossible to see. Once you have switched to manual volume control, you can set a level for each of the two mic inputs before you start recording. You can then monitor the input volume in the viewfinder display.

Although some high-end camcorders have four audio inputs, most camcorders have only two audio channels. Try to use one channel (normally channel 1) for the external mic and the other (channel 2) for recording ambient sound with the camera mic. If there are more than two sound sources, you need to control and mix (combine) them before they can be recorded on one of the two audio tracks. The necessary equipment to do so consists of the audio mixer, the audio console, and the audio cables and patch panel.

7.21 TABLE OF MICROPHONES

	MICROPHONE	TYPE AND PICKUP PATTERN	USE
Corporation	Sennheiser MKH 70	Condenser Supercardioid	Studio boom, fishpole. Good for EFP and sports.
Electronics, Inc.	Sony ECM 672	Condenser Supercardioid	Fishpole. Excellent for indoors.
Neumann GmbH	Neumann KM-184	Condenser Cardioid	Pencil mic. Used on fishpole for dialogue pickup.
Electro-Voice	Electro-Voice 635A or RE50	Dynamic Omnidirectional	Rugged hand mics. Good for all-weather ENG.
Shure, Inc.	Shure SM63L	Dynamic Omnidirectional	Fairly rugged. Excellent for ENG.
Electro-Voice	Electro-Voice RE16	Dynamic Supercardioid	All-purpose hand mic. Good outdoors (ENG/EFP).
Shure, Inc.	Shure SM58	Dynamic Cardioid	Hand mic for singer. Crisp, lively sound.
beyerdynamic, Inc.	Beyerdynamic M59	Dynamic Hypercardioid	Hand mic. Excellent for ENG.
Electronics, Inc.	Sony ECM 55 or ECM 77	Condenser Omnidirectional	Lavalier. Good voice pickup. Good studio mics that mix well with boom mics.
Electronics, Inc.	Sony ECM 88	Condenser Omnidirectional	Very small lavalier. Excellent quality. Low handling and wind noise.
Electronic Corporation	Sennheiser ME 2	Condenser Omnidirectional	Very small lavalier mic.

7.22 AUDIO FIELD MIXER

The audio mixer allows you to control the volume of a limited number of sound inputs and mix them into a single or stereo output signal. This mixer has three inputs with volume controls and one output with a master fader.

LED VU meter

Input volume controls   Master fader   Headphone jack

ATI Audio, Inc.

Audio Mixer

The audio mixer amplifies the weak signals that come from the microphones and other sound sources and lets you control the sound volume and mix two or more sound inputs. Actually, what you control and mix are not the sounds themselves but the signals, which are then translated back into actual sounds by the loudspeaker. **ZVL10** AUDIO→ Systems→ try it

A normal monophonic audio mixer has three or four XLR inputs and one output of the manipulated signal. A stereo mixer has two outputs, one for the left channel and another for the right. Normally, mixers have a rotary pot (for potentiometer) for each input and one master pot or *fader* (two for stereo mixers). They also have a monitor *jack* (outlet) for your earphones so that you can hear the outgoing signal. A *VU meter*, which measures in volume units the relative amplitude (loudness) of the incoming sound signals, helps you visually monitor the volume of each incoming source and the final line-out signal that leaves the mixer. **SEE 7.22** **ZVL11** AUDIO→ Consoles and mixers→ parts

Mic- and line-level inputs   Normally, professional mixers give you a choice between mic and line inputs, unless they do the switching internally. The difference between the two is that the mic-level input is for weak audio signals, such as those coming from a microphone. The line-level input is for relatively strong audio signals, such as from a video recorder (VR) or CD player. If you plug the output of a CD player into the mic input, a preamplifier will unnecessarily boost the sound; most likely, it will become grossly distorted. If you plug a microphone into the line input, you need to turn the volume control way up to hear anything and in so doing will inevitably cause extensive noise in the audio signal.

If you don't know whether an input source is suited for the mic-level input or the line-level input, do a brief test recording. If the recording sounds much too loud and distorted, you plugged a line-level source into a mic-level input. If you have to crank the volume up all the way just to hear anything, you plugged a mic-level source into a line-level input. If it sounds just about right and responds to the volume control as it should, you plugged the sound source into the correct input. **ZVL12** AUDIO→ Consoles and mixers→ signals

Controlling the volume   Controlling sound volume—or riding gain—is not only to make weak sounds louder and loud sounds softer but also to keep the sounds at a level where they do not get distorted. This is especially important when you work with digital audio. To increase the loudness of a sound, you turn the pot clockwise or push the horizontal fader up, away from you. To reduce the sound volume, you turn the pot counterclockwise or pull the fader down, toward you. The VU meter reflects the volume (gain) adjustment by oscillating along a calibrated scale. **SEE 7.23** Some audio mixers and consoles have VU meters with LED (light-emitting diode) displays instead of oscillating needles (see 7.22).

Adjust peak levels to fall near 0

7.23 VU METER

The volume-unit meter indicates the relative loudness of sound. The scale is given in volume units, ranging from –20 to +3 (upper scale), and percentages, ranging from 0 to 100 (lower scale).

If the volume is very low and the needle of the standard VU meter barely moves from the extreme left, or if the LED meter remains at the bottom of the scale, you are riding the audio "in the mud." When loud sounds make the needle hit the right side of the meter, you are "bending" or "pinning" the needle and should turn the volume down to avoid distortion.

When recording analog sound, try to keep the needle between 60 and 100 percent on the lower scale (or between –5 and 0 on the upper scale). Don't worry if the needle spills occasionally into the red, but keep it from oscillating entirely in this overload zone. Most LED meters change color when the sound is overmodulated, that is, when the audio signals are boosted too much. All of these systems indicate visually whether there is a sound signal in the system and how loud the sound is relative to a given volume scale.

When working with digital audio, however, you need to keep the volume lower than with analog audio. Because digital audio does not have any "headroom" that absorbs occasional bending-the-needle volume levels, keep the master fader at about –6 decibels (dB) instead of the 0 dB level. Newer machines lower the VU scale so that you can set the master fader at the accustomed 0 dB as the standard volume level. If the incoming volume is too high, it will clip the audio signal, which translates into sound distortion. If volume levels are low, you can always boost them to normal levels in postproduction without adding too much noise, but you cannot eliminate the distortion that resulted from recording at too high a volume. Overloading digital audio not only results in distorted sound but also adds considerable noise to the recording. **ZVL13** AUDIO→ Consoles and mixers→ control | try it

XLR pad   One way to prevent such high-volume distortion in digital sound is to use the XLR pad. This volume control looks like an XLR connector, with which you can join two balanced audio cables (see figure 7.26). By simply plugging the cable coming from the sound source into one end of the XLR pad, and another cable, which connects your audio to the camcorder or audio recorder, into the other end, you have pretty much eliminated the dreaded overload distortion.

Audio console line-out: 0 VU

VR input (recording level): 0 VU

© Cengage Learning 2011

7.24 CALIBRATING AUDIO CONSOLE AND VIDEO RECORDER VOLUME LEVELS

The VU meter on the VR input is adjusted to the 0 VU line-out signal of the console. Once calibrated, both VU meters must read 0 VU (or the designated standard operating level).

Sound calibration When the sound signals go through a mixer or the console before reaching the camcorder or an audio-recording device, you must adjust the recorder's volume meter so that it reads the identical volume units as on the mixer or console VU meter. This adjustment is called sound calibration. Generally, the audio technician feeds a 0 VU tone to the video recorder or other recording system. As mentioned before, some audio technicians suggest calibrating the system at a designated VU setting that is below the standard analog operating level of 0 VU. **SEE 7.24** `ZVL14` AUDIO→ Consoles and mixers→ calibration

Live field mixing Mixing means combining two or more sounds. You don't need a mixer if you simply interview somebody in the field: you plug the interviewer's hand mic into the appropriate input on the camcorder, turn on the camera mic for ambience, and start recording. But if you have a complicated audio assignment that requires more than two inputs or precise volume control beyond what the AGC or the camcorder volume controls can give you, a small mixer will come in handy.

The following guidelines are intended to assist you with field-mixing tasks, but observe this caveat: if at all possible, try to avoid intricate sound mixing in the field. It is usually easier to achieve a satisfactory mix if you record the various sound sources separately and then do the mixing in postproduction. That said, here are some of the most basic field-mixing guidelines:

■ Even if you have only a few inputs, label each one with what it controls: mic for the host and the guest, ambience mic, and so forth.

- Double-check all inputs from wireless microphone systems. They have a pesky habit of malfunctioning just before the start of an event.

- Always send a test tone at 0 VU (or whatever standard operating level you are working with) from the mixer to the video recorder before the actual recording. Adjust the VU meter on the VR (either the camcorder or a separate unit) so that it also reads 0 VU (or other standard). You have now calibrated the output from the mixer with the input of the recorder.

- Be sure to switch each input to the correct input level (mic or line). Many field productions have been ruined by somebody's not paying attention to the correct input setting.

- When working a mixer, set the master pot to 0 VU (or other standard), then adjust the volume of the various inputs for the proper mix. Watch the VU meter of the master pot (line-out). If it spills into the red zone, readjust the volume of the inputs but leave the master pot at the designated standard operating level.

- For field recording, use an XLR pad to avoid volume overload.

- If you have to do a complicated sound pickup in the field, protect yourself by feeding it not only to the camcorder but also to a separate audio recorder.

- Again, record digital sound at a lower level than analog sound. It is easier to boost a weak sound signal than to get the distortion out of an overmodulated one.

Audio Console

You won't usually need a large audio console for most routine television shows, such as interviews and news, although some productions in high schools and colleges require complex audio setups from time to time. For example, a video recording of a band or an orchestra requires an amazingly elaborate audio setup; a small audio console will no longer suffice. It is always easier to use a larger console for a small audio job than the other way around. This is why fairly large consoles are standard equipment in the audio control rooms and audio postproduction rooms of television stations, large corporate production centers, and major postproduction houses.

Even if a large audio console with its many buttons and levers resembles an exotic control panel in a sci-fi spaceship, there is no reason to be intimidated: the largest audio console operates similarly to a small mixer. Like the mixer, the audio console has inputs, volume meters and controls, mixing circuits, and outputs for the manipulated signal. Unlike the mixer, however, the console has many more inputs and outputs, slide faders instead of rotary pots, and a variety of additional quality controls as well as assignment and on/off switches.

The audio console is relatively large because, instead of the three or four inputs of the small mixer, it may have 24 or even 64. Each input has a separate slide fader and an array of quality controls and switches. Some of the larger consoles have a VU meter for each input channel. The console has additional subgroup faders that control the mix of various inputs before it gets to the two master faders that control the two

7.25 AUDIO CONSOLE

The audio console has many inputs (24 or more for large video productions), each of which has its own slide fader volume control, a variety of quality controls, various on/off and assignment switches, and a VU meter.

channels of the outgoing stereo signal. Each outgoing channel has its own VU meter. **SEE 7.25** Of course, if you work with 5.1 surround sound, you need six outgoing channels (five for the regular speakers placed in front and back, and one (the .1 subwoofer speaker) that takes care primarily of the very low sounds. A 7.1 system needs eight outputs.

An audio console lets you control the volume of all inputs, mix some or all of the input signals in various ways, and manipulate the sound signals of each input channel for the final mix. For example, with the quality controls you can add reverberation (echo) to the incoming sounds; reduce unwanted frequencies such as a hum or squeal; boost or attenuate (reduce) the high, middle, or low frequencies of each sound; and pan (move) a sound to a specific horizontal position between the two stereo speakers. Some controls allow you to adjust the strength of the signal input before it is amplified or to turn off all other inputs except the one you want to hear. You can also group some inputs into subgroups that can then be further mixed with other inputs or subgroups.

Why so many inputs? Because even a simple six-person panel discussion may use up to 10 inputs: six for the panel's microphones (assuming that each panel member has his or her own mic), one for the moderator's mic, one for the CD that contains the opening and closing theme music, and two more for the two servers (digital VRs) that play back program segments during the discussion.

Considering the many microphones and other sound equipment used in a rock concert, even 24 inputs seem modest. Large professional recording consoles are called in-line, which means that for each input there is a corresponding output. Many digital consoles are computer-controlled, which reduces their physical size despite their increased mixing capabilities. **ZVL15** AUDIO→ Consoles and mixers

Much professional audio postproduction mixing is done with a digital audio workstation (DAW), whose audio software takes care of the signal processing and facilitates volume control and mixing.

Cables and Patch Panel

Audio cables provide an essential link between the sound sources and the audio console or other recording equipment. Because cables have no moving parts or complicated circuitry, we tend to consider them indestructible. Nothing could be further from the truth. An audio cable, especially at the connectors, is vulnerable and must be treated with care. Avoid kinking it, stepping on it, or rolling a camera pedestal over it. Even a perfectly good cable may pick up electrical interference from lighting instruments and produce a hum in the audio—another reason for checking out the audio system before the director calls for a rehearsal.

Another potential problem comes from the various connectors that terminate the cables. All professional microphones and camcorders use three-conductor cables

Male Female
XLR connectors

Phone plug

RCA phono plug

Mini plug

Edward Aiona

7.26 AUDIO CONNECTORS
All professional microphones use the three-wire (balanced) cables with XLR connectors. Other audio connectors include the phone plug, the RCA phono plug, and the mini plug.

(called balanced cables) with three-conductor *XLR connectors*. They are relatively immune to outside interference from unwanted frequencies. With an XLR jack in a camcorder, you can use any professional audio cable to connect a high-quality microphone to the camera. Most consumer microphones and small camcorders use the smaller *RCA phono plug* or the *mini plug* for their (unbalanced) cables. Some audio cables terminate with the larger ¼-inch phone plug, which is used for short cable runs to connect musical instruments such as electric guitars. You can, of course, also transport digital audio signals with a USB 2.0 or 3.0, a FireWire (IEEE 1394), or an HDMI (High-Definition Multimedia Interface) cable over short distances. **SEE 7.26** **ZVL16** AUDIO→ Connectors

Adapters make it possible to hook up cables with different connectors. Although you should always have such adapters on hand, avoid using them as much as possible. As with video adapters, an audio adapter is at best a makeshift solution and always a potential trouble spot. **ZVL17** AUDIO→ Connectors→ overview

Using the patch panel will make your life easier by bringing the various sound inputs (microphones, CD players, remote inputs, and the audio tracks of the video recorder) into a desired order on the audio console. For instance, if the various audio sources correspond to widely dispersed faders on the console (such as the lavalier mic of the interviewer at fader 1, the CD player at fader 2, the VR playback at fader 3, and the second lav at fader 4), you may want to move the two lavaliers to adjacent faders, with the VR playback at fader 3 and the CD player at fader 4. Rather than change the cables to different inputs, you simply patch these sound sources so that they appear in the desired order on the console.

Patching can be done in two ways. The old (highly reliable) way is to connect with small cables the incoming signals (called outputs because they are carrying the outgoing audio signals that are to be connected with the audio console) to the various faders on the audio console (called inputs). **SEE 7.27** The most efficient way is to have a computer take over the signal routing, which accomplishes the same

KEY CONCEPT
Always check that the connectors on the cable fit the microphone output and the inputs at the other end (such as camcorder, mixer, or recording device).

KEY CONCEPT
Keep cable connections and adapters to a minimum; each one is a potential trouble spot.

7.27 PATCHING

The four audio sources (lav 1, CD player, VR playback, and lav 2) are rerouted through patching (lav 1, lav 2, VR playback, and CD player).

© Cengage Learning 2011

task faster and without additional cables and connectors. If something goes wrong, however, the computer patch is usually harder to trace than the physical one.

■ SOUND RECORDING

Sound, like video, can be recorded as analog or digital signals. Despite the inherent differences between analog and digital equipment, the old sound-recording rule still applies: careful attention to sound pickup and recording will often save you many frustrating hours of postproduction.

In most video productions, sound is recorded on the audio tracks of the videotape or nonlinear recording device (computer hard drive or memory cards) simultaneously with the video (see chapter 11). Ambitious projects sometimes require that the audio also be recorded on a separate audio recorder. This speeds up audio postproduction, where you may need to replace dialogue or add sound effects and background music to the existing track. Less ambitious audio postproduction, whereby you edit out various unwanted sounds or add a modest amount of sound, such as ambient sound or background music, is normally called *sweetening*. In audio postproduction you can also create an entirely new audio track and add it to the video that has already been shot and edited. Despite the amazing and readily available software for the postproduction of digital sound, you will still be surprised at just how time-consuming even relatively small sweetening jobs can be.

In most video productions, all audio is recorded on the audio tracks of the video recording or on some kind of tapeless recording device.

Digital Audio Recorders

You are certainly familiar with one of the most popular and highly effective small audio recorders: the iPod. With MP3 compression, you can store literally thousands of songs on its tiny hard drive.

Other digital audio recorders are so small you can put them in your pocket, yet they are powerful enough to capture and store hours of high-quality audio. These recorders are especially effective when doing fieldwork. Figure 7.28 shows one of these battery-operated wonder machines. It has two built-in stereo microphones that have an amazing reach, and a standard SD card on which you can store many hours of four-channel audio. **SEE 7.28**

If in a studio production you want to record audio in addition to, or separate from, the video recording, you can use any number of small but highly versatile

Stereo mics

Samson Technologies Corp.

Fostex Company

7.28 HANDHELD DIGITAL STEREO AUDIO RECORDER

This high-quality 4-track stereo recorder uses an SD card and accepts balanced XLR inputs. It is lightweight and small enough to fit in your pocket or purse.

7.29 DIGITAL AUDIO RECORDER

This digital audio recorder can simultaneously record eight tracks on a memory card. It also offers digital sound effects, has two XLR mic inputs and two headphone outputs, and can be connected to a computer and to CD and DVD players.

audio recorders. The digital recorder in figure 7.29 can record eight audio tracks on a memory card, let you add various sound effects, and finally transfer with a USB cable each pair of stereo tracks to a computer for editing or sweetening. **SEE 7.29** Unless you are specializing in audio recording or working with a DAW, such an audio recorder will most likely suffice for most of your video productions.

Optical Discs: CDs and DVDs

The principal optical audio-recording media used in general video production are the familiar CD (compact disc) and DVD (digital versatile disc). They are called "optical" because they use a laser beam for recording and playback on the 4¾-inch disc. The advantages of these recording media are that they are lightweight and easy to use, transport, and store. Compared with audiotape, both discs reproduce almost noise-free high-definition sound (assuming the recording was relatively noise-free in the first place). The DVD can record a much greater amount of data than the CD. The standard CD and DVD can be used only for a onetime recording of data. The rewritable ones can be used for multiple recordings, much like audio- or videotape, memory cards, and computer hard disks.

Although CDs and DVDs use different systems for writing (recording) and reading (playback) digital information, they are similar in operation.

Operational display   A highly accurate LED read-out system, which functions much like a counter, allows you to select a precise starting point regardless of where the segment may be buried on the disc.

7.30 OPERATIONAL DISPLAY FOR OPTICAL DISCS
The typical CD or DVD display consists of seven basic controls: *play, pause, stop, down* button, *up* button, *fast-rewind, and fast-forward.* The *down* button jumps to the beginning of the current track and to previous tracks. The *up* button jumps to the end of the current track and to subsequent tracks.

© Cengage Learning 2011

The standard CD and DVD displays consist of seven basic controls: *play, pause, stop, down* button, *up* button, *fast-rewind,* and *fast-forward.* Pressing the *down* button takes you to the beginning of the current track; repeated pressing skips to previous tracks. The *up* button takes you to the end of the current track; repeated pressing selects subsequent tracks. *Fast-rewind* moves the laser back until you release the button. *Fast-forward* moves the laser forward until you release the button. You can hear the audio in the fast-rewind and fast-forward modes. **SEE 7.30**

Despite all these spectacular achievements in digital audio recording, don't dismiss analog equipment just yet. It is still—or again—used by audio enthusiasts who are fascinated by the "warmer" quality of analog sound. You may still find analog audiotape and audiocassette recorders in operation in some sound studios; but for all practical purposes, analog audio equipment is no longer used in professional video operation.

■ AUDIO POSTPRODUCTION

At this point you probably won't be asked to do complicated sound postproduction work, but you should at least know something about it. Although the sound of most routine television shows (news, game shows, and soap operas) is captured during the production, there are just as many productions where the audio track is sweetened, partially reconstructed, made more complex by mixing various sound tracks, or constructed entirely in the postproduction phase. Most of this work is accomplished in an audio postproduction room.

Audio Postproduction Room

There is no specific formula that will tell you just what goes into such a room and where it should be placed. Each sound designer seems to have a slightly different idea of how to produce optimal sound for video. You will find, however, that most such audio postproduction rooms house a large console, a physical patchbay, various digital recorders, at least one digital audio workstation, a keyboard, and a sampler. All of these pieces of equipment are interconnected. **SEE 7.31**

Digital audio workstation   One of the key pieces of equipment in the postproduction room is the digital audio workstation. The typical DAW has a large-capacity hard drive and software that combines a digital audio-recording system with an audio console and editing system. **SEE 7.32** You can call up and operate with the mouse a

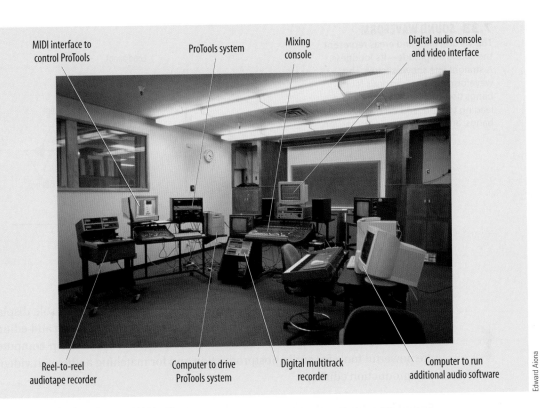

MIDI interface to control ProTools

ProTools system

Mixing console

Digital audio console and video interface

Reel-to-reel audiotape recorder

Computer to drive ProTools system

Digital multitrack recorder

Computer to run additional audio software

Edward Aiona

7.31 AUDIO POSTPRODUCTION ROOM

The audio postproduction room typically contains a digital audio console, audio recorders, a digital audio workstation, various MIDI connections, and a high-fidelity speaker system.

7.32 DIGITAL AUDIO WORKSTATION DISPLAY

Multiple computer interfaces display a variety of audio control and editing functions. They also activate hardware, such as audio consoles and recorders.

Avid Technology, Inc.

7.33 SOUND WAVEFORM

The vertical lines and areas represent the sound amplitude—its loudness. A straight line shows silence. This waveform illustrates various loud bangs (long spikes), a *vroom* sound leading to more and even louder bangs, and two thumps in succession.

© Cengage Learning 2011

virtual audio console and a great variety of editing controls. The console displays multiple audio tracks as waveforms for accurate sound manipulation and editing. But even relatively inexpensive audio software programs for desktop computers are powerful tools for audio postproduction and for matching audio with video in postproduction editing.

Sound waveform   The purple squiggly lines in the DAW interface in figure 7.32 are waveforms. A **waveform** is a graphic representation of a specific sound or combination of sounds that occur over a period of time. (The waveform on the cover of this book represents the words *video basics.*) The standard waveform shows the basic fluctuations of loudness of a sound—the dynamics—but not how high or low the sound is (its frequency).[1] The larger the vertical squiggles are, the louder the sound is. Silence shows up as a horizontal line with no squiggles above or below. Sudden loud sounds have long spikes. **SEE 7.33**

Once you have learned to interpret the sound waveform on the computer screen, you can select certain sound portions with great precision, delete some, or arrange them in any sequence. When editing, the best place to cut is, of course, where you can find a brief silence.

To synchronize the sound track with the video, the computer provides each video frame and the accompanying sound portion with a corresponding address. The most widely used address system is called the SMPTE time code. The displayed time code reads out hours, minutes, seconds, and frames (30 frames per second). (See chapter 12 for a more detailed explanation of the SMPTE time code.)

Automated Dialogue Replacement

Large postproduction rooms, like the ones for digital cinema, have an area specifically for automated dialogue replacement. Although it's sometimes called "automatic

---

1. See Stanley R. Alten, *Audio in Media,* 9th ed. (Boston: Wadsworth, 2011), pp. 421–30.

dialogue replacement," the process is anything but automatic. It requires a fairly large video projection that allows the talent to see the video playback of themselves while repeating their lines in perfect lip sync, perhaps with a dash or two of added emotion—all in the interest of improving the original audio.

SYNTHESIZED SOUND

If we can translate sound into digital information and then manipulate it, could we not use the computer to create digital information that can be translated into actual sound? Yes. The audio synthesizer, commonly called a keyboard, can generate a great variety of complex frequencies that we perceive as sounds produced by musical instruments. A single key can approximate the sound of a piano, an electric or acoustic guitar, a drum, a trumpet, and many more instruments. Such a keyboard, which you can easily carry under your arm, offers more sounds than a rock band and a symphony orchestra combined.

The computer can also be used to grab brief portions of a regular sound, such as a telephone ring, translate it into digital form, store it, and make it available for all sorts of manipulations. With the help of sampling software, you can repeat the telephone ring as often as you want, transform it into a shrill beat, speed it up or slow it down, play it backward, have it overlap, or distort it to the point that you no longer recognize the original sound.

> **KEY CONCEPT**
> Sounds and sound mixes can be entirely computer-generated.

SOUND AESTHETICS

Even the most sophisticated digital sound equipment is of little use if you cannot use your ears—that is, exercise some aesthetic judgment. Sounds can make us feel about pictures in a certain way and add energy to a scene. You can make the same scene appear high-energy or low-energy, happy or sad, simply by putting some happy or sad, or loud or soft, sounds behind it.

The basic aesthetic factors that can help you achieve an effective audio/video relationship are context, figure/ground, sound perspective, continuity, and energy and mood.

Context

In most studio sound-recording sessions, we try to eliminate as much of the ambient sound as possible. In the field, however, the ambient sounds are often as important as the principal ones: they help establish the general context of the event. If you shoot a scene at a busy downtown intersection, the environmental sounds of cars, horns, streetcars, and buses; people talking, laughing, and moving about; the doorman's whistle for a taxi; and the occasional police siren—all are important clues to where you are, even if you don't show the sound sources in the video portion.

Think of recording a small orchestra. If you do a studio recording, the coughing of one of the crewmembers or musicians during an especially soft passage would

> **KEY CONCEPT**
> Sounds can establish the event context.

certainly prompt a retake. Not so in the context of a live concert. We have learned to interpret the occasional coughing and other such environmental sounds as proof of the live quality of the event.

As pointed out previously, in normal field recording you should try to use one mic and audio track for the primary sound source, such as a reporter standing on a street corner, and another mic (usually the camera mic) and the second audio track for recording environmental sounds. Separating the sounds on different tracks as much as possible makes it easier to mix the two in the proper proportions in post-production editing.

Figure/Ground

One important perceptual factor is the figure/ground principle. This refers to our tendency to organize our environment into a relatively mobile figure (a person or car) and a relatively stable background (wall, houses, or mountains). If we expand this principle a little, we can say that we single out an event that is important to us and assign it the role of the figure while relegating all other events to the background or, as we just called it, the environment.

For example, if you are waiting for your friend and finally see her in a crowd, she immediately becomes the focus of your attention—the foreground—while the rest of the people become the background. The same happens with sound. We have the ability to perceive, within limits, the sounds we want or need to hear as the figure while pushing all other sounds into the background. For example, if you sit in a busy restaurant and listen to your friend telling you about her new video, you ignore mentally all the other people who are talking at the other tables.

When re-creating such a figure/ground relationship with sound, we usually make the "figure" somewhat louder or give it a distinct quality in relation to the ambient sounds. In the same way, we can easily bring a background sound up in volume to become the figure and relegate the other sounds to the ground. Fading down some sounds to relegate them as background and bringing up the volume of other sounds as foreground has become routine in many documentaries where there is a voice-over narration. In fact, you can get software that automates such figure/ground sound manipulations, a procedure known as "ducking audio."

KEY CONCEPT

The figure/ground principle in audio refers to making a selected sound or group of sounds (figure) louder and more distinct than the ambient sounds (ground).

Sound Perspective

Sound perspective means that close-up pictures are matched with relatively close sounds, and long shots are matched with sounds that seem to come from farther away. Close sounds have more presence than far sounds—a sound quality that makes us feel as though we are near the sound source. Faraway sounds seem to be more distant from us.

As you may recall, this desirable variation of sound presence is virtually eliminated when using lavalier mics. Because the distance between mic and mouth remains the same regardless of whether the performer is seen in a close-up or a long shot, the sound has the same presence. This is why you should use boom mics when controlling sound presence. The boom mic can be moved close to a performer during a close-up and must be somewhat farther away during a long shot to keep out of the picture—a simple solution to a potential audio problem.

KEY CONCEPT
Close-ups need closer sound presence than do long shots.

Continuity

Sound continuity is especially important in postproduction. You may have noticed the sound quality of a reporter's voice change depending on whether he or she was speaking on- or off-camera. In this case, the reporter used one type of microphone when on-camera and another when off-camera; the reporter also changed environments from on-location to the studio. This change in microphones and locations gives speech a distinctly different quality. Although this difference may not be too noticeable during the actual recording, it becomes readily apparent when the two audio sources are edited together in the final show.

What should you do to avoid such continuity problems? Use identical microphones for the on- and off-camera narration or at least ones that sound alike and, if necessary, mix the off-camera narration with some of the separately recorded ambient sounds. You can feed the ambient sounds to the reporter through earphones while recording the voice-over narration, which will help the reporter re-create the on-site energy.

Sound is also a chief element for establishing visual continuity. A rhythmically precise piece of music can help achieve continuity in a series of pictures that otherwise do not cut together very well. Music and sound are often the critical link among abruptly changing shots and scenes.

KEY CONCEPT
Sound is an important factor in providing shot continuity.

Energy and Mood

Unless you want to achieve a special effect through contradiction, you should match the general energy and mood of the pictures with sounds of similar energy and mood. Energy refers to all of the factors in a scene that communicate a certain degree of aesthetic force and power. The major ones are volume and rhythm. High-energy music, for example, is louder and has a more driving beat than low-energy music.

Mood refers to how the music makes us feel: happy, sad, excited, sleepy, uneasy, or frightened. Unless you want to create a conflict between video and audio, high-energy scenes, such as a series of big-screen close-ups of a rock band in action, can stand higher-energy sounds than a more tranquil scene, such as close-ups of lovers sitting by a lakeshore. A sad event is usually accompanied by low-energy music; a happy one with higher-energy music. But what, exactly, is happy and sad music? And what are the correct sound levels for high- and low-energy scenes? There are no clear-cut answers. You simply need to sense them. No musical chart or volume meter can substitute for your aesthetic judgment.

KEY CONCEPT
High-energy pictures should be matched with high-energy sounds; low-energy pictures, with low-energy sounds.

M A I N   P O I N T S

▶ **Sound Pickup Principle**

Microphones transduce (transform) the sounds we hear into electric energy—the audio signal.

▶ **Directional Characteristics of Mics**

Omnidirectional mics can hear equally well from all directions; unidirectional, or cardioid, mics can best hear sounds that come from the front. Hyper- and supercardioid mics make faraway sounds that lie in the pickup pattern appear close to the mic.

▶ **Mechanics of Mics**

Classified by how they are made, there are three types of mics: dynamic (the most rugged), condenser (high-quality but sensitive), and ribbon (high-quality and very sensitive).

▶ **Use of Mics**

Classified by how they are used, microphones can be divided into six types: small lavalier mics, which are clipped to the clothing of the performer; hand mics, which are carried by the performer; boom mics, which are suspended from a fishpole or a studio boom assembly; desk and stand mics, which are mounted on a tabletop stand or an adjustable floor stand; headset mics, which are worn by the performer and include earphones with a split audio feed; and wireless, or radio, mics, which broadcast the audio signal from a transmitter to a receiver. Treat all mics gently and test them before going on the air.

▶ **Sound Control**

When using a camcorder, AGC (automatic gain control) must be switched to manual volume control to ensure acceptable sound. Verify that the audio connectors fit their respective jacks. Carry adapters but use them only in an emergency.

▶ **Audio Mixer and Audio Console**

The mixer amplifies the incoming sound signals, controls the volume of each sound, and mixes (combines and balances) them in specific ways. A field mixer is small and normally has a maximum of four inputs. The audio console is much larger; it has many more inputs, each of which has a volume control and various quality and sound selection controls.

▶ **Sound Recording**

There are a great variety of digital audio recorders. They record on either hard drives or memory cards. Optical discs include read/write CDs (compact discs), and the higher-capacity DVDs (digital versatile discs).

▶ **Audio Postproduction**

Audio postproduction consists of sweetening, mixing various sound tracks, and creating new ones. The audio postproduction room contains a variety of sound equipment, most notably a digital audio workstation (DAW).

▶ *Sound Waveform*

The sound waveform is a graphic representation of the dynamics of various sounds as they progress in time. It facilitates sound editing.

▶ *Synthesized Sound*

Once sounds are in digital form, you can manipulate them with computer software. Computerized sound equipment, such as the keyboard, can create—synthesize—its own sounds.

▶ *Sound Aesthetics*

The basic aesthetic factors that can help you achieve an effective audio/video relationship are context, figure/ground, sound perspective, continuity, and energy and mood.

Z E T T L' S   V I D E O L A B

For your reference or to track your work, the *Zettl's VideoLab* program cues in this chapter are listed here with their corresponding page numbers.

KEY TERMS

additive primary colors Red, green, and blue. Ordinary white light (sunlight) can be separated into the three primary light colors. When these three colored lights are combined in various proportions, all other colors can be reproduced.

attached shadow Shadow that is on the object itself. It cannot be seen independent of (detached from) the object.

background light Illumination of the set pieces and the back-drop. Also called *set light*.

back light Illumination from behind the subject and opposite the camera; usually a spotlight.

baselight Even, nondirectional (diffused) light necessary for the camera to operate optimally. Refers to the overall light intensity.

cast shadow Shadow that is produced by an object and thrown (cast) onto another surface. It can be seen independent of the object.

color temperature Relative reddishness or bluishness of white light, as measured on the Kelvin (K) scale. The norm for indoor video lighting is 3,200K; for outdoors, 5,600K.

contrast The difference between the brightest and the darkest spots in a video image.

diffused light Light that illuminates a relatively large area and creates soft shadows.

directional light Light that illuminates a relatively small area and creates harsh, clearly defined shadows.

falloff The speed (degree) with which a light picture portion turns into shadow areas. *Fast falloff* means that the light areas turn abruptly into shadow areas and there is a great difference in brightness between light and shadow areas. *Slow falloff* indicates a very gradual change from light to dark and a minimal brightness difference between light and shadow areas.

fill light Additional light on the opposite side of the camera from the key light to illuminate shadow areas and thereby reduce falloff; usually done with floodlights.

floodlight A lighting instrument that produces diffused light.

foot-candle (fc) The unit of measurement of illumination, or the amount of light that falls on an object. One foot-candle is 1 candlepower of light (1 lumen) that falls on a 1-square-foot area located 1 foot away from the light source.

high-key lighting Light background and ample light on the scene. Has nothing to do with the vertical positioning of the key light.

incident light Light that strikes the object directly from its source. To measure incident light, point the light meter at the camera lens or into the lighting instruments.

key light Principal source of illumination; usually a spotlight.

LED lights *LED* stands for *light-emitting diodes*. A solid-state device that changes electric energy into light energy. Most computer screens use LEDs as the light source.

light plot A plan, similar to a floor plan, that shows the type, size (wattage), and location of the lighting instruments relative to the scene to be illuminated and the general direction of the light beams.

low-key lighting Fast-falloff lighting with dark background and selectively illuminated areas. Has nothing to do with the vertical positioning of the key light.

lux European standard unit for measuring light intensity. One lux is 1 lumen (1 candlepower) of light that falls on a surface of 1 square meter located 1 meter away from the light source. 10.75 lux = 1 foot-candle. Most lighting people figure roughly 10 lux = 1 foot-candle.

photographic principle The triangular arrangement of key, back, and fill lights. Also called *triangle,* or *three-point, lighting.*

reflected light Light that is bounced off the illuminated object. To measure reflected light, point the light meter close to the object from the direction of the camera.

RGB Stands for *red, green,* and *blue*—the basic colors of television.

spotlight A lighting instrument that produces directional, relatively undiffused light.

triangle lighting The triangular arrangement of key, back, and fill lights. Also called *three-point lighting* and *photographic principle.*

white-balance To adjust the color circuits in the camera to produce white color in lighting of various color temperatures (relative reddishness or bluishness of white light).

Light, Color, and Lighting

At this point you may ask why you should bother with reading a whole chapter on lighting when your cell-phone camera can practically see in the dark. The answer is easy: if you want to produce professional-looking video, you need to know at least the basic principles of lighting. It is true that the increased light sensitivity of video cameras has encouraged even some well-known video- and filmmakers to shoot scenes in available light without any additional lighting instruments; but, generally, good lighting still calls for deliberate illumination—to determine where and from what angle the light falls, whether the light should be soft or harsh, and what color it should have. Lighting also, if not especially, calls for the careful control of shadows and their relative transparency.

This chapter introduces you to the art of video lighting and the instruments you need to achieve good lighting for a variety of tasks. Once you have learned the basic lighting principles and practiced applying them, you can ignore them in cases where you want to achieve a special effect. **ZVL1** LIGHTS→ Light introduction

> **KEY CONCEPT**
>
> Lighting is deliberate illumination and shadow control.

▶ **LIGHT**
Directional and diffused light, light intensity and how to measure it, measuring incident and reflected light, and contrast

▶ **SHADOWS**
Attached and cast shadows and controlling falloff

▶ **COLOR**
Additive and subtractive mixing, the color television receiver and generated colors, and color temperature and white-balancing

▶ **LIGHTING INSTRUMENTS**
Spotlights, floodlights, and instruments for specific tasks

▶ **LIGHTING TECHNIQUES**
Operation of lights, lighting safety, studio lighting and the photographic principle, the light plot, last-minute lighting techniques, and field lighting

■ LIGHT

Learning about light and shadows seems like a strange assignment, considering that you have been seeing light and shadows all your life. But it makes more sense when you realize that what you see on a video or film screen is nothing but blobs of light and shadows and that lighting is the calculated interplay of these two elements.

Types of Light

No matter how the light is technically generated, you will work with two basic types: directional and diffused.

Directional light has a precise beam that causes harsh shadows. The sun, a flashlight, and the headlights of a car all produce directional light. You can aim directional light at a specific area without much spill into other areas.

Diffused light causes a more general illumination. Its diffused beam spreads out quickly and illuminates a large area. Because diffused light seems to come from all directions (is omnidirectional), it has no clearly defined shadows; they seem soft and transparent. A good example of diffused light occurs on a foggy day, when the fog operates like a huge diffusion filter for the sun. Observe the shadows in bright sunlight and on an overcast or foggy day; they are quite distinct and dense in sunlight but hardly visible in fog. The fluorescent lighting in elevators and supermarkets is a good example of diffused indoor light. It is used to minimize the harsh shadows on a face or an object and to illuminate large areas.

Light Intensity

An important aspect of lighting is controlling light intensity, or how much light falls onto an object. Also called light level, light intensity is measured in American foot-candles or in European lux. A foot-candle is simply a convenient measurement of illumination—the amount of light that falls on an object. One *foot-candle (fc)* is 1 candlepower of light (called a lumen) that falls on a 1-square-foot area located 1 foot away from the light source. The European measure for light intensity is *lux*—1 lumen of light that falls on a surface of 1 square meter that is 1 meter away from the light source (1 meter is a little more than 3 feet).

If you have foot-candles and want to find lux, multiply the foot-candle figure by 10. Twenty foot-candles is approximately 200 lux (20 × 10 = 200). If you have lux and want to find foot-candles, divide the lux number by 10. Two thousand lux is approximately 200 fc (2,000 ÷ 10 = 200). A room that has an overall illumination of 200 fc, or 2,000 lux, has quite a bit of light or, more technically, has a fairly high degree of light intensity. **ZVL2** LIGHTS→ Measurement→ meters

Baselight   Sometimes you may hear the lighting director (LD) or the video operator (VO) complain that there is not enough baselight. *Baselight* refers to general illumination, or the overall light intensity, such as the 200 fc in the room we just talked about. You determine baselight levels by pointing a light meter (which reads foot-candles or lux) from the illuminated object or scene toward the camera. To check the baselight of your living room, you would walk to the different corners of the room and point the light meter toward a real or imaginary camera position (probably in the middle of the room). **ZVL3** LIGHTS→ Measurement→ baselight

Although some camera manufacturers claim that their cameras can see in the dark, you need a certain amount of light to make the cameras see the colors and the shadows that you see when looking at the scene. In technical parlance you need to activate the imaging device and the other electronics in the camera to produce an optimal video signal at a given f-stop. Although newer cameras and lenses are much more sensitive than older ones and need less light, good, crisp video still demands a reasonable amount of illumination. A handheld camcorder may be able to produce recognizable pictures at light levels as low as 1 or 2 lux; but for high-quality pictures, you need more light. Top-of-the-line studio cameras may still require about 1,000 lux (100 fc) at an f-stop of about $f/8$ for optimal picture quality.[1]

Gain   If there is insufficient light even at the maximum aperture (lowest f-stop number), you need to activate the gain circuits of the camera. Most consumer camcorders do this automatically. On camcorders, studio cameras, and ENG/EFP (electronic news gathering/electronic field production) cameras, the gain is activated either via the camera control unit (CCU) or by a switch on the camera. The gain will boost the weak video signal electronically. High-definition cameras can tolerate a relatively high gain before they show picture "noise," that is, artifacts that show up as colored specks. When video quality is of primary concern, it is better to raise the baselight level than to activate the gain switch.

Measuring Illumination

In critical lighting setups, before turning on the cameras you may want to check whether there is enough baselight and whether the contrast between the light and dark areas falls within the acceptable limits (normally 50:1 to 100:1, depending on the camera; see Contrast on the following page). You can check this with a light meter, which simply measures the number of foot-candles or lux emitted by the lighting instruments—the ***incident light*** (what enters the lens or what comes from a specific instrument) or the ***reflected light*** (bouncing off the lighted object).

Incident light   An incident-light reading gives you an idea of the baselight level in a given area, which translates into how much light the camera receives from a particular location on the set. To measure incident light, stand next to or in front of the illuminated person or object and point the light meter toward the camera lens. Such a quick reading of incident light is especially helpful when checking the prevailing light levels at a remote location.

If you want a more specific reading of the light intensity from certain instruments, point the light meter *into the lights*. To check the relative evenness of the incident

---

1. An f-stop between $f/5.6$ and $f/8$ produces an optimal depth of field. This is why camera specifications use $f/5.6$ or $f/8$ as the norm for optimal light levels. Some manufacturers use $f/11$ in their specifications, with a higher baselight requirement (such as 200 fc). Of course, with larger apertures you can shoot with less light.

light, point the light meter toward the principal camera positions while walking around the set. If the needle or digital read-out stays at approximately the same intensity level, the lighting is fairly even. If the needle or read-out dips way down, the lighting setup has "holes" (unlighted or underlighted areas).

Reflected light   The reading of reflected light is done primarily to check the contrast between light and dark areas. To measure reflected light, stand close to the lighted object or person and point the light meter at the light and shadow sides from the direction of the camera. Be careful not to block the light whose reflection you are trying to measure. As mentioned before, the difference between the two readings will indicate the lighting contrast. Note that the contrast is determined not only by how much light falls on the object but also by how much light the object reflects back into the camera. The more reflective the object, the higher the reflected-light reading will be. A mirror reflects almost all of the light falling onto it; a black velour cloth reflects only a small portion.

Contrast

Contrast refers to the difference between the brightest and the darkest spots in a video image. Contrary to your eye, which can distinguish subtle brightness steps over a contrast ratio with a wide range, even high-end video cameras may be limited to a lower contrast range. Whereas some equipment salespeople might tell you that high-end video cameras can tolerate a contrast that is close to that of our vision, LDs and VOs say that too high a contrast is one of the most common obstacles to producing optimal video. Believe the people who use the cameras rather than sell them. Video professionals prefer a contrast ratio for studio cameras that does not exceed 100:1. The high number of the 100:1 contrast ratio indicates that the brightest spot in the scene is 100 times more intense than the darkest spot. Small digital camcorders will have trouble producing high-quality video that shows bright highlights as well as transparent shadows if the contrast ratio is higher than 50:1.

Measuring contrast   To measure contrast, point a reflected-light meter close to the bright side of the object, then close to the shadow side. (You will read more about measuring contrast in the next section.) The light meter reads the reflected light, first of the bright side (a high reading) and then of the shadow side (a low reading). If, for example, the light meter reads 800 fc in an especially bright area, such as one side of the reporter's face in direct sunlight, and only 10 fc in the dark background, the contrast ratio is 80:1 (800 ÷ 10 = 80). Even with a fairly good digital camcorder, this contrast may be too high for good pictures. **ZVL4** LIGHTS→ Measurement→ contrast

    High-end small camcorders and all professional cameras indicate just which picture areas are overexposed by showing a vibrating zebra-striped pattern over them. Most higher-end camcorders (handheld and shoulder-mounted) let you switch between a 100 percent and a 70 percent zebra setting. In the normal 100 percent mode, all picture areas that show a zebra pattern are overexposed. The 70 percent setting is used primarily to help you achieve correct skin tones. When the zebra stripes appear over the bright areas of the face, the exposure is correct.

As you know, the usual remedy for an overexposed image is to stop down the lens, that is, select a higher f-stop. But, while eliminating the white glare, you also compress the shadow areas into a dense, uniform black. So how can you control contrast?

- If you are outdoors, don't place the person in a sunny spot; move him into the shade. If that is not possible, lighten up the harsh shadows (as explained later in this chapter) or activate one of the neutral density (ND) filters that are built into the camcorder. They act like sunglasses, reducing the overall brightness without affecting the colors too much.

- Indoors you can reduce the light intensity by moving the lighting instrument farther away from the object, diffusing the light beam, or using an electronic dimmer to reduce the intensity of the main light source. (How to do all this is explained later in this chapter.)

- Remove overly bright objects from the scene, especially if you are operating with an automatic iris. A pure white object always presents a lighting hazard, no matter how high a contrast the camera can tolerate. The real problem is that even if the camera can manage a high contrast ratio, the average television set cannot always do likewise. **ZVL5** LIGHTS→ Measurement→ try it

◾ SHADOWS

Although we are quite conscious of light and light changes, we are usually unaware of shadows, unless we seek comfort in them on a particularly hot day or if they interfere with what we want to see. Because shadow control is such an important aspect of lighting, let's take a closer look at shadows and how they influence our perception.

Once you are aware of shadows, you will be surprised by the great variety that surround you. Some seem part of the object, such as the shadow on your coffee cup; others seem to fall onto other surfaces, such as the shadow of a telephone pole that is cast onto the street. Some shadows are dark and dense, as though they were brushed on with thick, black paint; others are so light and subtle that they are hard to see. Some change gradually from light to dark; others do so abruptly. Despite the great variety of shadows, there are only two basic types: attached and cast. **ZVL6** LIGHTS→ Light and shadow→ light

Attached Shadows

Attached shadows seem affixed to the object and cannot be seen independent of it. Take your coffee cup and hold it next to a window or table lamp. The shadow opposite the light source (window or lamp) on the cup is the attached shadow. Even if you wiggle the cup or move it up and down, the attached shadow remains part of the cup. **SEE 8.1**

Herbert Zettl

8.1 ATTACHED SHADOW
The attached shadow is always bound to the illuminated object. It cannot be seen separate from the object.

8.2 ATTACHED SHADOWS DEFINE SHAPE

Attached shadows help define the basic shape of the object. Without attached shadows, we perceive a triangle on the left; with attached shadows, we perceive a cone on the right.

© Cengage Learning 2011

Attached shadows help us perceive the basic form of an object. Without attached shadows the actual shape of an object may remain ambiguous when seen as a picture. In the figure above, the object on the left looks like a triangle; but when you see it with the attached shadows, the triangle becomes a cone. **SEE 8.2**

Attached shadows also contribute to perception of texture. A great amount of prominent attached shadows emphasizes texture; without them things look smoother. Attached shadows on a Styrofoam ball make it look like a moonscape; but when the attached shadows are removed through flat lighting, the ball looks smooth. **SEE 8.3 AND 8.4**

If you had to shoot a commercial for skin cream, you would want to light the model's face in such a way that the attached shadows are so soft that they are hardly noticeable. **SEE 8.5** But if you wanted to emphasize the rich, deep texture of the famous carving of the Aztec Sun Stone (generally known as the Aztec calendar), you would need to light for prominent attached shadows. **SEE 8.6** Highly transparent shadows would make the patterns in the stone hard to see. **SEE 8.7** **ZVL7** LIGHTS→ Light and shadow→ attached

> **KEY CONCEPT**
>
> Attached shadows reveal form and texture.

Because we normally see the main light source as coming from above (the sun, for example), we are used to seeing attached shadows below protrusions and

Herbert Zettl

8.3 ROUGH TEXTURE

Prominent attached shadows emphasize texture. The surface of this Styrofoam ball looks rough.

Herbert Zettl

8.4 SMOOTH TEXTURE

Here the attached shadows are almost eliminated, so the surface of the ball looks relatively smooth.

8.5 ATTACHED SHADOWS MINIMIZED
To emphasize the smoothness of the model's face, attached shadows are kept to a minimum.

8.6 ATTACHED SHADOWS EMPHASIZED
With the light coming from the side, the attached shadows on this Aztec Sun Stone are more prominent, and the rich, deep texture is properly emphasized.

8.7 ATTACHED SHADOWS MINIMIZED
With the light shining directly on the Sun Stone, the lack of attached shadows makes the intricate carvings look relatively flat.

indentations. When you lower the principal light source so that it illuminates an object, such as a face, from below eye level, we experience this departure from the norm as mysterious or spooky. There is probably not a single sci-fi or horror movie that does not use such a shadow-reversal effect at least once. **SEE 8.8** `ZVL8` LIGHTS→ Design→ horror

8.8 REVERSAL OF ATTACHED SHADOWS
The below-eye-level light source causes the attached shadows to fall opposite their expected positions. We interpret such unusual shadow placement as spooky or mysterious.

8.9 CAST SHADOWS

Cast shadows are usually cast by an object onto some other surface. In this case the cast shadows of the railing fall on the boards of the bridge.

Herbert Zettl

Cast Shadows

Unlike attached shadows, ***cast shadows*** can be seen independent of the object causing them. If you make some shadowgraphs on a wall, for instance, you can focus on the shadows without showing your hand. The shadows of telephone poles, traffic signs, or trees cast onto the street or a nearby wall are all examples of cast shadows. Even if the cast shadows touch the base of the objects causing them, they remain cast shadows and will not become attached ones. **SEE 8.9**

Cast shadows help us see where an object is located relative to its surroundings and often what the object that is causing the shadow looks like. They also help orient us in time, at least to some extent. Take another look at figure 8.9. The cast shadow of the bridge railing gives you more detail of how it is built than looking at the actual railing causing it. **ZVL9** LIGHTS→ Light and shadow→ cast

> **KEY CONCEPT**
>
> Cast shadows help tell us where things are and when events take place.

Falloff

Falloff indicates the degree of change from light to shadow. Specifically, it refers to the relative abruptness—the speed—with which light areas turn into shadow areas, or the brightness contrast between the light and shadow sides of an object. An abrupt change from light to dense shadow illustrates fast falloff; it indicates a sharp edge or corner. **SEE 8.10** Slow falloff shows a more continuous change from light to shadow; the gradual shading indicates a curved object. **SEE 8.11**

Fast falloff can also refer to a high contrast between the light and shadow sides of a face. When the shadow side is only slightly darker than the light side and the shadows are highly transparent, the falloff is slow. If both sides of the face are equally bright, there is no falloff. The perception of texture also depends on falloff. Fast-falloff lighting emphasizes wrinkles in a face; slow-falloff or no-falloff lighting hides them (see figure 8.5). **ZVL10** LIGHTS→ Falloff→ fast | slow | none | try it

> **KEY CONCEPT**
>
> Falloff defines the contrast between light and dark areas and how quickly light turns into shadow.

When generating lighting effects with a computer, the relationship between attached and cast shadows and the rate of falloff have to be carefully calculated. For example, if you simulate a light source striking the object from screen-right, the attached shadows must obviously be on its screen-left side (opposite the light source), and the cast shadows must extend in the screen-left direction. Such careful attention to shadow consistency is also important if you cut a live scene electronically into a photographic background (a process called chroma keying; see chapter 9).

Edward Aiona

Edward Aiona

8.10 FAST FALLOFF
The change of light to shadow areas on these buildings is very sudden. The falloff is extremely fast, indicating an edge or a corner.

8.11 SLOW FALLOFF
The attached shadow on this balcony gets gradually darker. The falloff is relatively slow, indicating a curved surface.

■ COLOR

In this section we focus on the basic process of color mixing, the color television receiver and generated colors, and color temperature and white-balancing.

Additive and Subtractive Color Mixing

Recall the discussion about the beam splitter that divides the white light transmitted by the lens into the three primary light colors—red, green, and blue *(RGB)*—and how we can produce all video colors by adding the red, green, and blue light in certain proportions. These are called *additive primary colors* because we mix them by adding one colored light beam on top of others.

If you had three identical slide projectors, you could put a red slide into one, a green slide in the second, and a blue slide in the third and aim them at the screen so that their beams overlapped slightly. **SEE 8.12** What you would perceive is similar to the three overlapping circles shown in the figure. The overlapped RGB light primaries

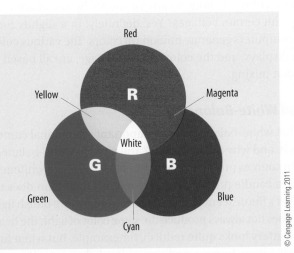

© Cengage Learning 2011

8.12 ADDITIVE COLOR MIXING
When mixing colored light, the additive primaries are red, green, and blue. All other colors can be achieved by mixing certain quantities of red, green, and blue light. For example, the additive mixture of red and green light produces yellow.

show that mixing red and green light adds up to yellow; red and blue mix to a bluish red called magenta; and green and blue combine to make a greenish blue called cyan. Where all three primary light colors overlap, you get white. By dimming all three projectors equally, you get a variety of grays. By turning them all off, you get black. By dimming any one or all projectors independently, you can achieve a wide variety of colors. For example, if the red projector burns at full intensity and the green one at two-thirds intensity with the blue projector turned off, you get a shade of orange. The more you dim the green projector, the more reddish the orange becomes.

You may remember from your finger-painting days that the primary colors were red, blue, and yellow and that mixing red and green paint together did not produce a clean yellow but rather a muddy dark brown. Obviously, paint mixes differently from light. When paint is mixed, its built-in filters subtract certain colors (light frequencies) rather than add them. We call this mixing process subtractive color mixing. Because the video system processes colored light rather than paint, we concentrate here on additive mixing.

Color Television Receiver and Generated Colors

The best way to explain the formation of a color video image is to use an old standard color television set. Instead of the three slide projectors we used for additive color mixing, a CRT (cathode ray tube) color television receiver uses three electron guns in the neck of the picture tube that shoot their beams at myriad red, green, and blue dots—pixels—on the inside of the television screen. As you recall from figure 3.2, one of the three guns hits the red dots, the other the green dots, and the third the blue dots. The harder the guns hit the dots, the more they light up. If the red gun and the green gun hit their dots with full intensity with the blue gun turned off, you get yellow. When all three guns fire at full intensity, you get white; at half intensity, you get gray. All three guns work overtime when you are watching a black-and-white show on a color television set. In the flat-panel displays, the same principle of additive color mixing applies, although the system of activating the pixels is quite different from the CRT one.

Because the video signal consists of electric energy rather than actual colors, couldn't we produce certain colors without a camera simply by stimulating the three types of color pixels with certain voltages? Yes, definitely! In a slightly more complex form, this is how computers generate millions of colors. The various colors in titles and other graphic displays, and the colors on a web page, are all based on the principle of additive color mixing.

Color Temperature and White-Balancing

In chapter 5 you learned that white-balancing is an important operational camera feature. But what exactly is it, and why is it necessary? You need to white-balance a camera because not all light sources produce light of the same degree of whiteness. As mentioned in chapter 5, a candle produces a more reddish light than does the midday sun or a supermarket's fluorescent lights, which give off a more bluish light. Even the same light source does not always produce the same color of light: the beam of a flashlight with a weak battery looks quite reddish, for example, but when fully charged the flashlight throws a more intense, and also whiter, light beam. The same color temperature change happens when you dim lights: the more you dim the lights, the more reddish they get. The camera needs to adjust to these differences to keep colors the same under different lighting conditions, a process called white-balancing.

Color temperature   The standard by which we measure the relative reddishness or bluishness of white light is called *color temperature*. The color differences of white light are measured on the Kelvin (K) scale. The more bluish the white light looks, the higher the color temperature and the higher the K value; the more reddish it is, the lower its color temperature and therefore the lower the K value.

Keep in mind that color temperature has nothing to do with how hot the actual light source gets. You can touch a fluorescent tube even though it burns at a high color temperature; but you wouldn't do the same with the incandescent lamp in a reading light, which burns at a much lower color temperature.

Because outdoor light is much more bluish than normal indoor illumination, two color temperature standards have been developed for lamps in lighting instruments: 5,600K for imitating or compensating outdoor illumination and 3,200K for indoor illumination. This means that when you use a 5,600K lamp in a lighting instrument, the light approximates the bluishness of outdoor light; the 3,200K lamps, on the other hand, emit a warmer, more reddish light. **ZVL11** LIGHTS→ Color temperature→ light sources

Because color temperature is measured by the relative bluishness or reddishness of white light, couldn't you raise the color temperature of an indoor light by putting a slightly blue filter in front of it, or lower the color temperature of an outdoor lamp by using a slightly orange filter? Yes, you can. Such color filters, called gels or color media, are a convenient way of converting outdoor instruments for indoor lighting and vice versa.

> **KEY CONCEPT**
>
> Color temperature, expressed in K (Kelvin), measures the relative reddishness or bluishness of white light. Reddish white light has a low color temperature; bluish white light has a high color temperature.

Most often, you will have to raise the color temperature of 3,200K indoor lights to match the bluish outdoor light coming through a window. Simply take a piece of light-blue plastic (available in most photo stores) and attach it to the front of the indoor instruments, then white-balance the camera again. Although the color temperatures of the outdoor light (coming through the window) and the indoor light (instruments) may not match exactly, they will be close enough for the camera to achieve a proper white balance. Similar filters are used inside some cameras for rough white-balancing.

White-balancing   Recall that *white balance* refers to adjusting the camera so that it reproduces a white object as white on the screen regardless of whether it is illuminated by a high-color-temperature source (the sun at high noon, fluorescent lamps, and 5,600K instruments) or a low-color-temperature source (candlelight, incandescent lights, and 3,200K instruments). When white-balancing, the camera adjusts the RGB signals electronically so that they mix into white. Most small camcorders have an automatic white-balancing mechanism. The camera measures more or less accurately the color temperature of the prevailing light and adjusts the RGB circuits accordingly.

Large camcorders and ENG/EFP cameras have a semiautomatic white-balance control that is more accurate than a fully automatic one. The disadvantage is that you must white-balance every time you move into a new lighting environment, such as from indoors to outdoors or from the fluorescent lights of a supermarket to the office that is illuminated by a desk lamp. The overriding advantage is that you white-balance a camera in the specific lighting in which you are shooting. When using a fully automatic white balance, you are never quite sure just what the camera considers to be white. As a result, the yellow lemons on the table might look green, and the white tablecloth appears light blue.

Higher-end camcorders allow you to use filters to perform a rough white balance under extremely reddish (low K value) or very bluish (high K value) light. The RGB mix is then fine-tuned with white-balance circuitry. Studio cameras and EFP cameras that are connected to a camera cable are white-balanced from the CCU or the RCU (remote control unit) by the video operator.

Proper white-balancing is very important for color continuity. For example, if you video-record a performer in a white shirt first outdoors and then indoors, his shirt should not look bluish in the outdoor scene or reddish in the indoor scene; it should look equally white in both. **SEE 8.13**

How to white-balance To white-balance a camera with a semiautomatic system, take a screen-filling close-up of a white card, a white shirt, or even a clean tissue and press the white-balance button. Some camera utility bags have a white patch sewn into them, giving you a handy white-balancing standard wherever you go. The viewfinder display (usually a flashing light) will tell you when the camera is seeing true white. Be sure that the white object fills the entire viewfinder and that it is located in the light that actually illuminates the scene you are shooting. For

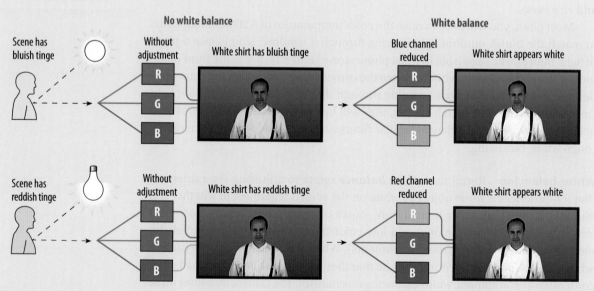

8.13 WHITE BALANCE
To counteract tinting caused by variations in color temperature, you must white-balance the camera. This adjusts the RGB channels to compensate for the unwanted color cast and make white look white.

example, don't white-balance the camera in bright sunlight outside the hotel and then proceed to video-record the fashion show in the hotel lobby. (If you do, you may find that the video colors are quite different from the actual colors the models wore.) You need to white-balance every time you move into a new lighting environment; even if the light seems the same to the naked eye, the camera will detect the difference. **ZVL12** ▸ LIGHTS→ Color temperature→ white balance | controlling | try it

◼ LIGHTING INSTRUMENTS

Despite the many lighting instruments available, there are basically only two types: spotlights and floodlights. *Spotlights* throw a directional, more or less defined beam that illuminates a specific area; they cause harsh, dense shadows. *Floodlights* produce a great amount of nondirectional, diffused light that yields transparent shadows. Some floodlights generate such slow falloff that they seem to be a shadowless light source. Television studio lights are usually suspended from a fixed lighting grid made of heavy steel pipes or from movable counterweighted battens. **SEE 8.14** Portable lights for ENG and EFP are lightweight and more flexible than studio lights but are generally less sturdy and powerful.

Spotlights

Most studio spotlights have a glass lens that helps collect the light rays and focus them into a precise beam. There are also special-purpose spotlights, which differ greatly in size and beam spread.

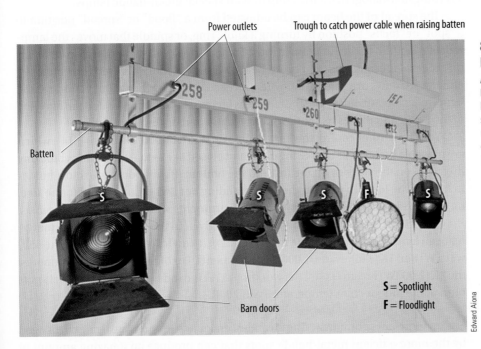

Power outlets

Trough to catch power cable when raising batten

Batten

Barn doors

S = Spotlight
F = Floodlight

Edward Aiona

8.14 STUDIO LIGHTING BATTEN WITH SPOTLIGHTS AND FLOODLIGHT
Lighting battens consist of a large grid of steel pipes that supports the lighting instruments. In this case, the batten can be lowered or raised using a counterweight system.

8.15 FRESNEL SPOTLIGHT

The Fresnel spotlight is the workhorse of studio lighting. Its lens creates a relatively sharp light beam that can be partially blocked by barn doors. This spotlight can be focused, tilted up and down, and panned sideways by turning the knobs with a lighting pole (a wooden pole with a metal hook at the end).

Panning mechanism controlled by pole-operated knob (see inset)

Gel and scrim holder

Fresnel lens

Other side:

Focus knob

Pan knob

Tilt knob

Colortran, Inc.

Fresnel spotlight   The workhorse of studio spotlights is the Fresnel (pronounced "fra-*nel*"). Its thin, steplike lens (developed by Augustin Jean Fresnel of France) directs the light into a distinct beam. **SEE 8.15** It can be equipped with an incandescent TH (tungsten-halogen) quartz lamp or with special metal-halide lamps.

The spread of the beam can be adjusted from a "flood" or "spread" position to a "spot" or "focus" position by turning a knob, ring, or spindle that moves the lamp-reflector unit. To flood the beam in most Fresnel spots, you move the lamp-reflector unit *toward* the lens. The light beam becomes slightly more diffused (less intense), and the shadows are softer than when focused. To focus the beam, you move the lamp-reflector unit *away from* the lens. This increases the sharpness and the intensity of the beam and makes its shadows fairly dense and distinct. **SEE 8.16**

You can further control the light beam with barn doors (see figure 8.14), which are movable metal flaps that swing open and closed like actual barn doors, blocking the beam on the sides or on the top and the bottom. Barn doors slide into a holder in front of the lens. To prevent them from sliding out and dropping, guillotine-like, on somebody, secure all of them to their instruments with safety chains or cables.

The size of Fresnel spotlights is normally given in the wattage of their quartz-halogen lamps. In the studio the most common incandescent Fresnels are the 650-watt (W) and 1K (1 kilowatt = 1,000W) instruments. For older, less sensitive cameras, the 2K (2,000W) Fresnel is still the workhorse. All incandescent studio Fresnel spots burn at the indoor color temperature of 3,200K.

Energy-efficient spotlights   The incandescent quartz Fresnels are being challenged by the more efficient metal-halide spots that can produce an amazing amount of light with lamps in the 100W to 500W range. **SEE 8.17**

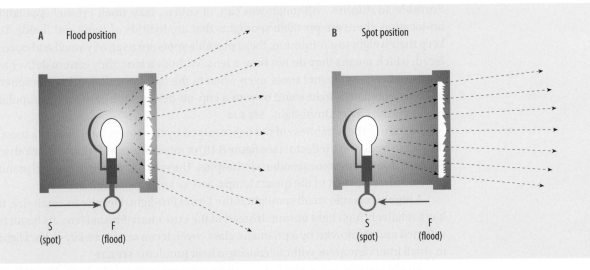

A **Flood position**

B **Spot position**

S (spot)   F (flood)

S (spot)   F (flood)

© Cengage Learning 2011

8.16 BEAM CONTROL OF FRESNEL SPOTLIGHT

A To flood (spread) the beam, turn the focus knob, ring, or spindle so that the lamp-reflector unit moves toward the lens.

B To spot (focus) the beam, turn the focus knob, ring, or spindle so that the lamp-reflector unit moves away from the lens.

A metal-halide lamp generates light by sending an electric arc through its high-pressure gas-filled tube. But these highly efficient lighting instruments have serious disadvantages. They operate only with a ballast to get them started, and some of the lamps flicker, which you can't see but the camera can. They still have trouble producing light of exactly the 3,200K indoor and 5,600K outdoor color temperature standards. And, unfortunately, they are usually quite expensive.

The HMI (hydragyrum medium arc-length iodide) instruments have been used for quite some time in the film industry and by large television stations. The HMI instrument emits a 5,600K outdoor light and consumes much less electricity compared with the incandescent equivalents. The reason why you usually don't find them in smaller video operations is that they are still expensive and need more setup time than their incandescent equivalents.

Whatever type of metal-halide instruments you may use, test them out on-camera before using them for a shoot. Some of them may generate a slight tint, such a blue or green. This subtle color shift may not be visible to the naked eye, but, like the flicker, it is certain to show up on-camera even if you have done some careful white-balancing.

The Arri Group

8.17 METAL HALIDE FRESNEL SPOTLIGHT

This metal-halide Fresnel spot has a built-in ballast. It has a very high light output with relatively low-wattage metal-halide lamps.

KEY CONCEPT

Spotlights produce a sharp, directional light beam and cause fast falloff.

Portable spotlights   Although you can, of course, take small Fresnel spotlights on-location, there are portable spotlights that are hybrids of spots and floods. To keep their weight to a minimum, these portable spots are relatively small and open-faced, which means they do not have a lens. Without a lens, they cannot deliver as precise a beam as Fresnel spots, even when in the focus position. All are designed to be mounted on a light stand or with a clip-on device. One of the more popular models is the Lowel Omni-light. **SEE 8.18**

To reduce the harshness of the light emitted by the quartz lamp, insert a metal diffuser in front of the reflector (see figure 8.18) or attach a piece of spun-glass cloth to the barn doors with some wooden clothespins. The spun glass, which can withstand the considerable heat of the quartz lamps, acts as an efficient diffuser.

A highly versatile small spotlight is the Lowel Pro-light. Despite its small size, it has a relatively high light output. Instead of the customary Fresnel lens, its beam is softened and reinforced by a prismatic glass cover. It can serve as a key or backlight in small interview areas without causing a heat problem. **SEE 8.19**

An old standby is the clip light, with its reflector built into its bulb. The PAR 38 lamp is especially popular for illuminating outdoor walkways and driveways. Clip lights are useful for supplemental illumination of small areas; you can easily clip them onto furniture, scenery, doors, or whatever the clip will fit. Metal housings with barn doors that fit over the clip light are also available. When using fluorescent clip lights, check whether they burn with a high or low color temperature. **SEE 8.20**

Diffuser screen

Lowel-Light Manufacturing, Inc.

8.18 LOWEL OMNI-LIGHT
This popular lightweight instrument doubles as a spot and a floodlight and is used mainly in ENG/EFP. You can plug it into any normal household outlet and hold it or fasten it to a light stand or any other convenient mounting device.

Lowel-Light Manufacturing, Inc.

8.19 LOWEL PRO-LIGHT
The Pro-light is a small, powerful (250W) ENG/EFP spotlight that can be handheld, clipped to the camera, or mounted on a light stand. With its lenslike prismatic glass, it produces an exceptionally even beam.

Metal housing

Gaffer grip or gator clip

Barn doors

Internal reflector lamp

Mole-Richardson Co.

8.20 CLIP LIGHT WITH BARN DOORS

Small spotlights, which use ordinary internal reflector lamps, are useful for illuminating small areas during field productions.

Floodlights

Floodlights have been used primarily to control falloff (that is, to fill in dense shadow areas) or to illuminate large areas with an even baselight. With today's lighting techniques, however, they also serve other functions, such as a key light—the principal light source in a standard lighting setup (see the following discussion of lighting techniques).

Floodlights have no lens and use large, relatively low-powered lamps because their purpose is to create highly diffused nondirectional illumination rather than a sharp beam. The diffused light creates soft and highly transparent shadows. When you illuminate an object with a floodlight, the falloff is automatically slower than with a spotlight. The more common studio floods are the scoop, the softlight, the fluorescent bank, and LED light panels.

Scoop   Named after its scooplike reflector, the scoop is an old-fashioned but highly useful floodlight. Scoops can be used as key lights as well as fill lights for dense shadow areas to slow down falloff and make shadows more transparent. They are ideal for lighting large areas with relatively even light. To diffuse the light beam even more, you can attach a spun-glass scrim to the front of the scoop. **SEE 8.21**

Softlight   Softlights are relatively large instruments with long tubelike lamps whose light bounces off a curved, light-diffusing reflector. The opening of the

Safety chain

Scrim holder with scrim

Edward Aiona

8.21 SCOOP WITH SCRIM

The scooplike reflector of this floodlight allows you to give its diffused beam some direction, which makes it a good fill light. With a scrim attached to its otherwise open face, it acts more like a broad.

Softlight
reflector/diffuser

Mole-Richardson Co.

8.22 SOFTLIGHT
This floodlight is covered with diffusing material and delivers extremely diffused light. It causes very slow falloff and renders shadows virtually invisible.

Lowel-Light Manufacturing, Inc.

8.23 FLUORESCENT BANK
The fluorescent bank consists of a series of fluorescent tubes. It produces very soft light with slow falloff.

reflector is covered with a diffusion material that scatters the light so much that it renders shadows virtually invisible. **SEE 8.22**

Softlights come in various sizes and burn at an indoor 3,200K color temperature. Most softlights are quite large and do not fit a cramped production space, but smaller softlights are the mainstay of news sets and interview areas. Some softlights have an attached gridlike contraption, called an egg crate, instead of the customary diffusion cloth. The squares of the egg crate diffuser give you a little more control over the direction of the softlight beam than does the diffusion cloth.

Fluorescent bank   The fluorescent bank, which consists of a row of fluorescent tubes, was one of the main lighting devices in the early days of television. After a hiatus the bank has made a comeback. It is highly efficient, produces extremely diffused light and slow falloff, and does not generate the heat of the other floodlights. You can get fluorescent banks that burn at approximately 5,000K for outdoor light or at 3,000K for indoor light. The manufacturers of fluorescent lights try hard to make the light look similar to that of incandescent floodlights, without the telltale greenish look of the fluorescents. Before you settle on a specific fluorescent bank, try it out: light a white object with the fluorescent bank, white-balance the camera, and video-record it for a minute or two. Then do the same with an incandescent instrument (such as a softlight or a scoop with a scrim). The object should look similarly white in both segments. Besides the color problem, the big disadvantage of all such lights is that the banks are still large and unwieldy, regardless of whether you use them in the studio or in the field. **SEE 8.23**   **ZVL13** LIGHTS→ Instruments→ studio

LED light panels   Thanks to the lower light requirements of improved sensors in digital video cameras, new ***LED lights*** are being manufactured that may eventually replace the incandescent floodlights and probably even the fluorescent instruments in current use. The reason for their rising popularity is that they can now be made large enough to be practical for major studio lighting functions.

LED lights operate on an illumination technology—the *light-emitting diode*—that is similar to the

8.24 LED LIGHT PANEL
This 12-by-12-inch LED light panel is dimmable, generates very little heat, draws little power for an amazingly high light output, and burns longer than any kind of incandescent lamp.

Small spotlights in the flood position

Light-diffusing tents

8.25 DIFFUSION TENT
Small portable lights, including spotlights, can be made into effective softlights by diffusing their beams with light tents.

way a computer screen works. When a computer screen is turned on, it can generate enough light to illuminate an object standing right next to it. If you colorize the screen, you can colorize a nearby white object without having to use color media.

LED panels have been used successfully for some time as camera lights or as floodlights to light small displays. But the larger panels (12-by-12 inches) emit enough light that they can take over most standard lighting functions. **SEE 8.24**

There are multiple advantages of LED lights: they last much longer than incandescent or fluorescent lamps; they use less power; they generate less heat than incandescent lights; they can generate both standard light temperatures (3,200K indoor and 5,600 outdoor); they can be dimmed without affecting the colors or the color temperature; they are flicker-free; and, compared with incandescent instruments, they are quite lightweight and their elements can be made to act more like a spotlight than a floodlight. The big disadvantage is that they are quite expensive.

8.26 CHINESE LANTERN
These floodlights produce highly diffused light over a large area.

Portable floodlights   When choosing a portable floodlight, look for one that is small, produces a great amount of diffused illumination, has a reflector that keeps the diffused light from spilling all over the area, can be plugged into an ordinary 120-volt (V) household outlet, and is lightweight enough to be supported by a light stand. You can, however, use any type of portable lighting instrument as a floodlight if you diffuse its beam.

When mounted inside an umbrella reflector, a Lowel Omni-light or even a small Fresnel spot can serve as a floodlight. Many portable lights come with light boxes, or light tents, which are tentlike diffusers that you can put over the portable light source to convert it to an efficient softlight. **SEE 8.25** Some diffusers look like Chinese lanterns and totally enclose the lamp. **SEE 8.26** **ZVL14** LIGHTS→ Instruments→ field

KEY CONCEPT

Floodlights produce general nondirectional illumination and cause slow falloff.

Special-Purpose Spotlights and Floodlights

There are numerous spotlights and floodlights that facilitate specific lighting tasks. The most popular are the ellipsoidal spotlight; the strip, or cyc, light; and a variety of small EFP floodlights.

Ellipsoidal spotlight   The ellipsoidal spotlight is used for special effects. It produces an extremely sharp, high-intensity beam that can be made rectangular or triangular with movable metal shutters. **SEE 8.27**

Some ellipsoidals have a slot next to the beam-shaping shutters that can hold a variety of metal sheets with patterned holes. Such metal sheets have acquired a variety of names, depending on the company that produces them or the LD who uses them. You may hear lighting people call them "gobos" (which can also mean the cutouts that are placed in front of a light source or camera) or "cucoloris" ("cookies" for short). Let's settle on *cookies*. When inserted in the slot of the ellipsoidal spot, the cookie pattern can be projected onto a dull-looking surface to make it more interesting. **SEE 8.28**

Strip, or cyc, light   The strip light is used primarily to illuminate cycloramas (the seamless background curtain that stretches along studio or stage walls), drapes,

8.28 COOKIE PATTERN
Some ellipsoidal spotlights double as pattern projectors. You can insert a variety of metal cutouts, called cookies, whose patterns are projected by the spotlight onto a wall or other surface.

Cooling vents

Shutters

Gel holder (for color filters)

Tilt adjustment

Lens

8.27 ELLIPSOIDAL SPOTLIGHT
The ellipsoidal spotlight produces an extremely sharp, bright beam. It is used to illuminate precise areas.

8.29 STRIP, OR CYC, LIGHT
These instruments are used primarily to illuminate cycloramas, drapes, and large scenic areas.

or large areas of scenery. They are similar to theater border lights and consist of rows of four to 12 quartz lamps mounted in long, boxlike reflectors. These strips are usually positioned side-by-side on the studio floor and shined upward onto the background. **SEE 8.29** There are LED strip lights available that can light up a cyc portion with a great many colors without the need for color gels.

Small EFP floodlight   The ENG/EFP task of lighting up an interior quickly and efficiently to get sufficient baselight has been greatly aided by small but powerful floodlights run off regular household current. **SEE 8.30** Much like clip lights, you can move them into position quickly and set them up in a matter of minutes. Trying to use a larger, more cumbersome studio light to illuminate the same area would probably take considerably longer. Don't touch the instruments once they are turned on; some of then get very hot and can cause serious burns.

Reflector

Lamp

Lowel-Light Manufacturing, Inc.

8.30 SMALL EFP FLOODLIGHT
This small EFP floodlight (Lowel V-light) runs off ordinary household current and can be used to illuminate small areas. When mounted inside an umbrella reflector, it serves as a softlight.

▮ LIGHTING TECHNIQUES

Now let's find out what to do with all these instruments. Start your lighting task with an idea of how you would like a person, scene, or display to look on the video screen, then choose the simplest way to achieve that look. Although there is no universal recipe that guarantees good lighting for every situation, there are established techniques that you can easily adapt to the specific task at hand. But do not become a slave to such methods. Although you may often wish you had more instruments, more space, and especially more time to do justice to the lighting, you should realize that the final criterion for video lighting is not how faithfully you imitate nature, or how closely you observe the standards as outlined in a book, but how it looks on the monitor and, especially, whether you get it done on time.

Let's take a look at some of the lighting basics: operation of lights, studio lighting, and field lighting.

Operation of Lights

Lighting presents some obvious hazards. Ordinary household current is powerful enough to kill. As just pointed out, the lamps, barn doors, and sometimes the instruments themselves get so hot that they can cause serious burns. If placed too close to combustible material, lighting instruments can cause fires. The instruments with barn doors are suspended far above studio floor areas and, if not properly secured, can come crashing down. Staring into a bright, high-intensity light beam can cause temporary vision problems. Even so, you don't need to be intimidated and give up lighting before getting started. You can easily eliminate these hazards by observing a few safety rules.

CHECKLIST: LIGHTING SAFETY

☑ **Electricity** Don't ever handle an instrument with wet hands, even if it is unplugged. Do not "hot-plug" an instrument; switch off the power before connecting or disconnecting the power cables or patch cords. Patch cords connect selected lighting instruments to specific dimmers. Wear gloves. Use fiberglass safety ladders rather than metal ones. Do not touch any metal while working with a power cable. If you need an adapter to connect a power cable or to plug it in, tape the connection with electrician's tape. Use only those instruments that are absolutely necessary. If you can, let the larger instruments warm up through reduced power before bringing the dimmer up full. Turn off the studio lights and use house lights for basic blocking rehearsals; this will keep the studio cooler and will also extend the life of the expensive bulbs. Do not waste electric energy.

☑ **Heat** The quartz lamps (quartz housing and a TH filament) get extremely hot. They heat up the barn doors and even the housing of the lighting instrument itself. Never touch the barn doors or the instrument with your bare hands once it is turned on. Use gloves or a lighting pole (a long wooden pole with a metal hook at one end) to adjust the barn doors or the instrument.

Keep instruments away from combustible materials, such as curtains, cloth, books, and wood paneling. If you need to place a lighting instrument close to such materials, insulate the materials with aluminum foil. Let lamps cool down before replacing them. This is the big advantage of fluorescent and LED lights: you won't burn your hand or objects close to the switched-on instrument even during hours of use.

☑ **Fingerprints** Don't ever touch quartz or metal-halide lamps with your fingers. Fingerprints or any other residue clinging to the quartz housing will cause the lamp to overheat at those points and burn out. In extreme cases, the weakened housing can explode because both types of lamps are highly pressurized. Use a tissue or, in case of emergency, your shirttail when exchanging lamps. Be sure the power is shut off before reaching into an instrument.

☑ **Hanging instruments** Before lowering movable battens, see to it that the studio floor is clear of people, equipment, and scenery. Because the tie-off rails, where the counterweighted battens are locked, are often hidden behind the cyclorama (so you can't see the studio floor), always give a warning before actually lowering the batten, such as "Batten 5C coming down!" Wait for an "all clear" signal before lowering the batten, and have someone watch the studio floor while you do so. Tighten all necessary bolts on the C-clamp. **SEE 8.31** Secure the instrument to the batten—and the barn doors to the instrument—with a safety chain or cable. Check the power connections for obviously worn or loose plugs and cables.

Whenever moving a ladder, watch for obstacles above and below. Don't leave a lighting wrench or other tool on top of a ladder. Never take unnecessary chances by leaning way out to reach an instrument. Whenever possible, have somebody steady the ladder for you.

Herbert Zettl

8.31 C-CLAMP
Use the C-clamp to fasten heavy lighting instruments to the lighting battens. Even when tightly fastened to the batten, the C-clamp allows a lighting instrument to be rotated.

☑ **Eyes** When adjusting an instrument, try not to look directly into the light. Work from behind, rather than in front of, the instrument. This way you look with the beam, rather than into it. If you have to look into the light, do it very briefly and wear dark glasses.

Studio Lighting

Now you are ready to do some actual lighting assignments. Although you may struggle with lighting at remote locations more often than you do in studio work, you will find that learning to light is easier in the studio than in the field. The art of lighting is neither mysterious nor complicated if you keep in mind its functions: to reveal the basic shape of the object or person, to lighten or darken the shadows, to show where the object is relative to the background, to give the object or person some sparkle and the whole scene a specific mood.

Photographic principle, or triangle lighting Still photographers have taught us that all of these functions can be accomplished with three lights: the *key light*, which reveals the basic shape; the *fill light*, which fills in the shadows if they are too dense; and the *back light*, which separates the object from the background and provides some sparkle. The various lighting techniques for video and motion pictures are firmly rooted in this basic principle of still photography, called the *photographic principle*, or *triangle lighting*. Some lighting people have yet another name for the photographic principle: three-point lighting. **SEE 8.32**

Key light In the studio a slightly diffused Fresnel spot is normally used for the key light. A Fresnel lets you aim the beam at the object without too much spill into other set areas. But you can also use other instruments for a key light, such as an Omni-light, a scoop, an LED light panel, or even a light that is reflected off a white card. As you can see, the key light is not defined by the instrument used but by its function: to reveal the basic shape of the object. The key light is usually placed above and to the right or left of the front of the object. **SEE 8.33** Note that when a spotlight is used as a key, it produces fast falloff (a dense attached shadow); when you use a floodlight, the falloff is slower, and the shadows are more transparent. **ZVL15** LIGHTS→ Triangle lighting→ key

© Cengage Learning 2011

8.32 BASIC PHOTOGRAPHIC PRINCIPLE

The basic photographic principle uses a key light, a fill light, and a back light. They are arranged in a triangle, with the back light at its apex, opposite the camera.

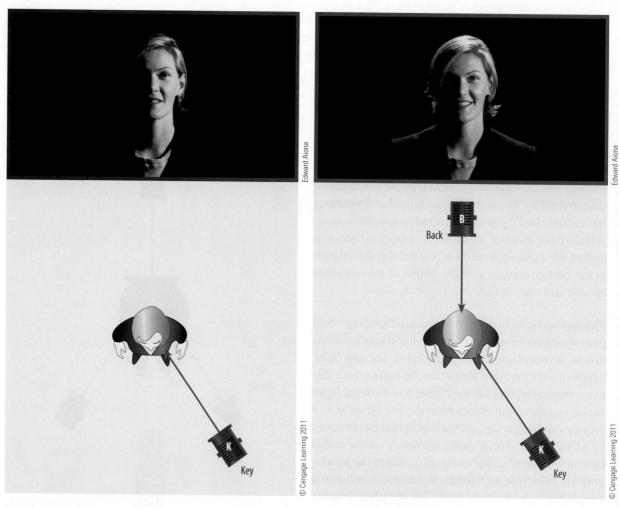

Edward Aiona

© Cengage Learning 2011

8.33 KEY LIGHT

The key light is the principal light source. It reveals the basic shape of the object. A spotlight is generally used as a key.

8.34 BACK LIGHT ADDED

The back light outlines the subject against the background and provides sparkle. Focused spots are used as back lights.

Back light   To outline the subject more clearly against the background, and especially to give the hair—and with it the whole picture—some sparkle and luster, you need a back light. Some lighting people believe that it is the back light in particular that gives the lighting its professional polish. **SEE 8.34**

As the name suggests, the back light falls on the back of the subject's head. You place it opposite the camera above and directly behind the subject. Because the area to be illuminated by the back light is quite limited, use a Fresnel spot. To keep the back light from shining into the camera or being in the shot, place it fairly high behind the subject.

Some LDs insist on having the back light burn with the same intensity as the key. Such a rule makes little sense because the intensity of the back light depends on the relative reflectance of the object or subject. A blond woman wearing a white blouse certainly needs a less intense beam than a man in a dark suit who has curly black hair. **ZVL16** LIGHTS→ Triangle lighting→ back

Fill light   To slow down falloff and thereby render dense shadows more transparent, you need a fill light. A floodlight is generally used, but you can of course also use a Fresnel (or any other spotlight) for fill. Obviously, you place the fill light on the side opposite the key light and aim it toward the shadow area. **SEE 8.35** **ZVL17** LIGHTS→ Triangle lighting→ fill

The more fill light you use, the slower the falloff. If the fill light is as strong as the key light, you have eliminated the attached shadow and, with it, any falloff. Many news and interview sets are deliberately lighted flat with floodlights (such as LED panels), with equally strong softlights for key and fill, to render the close-up faces of the newspeople and the guests relatively wrinkle-free (but, unfortunately, also flat). You still need spot lights for the back lights, however.

Background light   Unless you want a dark background, you need additional light to illuminate the background or set. This additional source is called the ***background light*** or set light. For a small set, you may need only a single Fresnel spot or scoop. **SEE 8.36** A large set may require a few more instruments, each of which illuminates a specific set area. To keep the attached shadows of the background on the same side as the foreground shadows, the background light must be on the same side of the camera as the key light.

You can also use the background light to provide some visual interest to an otherwise dull background: you can produce a "slice" of light, a prominent cast shadow that cuts across the background, or a cookie pattern. To suggest nighttime when lighting an interior set, keep the background generally dark and illuminate only small portions of it. If you want to evoke daylight, illuminate the background evenly. You can colorize a neutral gray or light background simply by putting color gels in front of the background lights. Colored light can save you a lot of painting. **ZVL18** LIGHTS→ Triangle lighting→ background

Adapting the lighting triangle   Whenever possible, put up the set where the lights are rather than move the lights to the set location. If, for example, you have to light a simple two-person interview in the studio, look up at the lighting grid and find a key, fill, and backlight triangle and place the chair in the middle of it. Even if you can't find another lighting triangle for the other chair, you are still ahead—half of the

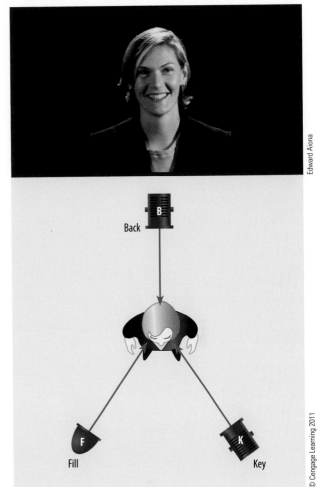

Edward Aiona

© Cengage Learning 2011

8.35 FILL LIGHT ADDED
The fill light slows down falloff and renders shadows more transparent. Floodlights are generally used to fill in dense shadows.

8.36 BACKGROUND LIGHT ADDED

The background, or set, light illuminates the background and various set areas. Spots or floodlights are used on the same side as the key.

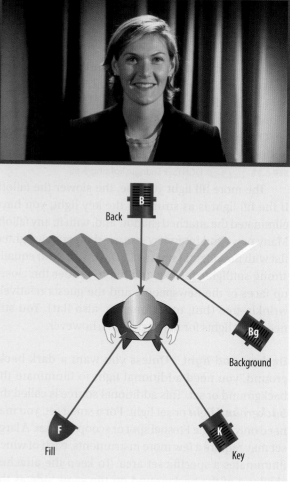

lighting is already done. You will find that you cannot always apply the photographic principle so that the three instruments form the prescribed triangle. This is perfectly normal. Realize that the lighting triangle is a basic principle, not a mandate.

Always try to accomplish a lighting setup with as few instruments as possible. If the falloff from a diffused key light is slow enough (the shadow side is not too dense), you may not need a fill light. Even when doing studio lighting, you may find that a reflector is more effective for filling in shadows than setting up a fill light. (We discuss the use of reflectors in the context of field lighting later in this chapter.) Sometimes the key light will spill over onto the background and eliminate the need for a set light.

In any case, don't be a slave to the photographic principle. Sometimes a single Fresnel aimed at the windshield of a car is all you need to produce a convincing nighttime effect for the car interior; at other times you may need four or five carefully placed instruments to re-create the effect of a single candle. The effectiveness of the lighting is determined not by how faithfully you observe traditional lighting conventions but by how the scene looks on the monitor. Always keep in mind that you light for the camera. **ZVL19** LIGHTS→ Triangle lighting→ try it

KEY CONCEPT

The major criterion for good lighting is how it looks on the video monitor.

8.37 HIGH-KEY LIGHTING
High-key lighting shows a bright scene with an abundance of diffused light. The background is usually light.

8.38 LOW-KEY LIGHTING
Low-key lighting shows dramatic, selective lighting with fast-falloff attached and prominent cast shadows. The background is usually dark.

High-key and low-key lighting Sometimes you will hear the terms *high-key* and *low-key* lighting. This has nothing to do with the vertical positioning of the key light. Rather, it describes the overall lighting effect and its general feel. A scene with ***high-key lighting*** has an abundance of bright, diffused light, resulting in slow-falloff or flat lighting. The background is usually light and projects a high-energy, upbeat feeling. Game shows and situation comedies are usually lighted high-key. Because of the slow falloff, high-key lighting is also used for commercials that advertise beauty products. **SEE 8.37** `ZVL20` LIGHTS→ Design→ high key

A scene with ***low-key lighting*** is much more dramatic; it uses relatively few spotlights to create selective lighting with fast-falloff attached shadows and prominent cast shadows. The background and, wherever possible, the floor areas are kept dark. Most outdoor night scenes exhibit low-key lighting. It is also frequently used in dramatic scenes in soap operas, in mystery and crime shows, and sometimes in sci-fi movies. **SEE 8.38** `ZVL21` LIGHTS→ Design→ low key

Light Plot

For all but routine shows, you need to prepare a ***light plot***. Some light plots are rough sketches to indicate the approximate positions of lights; arrows indicate the approximate directions of their beams. **SEE 8.39** Others are drawn on a floor plan grid, which shows the background scenery, the major action areas, and the principal camera positions. Detailed light plots show the position, type, and functions of the lighting instruments needed. **SEE 8.40**

Last-Minute Lighting Techniques

When you are called upon to do some eleventh-hour lighting, do not whine about artistic integrity or lack of time. Simply turn on as many floodlights as possible and try to place some back lights to give the scene some sparkle. This is not the time to fret about triangle principles or falloff. Every so often such an emergency technique will result in surprisingly good lighting—but don't rely on it.

8.39 SIMPLE LIGHT PLOT SKETCH FOR TWO-PERSON INTERVIEW

Most light plots are rough sketches that indicate the types of lights used (spots or floods), their approximate positions, and the general direction of their beams.

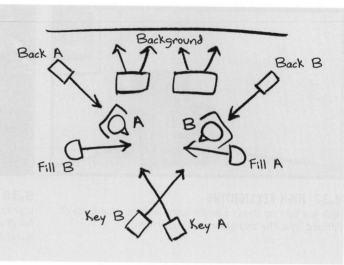

8.40 DETAILED LIGHT PLOT FOR TWO-PERSON INTERVIEW

This light plot shows the type and the position of the lighting instruments used and the approximate directions of their beams. Sometimes light plots even indicate the size (wattage) of the instruments. Note that there are two overlapping lighting triangles—one for person A and the other for person B.

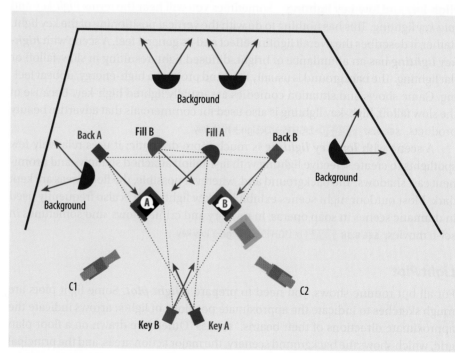

Field Lighting

Whereas studio lighting is done exclusively with various types of instruments, field, or location, lighting often extends to the control or augmentation of available light. When shooting outdoors you are pretty much dependent on available light. Your lighting job is to manipulate sunlight so that it yields, at least to some extent, to the basic lighting principles. When shooting indoors you can apply all studio lighting principles, except on a smaller scale. Windows often present a problem because the light entering from outside is usually brighter than the indoor light and has a much higher color temperature. But light from windows can also be an important illumination source.

Outdoors—overcast and shadow area A foggy or overcast day is ideal for outdoor shooting. The fog and the clouds act as giant diffusion filters: the giant and brutally bright spotlight of the sun becomes a huge but gentle softlight. The highly diffused light produces slow falloff and transparent shadows. The camera likes such low-contrast lighting and produces crisp and true colors throughout the scene. The scene is basically illuminated by high-intensity baselight. Be sure to white-balance the camera before video-recording; the light on an overcast day has a surprisingly high color temperature (bluish tint).

A large shadow area will provide you with similarly slow-falloff lighting. Whenever possible, put the on-camera people in the shade. Besides the gentle shadows, you will have no contrast problems unless you include part of the sunlit area in the picture. As you can see, this is a quick solution to a potentially difficult lighting situation.

Bright sunlight When forced to shoot in bright sunlight, you are not so lucky. The bright sun acts like a giant high-intensity spotlight, which renders the falloff appropriately fast; the shadows are very dense, and the contrast between light and shadow sides is extremely high. This extreme contrast can present a formidable exposure problem. If you close down the iris (high f-stop setting for a small aperture) to prevent too much light from overloading the sensors, the shadow areas will turn uniformly dark and dense and will show no detail. If you open up the iris to see some detail in the shadow areas, you will overexpose the bright areas. The automatic aperture in a camcorder is of no help in this situation: it simply adjusts to the brightest spot in the scene and renders all shadow areas equally dark. Even the most sophisticated camera cannot adjust itself to accommodate these conditions.

There are two things you can do. As mentioned earlier, you can first use an ND (neutral density) filter on the camera to reduce the overly bright light without affecting the colors. Second, you can provide enough fill light to slow down the falloff, reduce the contrast, and make the attached shadows more transparent without overexposing the bright areas. But where in the field can you get a fill light strong enough to offset the sun?

In expensive and elaborate productions, high-intensity spotlights (usually HMI lights) that burn at 5,600K are used as outdoor fill lights. Fortunately, you can also use the sun to serve simultaneously as both key and fill lights—all you need is a reflector to bounce some of the sunlight back toward the shadow area. **SEE 8.41** You can use a sheet of white foam core or a white card as a reflector, or use crumpled aluminum foil taped to a stiff backing. You can also use a number of commercially available reflectors that fold up and prove effective over considerable distances. The closer you hold the reflector to the object, the more intense the fill light will be. Some LDs and DPs (directors of photography) use multiple reflectors to reflect light into areas that face away from the light source. In this case the reflector becomes the principal light source. With good reflectors (mirrors), you can even guide sunlight indoors to light up a room or hallway without any lighting instruments.

KEY CONCEPT

Reflectors can replace lighting instruments.

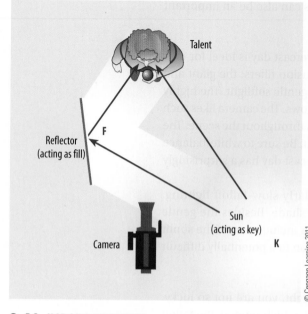

8.41 USE OF A REFLECTOR

The reflector acts like a fill light: it bounces some light back toward the dense shadow areas and slows down falloff.

Avoid shooting against any bright background, such as a sun-drenched white wall, the ocean, or a lake. Anyone standing in front of it will be rendered in silhouette unless you use huge reflectors or high-intensity fill lights. Whenever possible find some shade in which to position the subject. When shooting at a lakeshore or the ocean beach, use a large umbrella to create the necessary shadow area. The umbrella will not only make your lighting job considerably easier but also provide some visual interest. 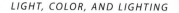 LIGHTS→ Field→ outdoor | use of reflectors

Indoors without windows   If the room is adequately illuminated, try to shoot with available light and see how it looks on the monitor. We discussed earlier that the high light-sensitivity of camcorders and ENG/EFP cameras enables DPs to shoot much more often in available light than was previously possible. The basic rule still applies for available light: if it looks good to you, there is no need for additional instruments.

Remember to white-balance the camera to the available light before starting to shoot. Most indoor lighting can be easily improved by adding some back lights in the appropriate areas. Potential problems include light stands that show up on-camera or a back light that cannot be positioned high enough to be out of camera range. In this case, place the instrument somewhat to the side, or use some 1 × 2 lumber to create a temporary support for it. Move the back light close enough to the subject to keep it out of camera view.

When lighting a person who remains stationary in a room, as in an interview, you use the same photographic principle as in the studio except that you now have to place portable lights on stands. Try to have the key or fill light double as the background light. To avoid the infamous reddish or white hot spot on the subject and to make the light look generally softer, attach spun-glass scrims to all three instruments. You can use wooden clothespins to attach the scrims to the barn doors. Floodlights, such as LED panels, are ideal instruments for achieving good key and fill lighting. For the backlight use a small spotlight.

If you have only two lights with which to light a person indoors, you can use one as the key, the other as the back, and a reflector to act as the fill. **SEE 8.42** You can also place a softlight for the key (light diffused by a light tent) almost directly opposite the person to avoid a dense shadow side, then use the second light as a back light.

If you have just one lighting instrument, such as an Omni-light, you can use it as a key, with the reflector acting as the fill. In such a setup, you must necessarily sacrifice the back light. If you diffuse the key light and move it closer to the camera than it is in figure 8.42, however, you can light the face almost straight on. Then use the reflector in the back (out of camera range) to provide the all-important back light.

8.42 TWO-POINT INDOOR LIGHTING
To achieve effective triangle lighting with only two lights, use one for the key light and the other for the back light. Fill light is achieved with a reflector.

© Cengage Learning 2011

To light an ordinary-sized room so that you can follow somebody walking through it, use the portable lights in the flood position and reflect them off the ceiling or walls, or diffuse their beams with scrims. If available, use a light-diffusing umbrella. Aim the instrument into the umbrella, with the opening of the umbrella toward the scene, or at reflectors rather than directly toward the action area. You can apply the same technique for lighting a large interior except that you need more or higher-powered instruments. The idea is to get as much baselight (highly diffused overall light) as possible with a minimum of instruments.

Indoors with windows   By now you know that windows can present a formidable lighting problem. Even if you don't shoot against them, they admit a great amount of high-color-temperature light. If you try to augment the bluish 5,600K outdoor light with normal indoor 3,200K lighting instruments, the camera will have trouble finding the correct white balance. The simplest way to match the lower 3,200K indoor color temperature with the prevailing 5,600K outdoor color temperature is to attach a light-blue gel (color media) to the indoor lighting instruments. The blue gel helps raise their color temperature to approximate the 5,600K outdoor light. Even if it is not a perfect match, the camera can be properly white-balanced for both the light coming through the window and the indoor lighting instruments.

> **KEY CONCEPT**
> In the field, light for visibility rather than artistic impact.

8.43 WINDOW USED AS BACK LIGHT

In this interview setup, the lighting is done with a single instrument. A diffused Lowel Omni-light with a light-blue gel acts as the key. The back light is provided by the window, which is kept out of camera range.

The best way to cope with windows is to avoid them: draw the curtains and use a normal triangle lighting setup. Many times, however, you can use the window light as a back light or even as a key. For example, when using the window as a back light, you need to position the subject in such a way that the light strikes from the side and the back. Then position the key light and the camera. **SEE 8.43** Obviously, the window should be off-camera. By changing the window from a hazard to an asset and with only one lighting instrument in the room, you have achieved a professional lighting setup. What about the fill light? The spill from the window and the diffused key light should be enough to provide for relatively slow falloff. If not, you can always use a reflector to bounce some of the key light back as fill. **ZVL23** LIGHTS→ Field→ indoor | mixed

GUIDELINES: FIELD LIGHTING

☑ **Scout ahead** Check out the location and determine the lighting requirements before the actual shooting date. Establish a contact person and get his or her name, address, and all phone numbers. Check the breaker box and determine the available power, the nature of the outlets, and the extension cords needed. Have adapters available that fit the various outlets.

☑ **Be prepared** Always take with you a few rolls of gaffer's tape, a roll of aluminum foil, gloves, a wrench, some wooden clothespins (plastic ones melt), and a fire extinguisher.

☑ **Don't overload circuits** Once on-location don't overload the circuit. Although a normal 15-amp household outlet will accommodate 1,500 watts of lighting instruments, do not plug more than 1,000 watts into a single circuit. Realize that several outlets may be on the same circuit even if they are in different corners of the room. To test which outlets are on the same circuit, plug a light into various outlets and turn off the breaker. If the light goes out, you are on the designated circuit. If the light stays on, the outlet is connected to another circuit. Keep in mind that even long extension cables can add to the circuit load.

☑ **Don't waste lamp life** Turn on the lights only as needed. The incandescent quartz lamps for portable lighting instruments have a limited life span. Turning off the lights as much as possible will preserve energy, extend the life of the lamps, and reduce the heat in the performance area.

☑ **Secure the light stands** Be especially careful when placing lighting instruments on portable stands. Secure all light stands with sandbags so they won't tip over when somebody brushes against them. Route extension cords out of the main traffic pattern. If you have to lay them across a hallway or threshold, tape them securely in place (here is where the gaffer's tape comes in handy) and put a rug or rubber doormat over them.

☑ **Move cords carefully** Don't pull on an extension cord that is connected to a lighting instrument; light stands tip over easily, especially when fully extended.

☑ **Be time conscious** Don't underestimate the time it takes to set up even simple location lighting.

M A I N   P O I N T S

▶ *Light and Shadow Control*
   Lighting is the deliberate illumination of a performance area and the control of attached and cast shadows.

▶ *Types of Light and Light Intensity*
   The two basic types of light are directional and diffused. Directional light is focused and causes harsh shadows. Diffused light is spread out and creates soft shadows. Light intensity is measured in foot-candles (fc) or European lux. There is approximately 10 lux per foot-candle.

▶ *Contrast and Measuring Light*
   Contrast is the difference between the darkest and the brightest areas in the video image. This contrast is often expressed as a ratio, such as 60:1, which means that the brightest spot is 60 times the intensity of the darkest spot. Many cameras tolerate a

relatively limited contrast ratio, ranging from 50:1 to 100:1. When measuring contrast, the light meter must read reflected light. When measuring baselight levels, the meter reads incident light.

▶ *Shadows and Falloff*

There are two types of shadows: attached and cast. Attached shadows are affixed to the object; they cannot be seen independent of it. Cast shadows can be seen independent of the objects that cause them. Falloff indicates the change from light to shadow and the contrast between light and shadow areas. Fast falloff means that the light area changes abruptly into dense shadow area; the contrast is high. Slow falloff means that the light turns gradually into the shadow side; the contrast is low.

▶ *Colors and Color Temperature*

Colors are generated through additive color mixing. All colors are mixed by adding the primary light colors—red, green, and blue (RGB)—in various proportions. Color temperature refers to the relative reddishness or bluishness of white light. White-balancing adjusts the camera to the color temperature of the prevailing illumination so that the camera will reproduce a white object as white on the video screen.

▶ *Lighting Instruments*

Lights are usually classified into spotlights and floodlights, and studio and portable lights. Spotlights produce a sharp, focused beam; floodlights produce highly diffused, nondirectional illumination. Studio lights are normally suspended from the ceiling. Portable lights are smaller and supported by collapsible light stands.

▶ *The Photographic Principle, or Triangle Lighting*

Lighting functions can usually be achieved with the basic photographic principle: a key light (principal light source), a fill light (fills in dense shadows), and a back light (separates the subject from the background and gives it sparkle). This is also known as three-point lighting. Reflectors frequently substitute for fill lights. The background light is an additional light used for lighting the background and the set area. In field, or location, lighting, it is often more important to provide sufficient illumination than careful triangle lighting. In the field floodlights are used more often than spotlights.

▶ *High-Key and Low-Key Lighting*

High-key lighting uses an abundance of bright, diffused light, resulting in slow-falloff or flat lighting; the high-key scene generally has a light background and an upbeat mood. Low-key lighting uses few spotlights to create fast-falloff lighting and prominent cast shadows; it illuminates only selected areas and projects a dramatic mood.

▶ *Windows*

In EFP lighting, a window can serve as a key or a side-back light, so long as it is off-camera. All indoor incandescent instruments must have light-blue color media attached to match the color temperature of the outdoor light coming through the window.

ZETTL'S VIDEOLAB

For your reference or to track your work, the *Zettl's VideoLab* program cues in this chapter are listed here with their corresponding page numbers.

PART

V

Production Environment: Studio, Field, and Synthetic

When you look at some of the clips you shot with an HDTV pocket recorder at your friend's home, you probably wonder why we still use studios. After all, the highly portable camcorders and lights and the wireless microphones make it possible to originate a video program anywhere, indoors or out—even in outer space. In tandem with portable transmission equipment and satellite uplinks, you don't need to re-create a street corner in the studio—you can go to the actual street corner as the background for your interview. This is true so long as it doesn't rain, the street noise doesn't obliterate your guest's answers, and you don't have kids making faces in the background of your shot.

Studios provide optimal production control and efficiency. It is, after all, much easier to cut between interviewer and guest with a switcher than to take two camcorders on-location and then do extensive editing to insert close-ups and reaction shots. On the other hand, you would have a hard time fitting a football game into even a large studio. In this case, you need to pack much of the studio's control equipment into a truck and bring it to the stadium.

Part V explains the relative advantages of the studio and field production environments and briefly touches on synthetic, computer-generated imaging.

KEY TERMS

cyclorama A U-shaped continuous piece of canvas or muslin for backing of scenery and action. Also called *cyc*. Hardwall cycs are permanently installed in front of one or two of the studio walls.

flat A piece of standing scenery used as a background or to simulate the walls of a room. There are hardwall and soft-wall flats.

floor plan A diagram of scenery, properties, and set dressings drawn on a grid.

IFB Stands for *interruptible foldback* or *feedback*. A prompting system that allows communication with the talent while on the air. A small earpiece worn by on-the-air talent carries program sound (including the talent's voice) or instructions from the producer or director.

ingest The selection, coding, and recording on a large server of various program feeds.

intercom Short for *intercommunication system*. Used for all production and engineering personnel involved in a show. The most widely used system has telephone headsets to facilitate voice communication on several wired or wireless channels. Includes other systems, such as IFB and cellular telephones.

master control Controls the program input, storage, and retrieval for on-the-air telecasts. Also oversees the technical quality of all program material.

monitor High-quality video display used in the video studio and control rooms. Cannot receive broadcast signals. Also refers to flat-panel camera viewfinders.

PL Stands for *party line, phone line,* or *private line*. Major intercommunication device in video studios.

props Short for *properties*. Furniture and other objects used by talent and for set decoration.

SA Stands for *studio address system*. A public address loud-speaker system from the control room to the studio. Also called *studio talkback* and *PA* (public address) *system*.

studio control room A room adjacent to the studio in which the director, producer, production assistants, technical director, audio engineer, and sometimes the lighting director perform their production functions.

Production Environment: Studio

The video production studio provides an environment that is independent of the weather and the restrictions of an outdoor location. It affords optimal production control. The studio facilitates the coordination and the effective use of all major production elements—cameras, lighting, sound, scenery, and the actions of production personnel and performers—making video production highly efficient.

After visiting a few studios in television stations, independent production houses, or colleges, you will soon discover that despite their differences in size and layout they all contain similar installations and equipment. Television studios are designed to facilitate the interaction of the installations and the team members for a great variety of production activities. Knowing about how a studio and its facilities function will help you make optimal use of them.

▶ **VIDEO PRODUCTION STUDIO**
Physical layout and major installations

▶ **STUDIO CONTROL ROOM**
Image control and sound control

▶ **MASTER CONTROL**
Automated workflow and quality control, content ingest, and storage and archiving

▶ **STUDIO SUPPORT AREAS**
Scenery and property storage, and makeup and dressing rooms

▶ **SCENERY, PROPERTIES, AND SET DRESSINGS**
Softwall and hardwall flats; modules, drops, and set pieces; set and hand props; and set dressings

▶ **SET DESIGN**
Process message, floor plan, prop list, and setup

▇ VIDEO PRODUCTION STUDIO

Video production studios are designed not only for multicamera productions and teamwork but also to provide an optimal environment for single-camera video and digital cinema productions. Most studios are fairly large rectangular rooms with smooth floors and high ceilings from which the lighting instruments are suspended. They have a number of other technical installations that facilitate a great variety of productions and help make them highly efficient. **SEE 14.1**

Physical Layout

When evaluating a production studio, you should look not only at the electronic equipment it houses but also at its physical layout—its size, floor and ceiling, doors and walls, and air-conditioning.

Size   If you do a simple interview or have a single performer talk to the audience on a close-up, you can get by with amazingly little studio space. But if you plan a more ambitious project, such as a large panel discussion or the video-recording of a music show or drama, you need a larger studio. In general, it is easier to produce a small show in a large studio than a large show in a small one. But you will quickly learn that large studios are usually harder to manage than small ones. Somehow large studios require more energy to get a production started than do smaller ones; they necessitate longer camera and audio cables, more lighting instruments, and usually more crew. If you have a choice, use a studio that fits your production needs.

Floor and ceiling   A good studio must have a hard, level floor so that cameras can travel freely and smoothly. Most studio floors are concrete that is polished or covered with hard plastic or seamless linoleum.

14.1 VIDEO PRODUCTION STUDIO

A well-designed studio provides optimal control for multicamera and single-camera video productions. It facilitates teamwork and the coordination of all major production elements.

Edward Aiona

One of the most important design features of a good studio is adequate ceiling height. The ceiling must be high enough to accommodate normal 10-foot scenery and to provide enough space for the lighting grid or battens. Although you may get by with a minimum ceiling height of 14 feet for a very small studio, most professional studios have ceilings that are 30 or more feet above the studio floor. Such a high ceiling makes it possible to suspend the lighting instruments above even tall scenery and leaves adequate space above them for the heat of the lighting instruments to dissipate.

Doors and walls   Studio doors seem rather unimportant until you have to move scenery, furniture, and large equipment in and out. Undersized studio doors can cause a great deal of frustration for the production crew and frequently damage to equipment and scenery. Good studio doors must also be soundproof enough to keep all but the loudest noises from leaking into the studio.

The studio walls and ceiling are normally treated with sound-absorbing material to "deaden" the studio. A fairly "dead" studio minimizes reverberation, which means that it keeps the sounds from bouncing indiscriminately off the walls.

At least two or three sides of the studio are normally covered with a *cyclorama*, or cyc—a continuous piece of muslin or canvas suspended from a pipe or heavy curtain track. The light-gray or light-beige cyc serves as a convenient neutral background for a variety of setups. It should be light enough so that you can tint it with colored lights. A ground row, which is a curved piece of scenery placed on the studio floor in front of the cyc, helps blend the vertical cyc into the studio floor to form a seamless background. **SEE 14.2**

Some cycloramas are suspended from a double track, with the front track holding a variety of additional curtains, called drops. The most frequently used drops are the chroma-key backdrop, which consists of a large chroma-key blue or green piece of cloth, and the black drop, used for special lighting effects.

Many studios have a built-in hardwall cyc, which covers part of a studio wall. The ground row is part of the hardwall cyc. **SEE 14.3** The advantages of a hardwall cyc are that it does not wrinkle or tear even after longtime use and it can easily be repainted. The disadvantages are that it has a high degree of sound reflectance, often causing unwanted echoes, and it takes up considerable studio space.

Air-conditioning   Many studios suffer from air-conditioning problems. Because the lighting instruments generate so much heat, the air-conditioning system must work overtime. When operating at full capacity, all but the most expensive systems create air noise, which is inevitably picked up by the sensitive studio mics and duly amplified in the audio console. You must then decide whether to keep the air-conditioning going despite the noise it makes or to turn it off and make talent, crew, and equipment sweat.

Cyclorama

Ground row

© Cengage Learning 2011

14.2 GROUND ROW
The ground row is a curved piece of scenery that is placed on the studio floor in front of the cyclorama to blend the two into a seamless background.

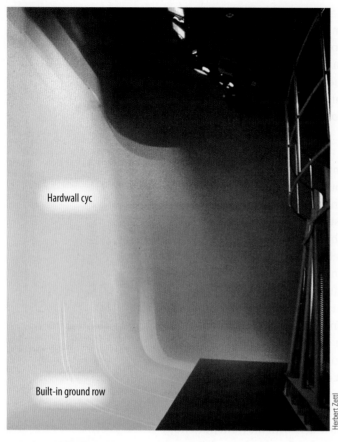

Hardwall cyc

Built-in ground row

Herbert Zettl

14.3 HARDWALL CYC
The hardwall cyc is constructed of fiberboard and placed in front of one of the studio walls. The ground row is built-in.

Major Installations

Regardless of size, all studios have similar basic technical installations, which include lights, electrical outlets, intercommunication systems, monitors, and studio speakers.

Lights   Most of the lighting instruments used in a video production studio are suspended from a lighting grid or movable battens, as shown in figure 14.1. Hanging the lighting instruments above the scenery and action keeps the lights out of camera range, allows the cameras and the people to move about freely, and, if it is a permanent set, minimizes the time needed for lighting it.

Some studios still have a physical lighting patchboard (which routes lights to specific dimmers) and even the actual dimmer controls in the studio itself. When using computerized lighting control units, you may find the main control unit in the control room and an additional remote lighting control in the studio. The one in the control room is used for the actual studio production; the one in the studio is for setup and rehearsals. The patching—the assignment of lighting instruments to dimmers—is usually done with computer software.

Electrical outlets   You may not consider wall outlets an important factor in studio design until you discover that there are not enough of them or that they are in the wrong places. There should be several groups of outlets for cameras, microphones, monitors, intercommunication headsets, and regular AC power distributed along all four walls. If all the outlets are concentrated on only one wall, you will have to string long power cables and extension cords throughout the studio to get the equipment into the desired positions around the scenery.

All outlets must be clearly marked so that you do not plug equipment into the wrong outlet. This labeling is especially important when the outlets are behind the cyc, where it is usually dark and there is little space to maneuver.

Intercommunication systems   Reliable *intercom* systems are one of the most important technical installations. Normal studio intercoms use PL and IFB systems. The *PL* (party line, phone line, or private line) system allows all production and engineering personnel to be in constant voice contact with one another. Each member of the production team and the technical crew wears a headset with a microphone for efficient communication. Such systems can be wired (through the camera cables or separate intercom cables) or, in larger studios, wireless. Most PL systems operate on at least two channels so that different groups can be addressed separately.

Producers and directors make frequent use of the **IFB** (interruptible foldback or feedback) system, which allows them to communicate directly with the talent, who wear tiny earpieces instead of headsets while on the air. Such instant communication from the control room to the talent is especially important during news and interviews.

Monitors   As you recall, a **monitor** is a high-quality video display that cannot receive broadcast signals. You need at least one fairly large monitor in the studio that shows the line-out pictures—the video that goes to the video recorder (VR) or transmitter—to everyone on the floor. By viewing the line-out picture, the crew can anticipate a number of production tasks. For example, the operator of the camera that is not on the air can vary its shot so that it does not duplicate that of the on-the-air camera; the floor manager can see how close he can be to the talent for the necessary hand signals without getting into camera range; and the microphone boom operator can test how far the mic can be lowered before it gets into the shot.

News- and weathercasters often work with several studio monitors that carry not only the line-out pictures but also the remote feeds and the video playbacks. Because the weathercaster actually stands in front of a plain chroma-key backdrop when pointing to the (nonexistent) weather map, the monitor, which shows the complete key including the map, is essential for guiding the talent's gestures. For audience participation shows, you need several monitors to show the audience what the event looks like on-screen. When the camera is on the audience, it always entices some people watching the monitors to wave at themselves, probably to confirm that they are indeed on television.

Studio speakers   The studio speakers do for the program sound what the video monitors do for the picture portion. The studio speakers can feed the program sound or any other sounds—music, telephone rings, crashing noises—into the studio to be synchronized with the action. They can also be used for the **SA** (studio address system, also called PA, for public address system), which allows the control room personnel (usually the director) to talk to the studio personnel who are not on headsets. The SA is obviously not used on the air, but it is helpful for calling the crew back to rehearsal, reminding them of the time remaining to air time, or advising them to put on their PL headsets.

◼ STUDIO CONTROL ROOM

The **studio control room**, housed in a separate area adjacent to the studio, is designed to accommodate the people who make the decisions while production is under way as well as the equipment necessary to control the video and audio portions of the production.

The people normally working in the control room are the director, the producer, and their associates; the technical director (TD); the CG (character generator) operator; the audio engineer; and sometimes the lighting director (LD) and even the video operator (VO).

The control room equipment is designed and arranged to coordinate the total production process. Specifically, it facilitates the instantaneous editing (selection and sequencing) of video images, the selection and the mixing of sound inputs, and the lighting control. The control room of news studios also houses the control equipment for robotic cameras. Some control rooms have windows that let the control room personnel see what is going on in the studio. More often, however, you will find that the only way you can see what's happening in the studio is by watching the monitors that show the various camera points of view. A studio that is used primarily for instruction, however, should have a large window. Such a window will greatly help students translate what appears on the control room monitors into actual studio traffic.

Image Control

The image control section contains the equipment necessary to select and sequence the video inputs, to coordinate the video with the audio, and to communicate with the production people, technical crew, and talent. In news studios it also includes the operation of robotic cameras (see figure 10.14).

Monitors   Recall for a moment the video switcher (explored in chapter 10). Each of the buttons on the program bus represents a separate video input. But how can you tell which pictures to choose from all the inputs? Wouldn't you need a separate monitor for each major video input? Yes, indeed. This is why a control room requires a large bank of monitors. **SEE 14.4**

Even a small control room requires a surprising number of monitors. Let's count them and identify their functions. **SEE 14.5**

Preview	1	
Line	1	
Air	1	If an on-the-air or cable station studio, this monitor will show what the home viewer sees
Camera preview	4	One for each camera; camera 4 can also be switched to remote
VRs	3	One for each playback VR
CG	1	
Electronic still store system	1	
Special effects	1	
Remote	1	Remote feeds; can also be used for additional camera
Total	14	Monitors

These monitors are stacked in a variety of configurations in front of the director and the TD. The preview (or preset), line, and air monitors are generally larger than the rest of the preview monitors. They usually have the wide-screen 16 × 9 HDTV (high-definition television) aspect ratio, even if the rest of the preview monitors

Previews for 6 cameras | Clock | Remote feeds | Digital effects previews | Previews for video recorders

Preview monitor | Video servers | Line or program monitor | CG and ESS system | Preview monitor

Edward Aiona

14.4 CONTROL ROOM MONITOR STACK

The control room monitors show all available video sources, such as the studio cameras, remote video, video recorders, servers, CG, electronic still store (ESS) system, and special effects. The large color monitors show the preview video (the upcoming shots) and the line-out (what is being sent to the VR and/or the transmitter).

14.5 SIMPLE MONITOR STACK

Even this simple control room display requires 14 monitors: three large 16 × 9 monitors for preview, line, and air; four camera previews, one of which is switchable to remote; three for VRs; and one each for CG, ESS, special effects, and remote. Except for the 16 × 9 preview, line, and air monitors, all are 4 × 3 displays.

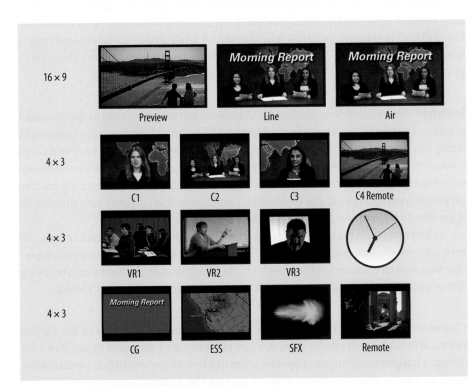

16 × 9 — Preview | Line | Air

4 × 3 — C1 | C2 | C3 | C4 Remote

4 × 3 — VR1 | VR2 | VR3

4 × 3 — CG | ESS | SFX | Remote

Edward Aiona

have 4 × 3 screens. If the stack is relatively simple, some control rooms divide a large flat-panel screen into various monitor displays. Many different configurations are possible with such a multiview display.

You may wonder how anybody can ever watch all these monitors at the same time during a multicamera show. Actually, you don't pay full attention to all of them all the time; you scan the active ones, much like looking at your rearview mirrors while driving, and then focus your attention on the monitors that carry the video most important to you. Nevertheless, you must always be aware of what the rest of the monitors are showing. After some practice you will be able to see more and more monitors, much like a maestro's reading a complex score while conducting an orchestra.

Intercom   The director also has easy access to a variety of intercom switches that control the PL, SA, and IFB systems. The associate director (AD), who sits next to the director in large productions, uses the same switches. The producer, who may sit next to or behind the director, will normally have a duplicate set of intercom switches; this extra set enables the producer to communicate with the talent and the production people without interfering with the director.

Program sound   In addition to watching the preview monitors, giving instructions to production people, and listening to the PL, the director must also listen to the program audio to coordinate the video portion with the sound. A separate volume control enables the director to adjust the control room speakers, called audio monitors, without affecting the volume of the program sound that goes to the line-out. You will find that listening to the program sound while doing all the other things is one of the hardest tasks for a rookie director. (We discuss directing more thoroughly in chapter 17.)

Switcher   You already learned that the video switcher is located next to the director's position. But why? This proximity enables the TD (technical director, who is normally doing the switching) to use the same monitor stack as the director and remain in close contact. Sitting close together helps the director and the TD communicate not only through the PL system but also through hand signals. For instance, by moving an arm at a certain speed, the director can indicate to the TD how fast a dissolve or wipe should be. **SEE 14.6** **ZVL1** SWITCHING→ Switching introduction

When fast cutting is required, some directors snap their fingers rather than call for a take once a shot has been readied. Such physical cues are faster and more precise than verbal ones. In smaller productions directors may do their own switching (labor unions permitting), a practice not recommended for complex shows.

Character generator   The CG and the CG operator are also located in the control room. Although most of the titles are usually prepared ahead of time, there are always changes to be made. Especially during live or live-recorded productions, such as sports, the CG operator must update the scores and prepare statistics

14.6 DIRECTOR/ TD PROXIMITY IN CONTROL ROOM
The production switcher is located next to the director's position for optimal communication between director and TD.

Production switcher

TD operating switcher

Director

during the game; or the producer or director may call for titles that have not been preprogrammed. With the CG operator in the control room, such changes are readily communicated and quickly made.

Clocks and stopwatches   These timing tools are essential in broadcast operations, where programs are aired according to a second-by-second schedule. But even if your productions are video-recorded for postproduction, the clock will tell you whether the recording session is going according to the production time line, and the stopwatch will guide you when inserting other recorded material. Digital stopwatches—actually little clocks—give you a choice of running forward from the start of the program or backward from the end-time. When running backward the stopwatch will display the time actually left in the program. Some directors prefer the analog clock and stopwatch because they can "look ahead" by watching the hands of the clock moving and thus pace the remaining program more accurately.

Lighting control and CCUs   Some control rooms house the lighting control (dimmers) and/or the CCUs (camera control units) for each camera. The advantage of having this additional equipment in the control room is that all image control is in a single location, helping communication among the various technicians. The disadvantage is that the control room gets quite crowded with additional equipment and people.

14.7 AUDIO CONTROL BOOTH

The television audio control booth contains a variety of audio control equipment, such as the control console, a patchbay, various digital record and play equipment, loudspeakers, intercom systems, and a video line monitor.

Video monitors · Audio monitor · Patchbay · VU meter (volume indicators) · Sound quality controls · Volume controls

Edward Aiona

Sound Control

The sound control is the audio booth attached to the video control room. It is usually isolated from the video control room so that the audio engineer is not disturbed by all the talk. Most audio booths have a window that allows the audio engineer to see the activities in the control room and, ideally, even the director's preview monitors. Well-equipped audio booths have both a preview and a line monitor. The preview monitor aids the audio engineer in anticipating and executing tight audio cues. The audio engineer is further aided by a marked script or show format, whose cue lines prepare him for upcoming audio and help him react more quickly to the director's cues.

The audio booth normally contains an audio console, a patchbay, a computer, and various digital recording and playback devices. The audio engineer can listen to the director via a PL headset or a small cue speaker and can talk to the control room and the studio through the PL and SA systems. The program sound is monitored though high-quality program speakers. **SEE 14.7**

■ MASTER CONTROL

If you use the studio strictly for producing video-recorded programs, you don't need a master control room, assuming that the CCUs are located somewhere in the studio control room. But all television stations and most larger nonbroadcast production houses have an equipment and communication center called ***master control***. If you are in the business of telecasting programs over the air or on cable or via Internet streaming, master control becomes an essential electronic nerve center.

The basic functions of master control in broadcast operations are overseeing the automated workflow and the technical quality of all program material slated for transmission, the content ingest from various internal and external program sources, and the storage and archiving of recorded content.

Master control normally houses the studio CCUs, video recorders, video servers, ESS systems, and various routing switchers and installations that monitor the technical quality of every second of programming that is broadcast on the air, though cable, or via Internet streaming. Master control for nonbroadcast operations may contain equipment that is usually housed in a studio control room, such as CCUs, video recorders and servers, and monitors and intercom systems.

Workflow and Quality Control

Master control monitors every studio production and supplies additional video clips from both stored and external sources. Its main function is to select for each program day specific live feeds or content from video servers, check their technical integrity, and route the selected programs to the transmitter, cable, or other distribution channel, such as the Internet.

The daily program sequence is dictated by the program log, which lists what programs go on the air at what time. The program log shows every second of programming aired on a particular day as well as other important information, such as the title and the type of each program and its origin (local live, server, or network or satellite feed). The log is distributed throughout the station via computer and sometimes also as hard copy. **SEE 14.8**

The actual on-the-air switching of broadcast content is mostly done by computer. In case the computer system goes down, however, an operator monitors

HSE NUMBER	SCH TIME	PGM	LENGTH	ORIGIN VID	AUD
N 3349	10 59 40	NEWS CLOSE	015	VR4	VR4
S11	10 59 55	STATION BR	005	ESS	CART20
E 1009	11 00 00	GOING PLACES 1	030	VR5	VR5
C5590	11 00 30	FED EX	010	VR2	VR2
C 9930-0	11 00 40	HAYDEN PUBLISHING	010	VR18	VT18
C 10004	11 00 50	SPORTS HILIGHTS	005	ESS	CART21
PP 99	11 00 55	STATION PROMO SPORTS	005	SVR2	SVR2
E 1009	11 01 00	GOING PLACES CONT 2	1100	VR5	VR5
C 9990-34	11 12 00	HYDE PRODUCTS	030	VR34	VR34
C 774-55	11 12 30	COMPESI FISHING	010	VR35	VR35
C 993-48	11 12 40	KIPPER COMPUTERS	010	VR78	VR78
PS	11 12 50	RED CROSS	005	ESS	CART22
PP 1003	11 12 55	STATION PROMO GOOD MRNG	005	SVR2	SVR2
E 1009	11 13 00	GOING PLACES CONT 3	1025	VR5	VR5
C 222-99	11 23 25	WHITNEY MOTORCYCLE	020	VR33	VR33
C 00995-45	11 23 45	IDEAS TO IMAGES	010	VR91	VR91
PS	11 23 55	AIDS AWARENESS	005	ESS	CART02
E 1009	11 24 00	GOING PLACES CONT 4	100	VR5	VR5
N 01125	11 25 00	NEWSBREAK ***LIVE	010	ST1LV	ST1
C 00944-11	11 25 10	ALL SEASONS GNRL FOODS	030	VR27	VT27
N 01125	11 25 40	NEWS CONT***LIVE	200	ST1LV	ST1
C 995-89	11 27 40	BLOSSER FOR PRESIDENT	020	VR24	VR24
PP 77	11 28 00	NEXT DAY	010	VR19	VR19

© Cengage Learning 2011

14.8 PROGRAM LOG

The program log is a second-by-second list of all programs telecast during a broadcast day. It shows the scheduled (start) times, program title and type, video and audio origin (server, tape, live, or feed), house number, and other pertinent broadcast information.

14.9 MASTER CONTROL SWITCHING AREA

Master control serves as the final video and audio control for all program material before it is broadcast or distributed by the station's transmitter, a satellite, cable, or the Internet. Computers run most master control functions, with the master control technician overseeing the automated functions and assuming manual control in case of system failure.

Computer log display   Manual master control switcher

Edward Aiona

the automatic switching and is ready to press into service the manual master control switcher. **SEE 14.9**

Content Ingest

Content **ingest** refers to program input. Somehow the industry fell in love with this term, which stuck against all odds and respect for language. Master control keeps track of all incoming content, regardless of whether it arrives via satellite, cable, Internet, or mail. As ingest operator, you are responsible for logging all incoming program feeds, giving them identification codes (occasionally still called "house numbers"), and recording the priority feeds on a video server. Fortunately, much of this work is automated by computer. Isn't ingest a form of capture? Yes, but *capture* refers more to transferring camera source footage onto the hard drive of a nonlinear editing program, whereas *ingest* refers to selecting relevant programs from the various program feeds, translating them into specific data files, and storing them on high-capacity hard drives of large video servers.

Storage and Archiving

You have probably noticed that storing all of the videotapes, CDs, and DVDs you have collected is already quite difficult, especially if you want to quickly find a specific disc. Just think how challenging that job must be for a television station that deals with hundreds of pieces of new program content every day. Much of such content needs to be cataloged and stored for easy retrieval. Also, somebody must take care of archiving the ever-growing video library so that a specific piece of content, such as the president's latest speech, can be quickly retrieved if necessary for the evening newscast. Fortunately, these activities are also made somewhat more manageable by workflow software.

■ STUDIO SUPPORT AREAS

No studio can function properly without support areas that house scenery, properties, and makeup and dressing rooms. Unfortunately, even large and relatively new studios usually lack sufficient support areas. As a consequence the studios themselves become partial storage areas for scenery and sometimes even serve as makeup and dressing rooms.

Scenery and Property Storage

One of the most important aspects of scenery and property storage is ease of retrieval. The floor crew must be able to find and pull each piece of scenery without having to dig it out from under all of the others. The prop areas and the storage boxes must be clearly labeled, especially if they contain small hand props.

Makeup and Dressing Rooms

Wherever you apply makeup, it must be done in lighting conditions that are identical to those in the studio. Most makeup and dressing rooms have two types of illumination: indoor lighting (with a color temperature standard of 3,200K) and outdoor lighting (5,600K). Because the indoor standard has a warmer, more reddish light than the cooler, more bluish light of outdoors, you should always check your makeup on-camera in the actual performance area before the dress rehearsal and again before the performance. (Color temperature is explained in chapter 8.)

■ SCENERY, PROPERTIES, AND SET DRESSINGS

You may wonder why the networks have such gigantic news sets for a single anchor, who usually appears on a loose close-up throughout the newscast. Although you see the whole set for only a few seconds during the opening and the closing, it is supposed to signal that the news department is large, well equipped, and high-tech and that the news the anchor delivers is significant. Yes, you could certainly do the same newscast just as successfully on a much smaller set.

Nevertheless, scenery and properties are used primarily to create a specific environment in which the action takes place, but they also reflect the nature of the event. The bookcases filled with matching volumes in an interview set may be a cliché, but they instantly communicate a lawyer's office. When dealing with scenery and properties in video production, you must always keep in mind that it is the camera that looks at the scenic environment, not the crew or the casual studio visitor. The set must be detailed enough to withstand the close-up scrutiny of an HD (high-definition) camera yet plain enough to avoid clutter that can detract from the performers. Careful attention to set detail is especially important when using HDTV cameras. The high resolution of HDTV makes even background detail more visible. The set must also allow for optimal camera movement and angles, microphone placement and mobility, appropriate lighting, and maximum action by the talent. It is also a major factor in setting style.

> **KEY CONCEPT**
>
> Scenery must create a certain environment and allow for optimal lighting, audio pickup, and camera movement.

Scenery

Although the design and the construction of scenery require specific training and skills, you should know what standard set units are and how to use them for creating simple environments. Here we discuss softwall flats; hardwall flats; set modules; seamless paper and painted drops; and set pieces, platforms, and wagons.

Softwall flats   A *flat* is a freestanding piece of scenery used as a background or to simulate the walls of a room. Softwall flats are background units constructed of a lightweight wood frame covered with muslin. The wood frame consists of 1 × 3 lumber that is glued together and reinforced at the corners by ¼-inch plywood pieces. To keep the frame from twisting, it is further strengthened by two diagonal braces and a toggle rail in the middle. If the studio floor is hard, you can put metal or plastic gliders on the bottom rail of the flat so that you can push it around without damaging the flat or the floor or yourself. **SEE 14.10**

The traditional and still most practical way to tie softwall flats together is by using lashlines. When joining flats, you actually lash two pieces of scenery together with a clothesline that is attached to the right top rail of each flat and pulled through cleats, similar to lacing the hooks of a boot. **SEE 14.11**   Flats are supported by jacks—wood braces that are hinged, tied, or fastened to the flats with C-clamps—and are weighted down and held in place with sandbags or metal weights.

Standard softwall flats have a uniform height but various widths. The height is usually 10 feet, or 8 feet for small sets or studios with low ceilings; width ranges from 1 to 5 feet. When two flats are permanently hinged together, they are called twofolds or books (because they open like a book); three flats hinged together constitute a threefold.

Softwall flats are easy to move, assemble, and store, but their simple construction is also a disadvantage: they tend to shake when you close a door or window on

14.10 SOFTWALL FLATS
Softwall flats are made of 1 × 3 lumber and covered with muslin.

Wood frame

Cleats for joining flats

Canvas or muslin cover

Lashline

Sandbag

Herbert Zettl

the set or if someone or something brushes against them. They are ideal for rehearsal and for less demanding productions.

Hardwall flats   Most professional video production sets are constructed with hardwall flats. They are usually built for a specific set and do not always conform to the standard dimensions of softwall scenery. Although there is no standard way to build hardwall scenery, most flats are constructed with a sturdy wood or slotted-steel frame (which looks like a big erector set) and covered with plywood or pressed fiberboard. Most hardwall scenery is moved with the help of built-in casters and joined with bolts or C-clamps. **SEE 14.12**

The advantage of hardwall scenery is that it is extremely sturdy; if a scene calls for slamming the door, you can do so without fear of shaking the whole set. You can also attach pictures or posters the way you would on a real wall. The disadvantages of hardwall flats are that they are expensive to build, difficult to move and set up, and even harder to store. Hardwall scenery is also apt to reflect sound and cause unwanted reverberations.

Set modules   Smaller video production companies, whose scenery demands are usually limited to news, interviews, office sets, or environments in which products are displayed and demonstrated, often use set modules. A set module is a series of hardwall flats and three-dimensional set pieces whose dimensions match whether they are used vertically (right-side up) or horizontally (on their sides). They can be assembled in different combinations, similar to building blocks. For example, you might use a modular hardwall set piece as a hardwall flat in one production and as a desktop in the next. Or you might dismantle a modular desk and use the boxes (representing the drawers) as display units. A wide variety of set modules are commercially available.

Herbert Zettl

14.11 FLATS JOINED BY LASHLINE
Softwall flats are connected by lashing them together with a clothesline, called a lashline. The lashline is woven around alternating metal cleats and secured with a slipknot.

Edward Aiona

14.12 HARDWALL SCENERY
Hardwall scenery is built with a sturdy wood or metal frame that is covered with plywood or fiberboard. Most hardwall scenery has built-in casters or is placed on small wagons for mobility. This is the back of a windowseat.

Seamless paper and painted drops   As you recall, the cyclorama is a large, plain, seamless drop that serves as a neutral background (see figure 14.2). In the absence of a cyc, you can construct a limited neutral area with a roll of seamless paper (usually 9 feet wide by 36 feet long) simply by unrolling it and stapling it horizontally on softwall flats. Seamless paper rolls come in a variety of colors and are relatively inexpensive. Painted drops, on the other hand, usually refer to rolls of paper or canvas with realistic or, more often, stylized background scenes painted on them. You can also create believable backgrounds electronically. (Synthetic environments are discussed in chapter 15.)

Set pieces, platforms, and wagons   Set pieces consist of freestanding three-dimensional objects, such as pillars, pylons (which look like three-sided pillars), sweeps (large, curved pieces of scenery), folding screens, steps, and periaktoi (plural of *periaktos*). A periaktos is a three-sided standing unit that looks like a large pylon; it moves and swivels on casters. **SEE 14.13** Set pieces are often constructed in modular dimensions so that they can be fitted together in different combinations. Some set pieces, such as pillars and pylons, are unstable and must be secured so that they do not tip over when bumped by crew, talent, or equipment. It is always better to overbrace than underbrace a set.

Platforms are elevation devices. Normal platforms are 6 inches, 8 inches, or 12 inches high and can be stacked. Platforms are often used for interview and panel discussion sets so that the cameras see the participants straight-on rather than look down on them. When used for interviews, the entire platform should be covered

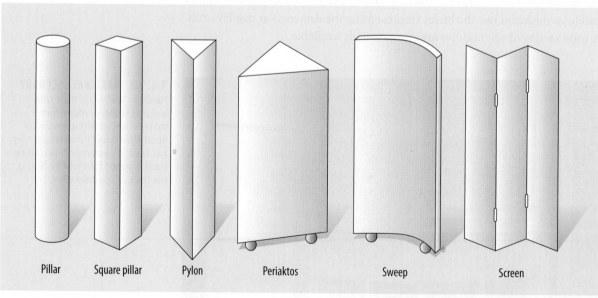

Pillar   Square pillar   Pylon   Periaktos   Sweep   Screen

14.13 SET PIECES
Set pieces are freestanding three-dimensional scenic objects used as background or foreground pieces.

with carpeting. As well as making the set more attractive, the carpeting absorbs the hollow sounds from people moving on the platform. You can further deaden such sounds by filling the platform interior with foam rubber or foam spray. Some 6-inch platforms have four heavy casters, converting the platforms into wagons that can support and move scenery from one place in the studio to another.

Properties

In video production properties—**props** for short—and set dressings are often more important than the background scenery for signifying a particular environment. You will work with two kinds of properties: set props and hand props.

Set props   Set props include the furniture you use on a set, such as the chairs for an interview, the table for a panel discussion, the desk from which the corporate manager delivers her weekly address, the bookcase and the file cabinet for the office set, and the inevitable couch in situation comedies.

When choosing set props, look for functional furniture that can be used in a variety of settings. Small, simple chairs, for example, are more useful and versatile than large upholstered ones. Most regular couches are too low and make sitting down and getting up look awkward on-camera. You can easily remedy this problem by padding the seats or elevating the entire couch. Some set props, such as news desks or panel tables, are custom-made. As with the news set, do not go overboard with such custom furniture, especially if most of the scenes show only medium shots or close-ups of the performers.

Hand props   Hand props are items actually handled by the talent—cell phones, laptop computers, dishes, silverware, books, magazines, glasses, and flowers. Hand props must work and they must be real. A bottle that doesn't open on cue can cause costly production delays. Because hand props are an extension of the talent's gestures and actions, and because of the close scrutiny of the video camera, you cannot get by with fake props. A papier-mâché chalice that looks regal on the theater stage looks ridiculous on the video screen. Equally silly is laboring under the weight of an empty suitcase. Whereas the theater audience may have some sympathy for your toil, the television viewer will more likely consider it a comic routine or a production mistake.

If you have to use a handgun, never use an actual firearm; try to get a prop gun. Shooting blanks at close range can be as deadly as if you were to use a bullet. This is one place where you can pretend; rather than pull the trigger, you can simply add a popping sound by pricking a balloon. The balloon pop is uncomfortably similar to the sound of a handgun going off and can be more accurately synchronized with the action than a recorded effect. If you add the sound in postproduction, you can quite readily match the pop with the action.

When using food, make certain that it is fresh and that the dishes and the silverware are meticulously clean. Liquor is generally replaced with water (for clear spirits), tea (for whiskey), or soft drinks (for white and red wine). With all due respect for realism, such substitutions are perfectly appropriate.

Set Dressings

Set dressings include things that you would place in your own living quarters to make them look attractive and to express your taste and personal style. Although the flats may remain the same from one type of show to another, the dressing gives each set its distinguishing characteristics and helps establish the style of the environment. Set dressings include curtains, pictures, sculptures, posters, lamps, plants, decorative items for a desk and bookshelves, or a favorite toy that survived childhood. Secondhand stores and flea markets provide an unlimited source for such things. In case of emergency, you can always raid your own living quarters or office. As with props, set dressings must be realistic so that they can withstand even the probing eye of an HD camera.

◼ SET DESIGN

Although you may never be called upon to design a set, you will certainly have to tell the set designer what environment you envision and why. You will also have to know how to interpret a set design so that you can evaluate the set relative to the program objective and the technical requirements, such as lighting, audio pickup, and camera and talent movement.

Process Message

Once again, a clear statement of the desired process message will guide you in designing the appropriate environment. For example, if the objective of an interview is to have the viewer get to know the guest as intimately as possible and probe her feelings and attitudes, what kind of set do you need? Because you should show the guest in close-ups throughout most of the show, you don't need an elaborate interview set. Two simple chairs in front of an uncluttered background will do just fine.

On the other hand, if the objective is to have the viewer see how the guest uses the physical environment of her office to reflect her power, you had better conduct the interview on-location from the guest's actual office or on a studio set that closely resembles it.

As with all other medium requirements, in designing or evaluating a set you must have a pretty good idea of what it is you want the viewer to see, hear, and feel. Once you have interpreted the process message as to scenic requirements, you need to translate the scene design into a floor plan of an actual studio set.

Floor Plan

The *floor plan* is a diagram of scenery and set properties drawn on a grid, called a floor plan pattern, that resembles the usable floor space in the studio. To help you locate a certain spot on the studio floor, the floor plan pattern normally has the lighting grid superimposed, much like the orientation squares of a map. By using the lighting grid, the floor plan pattern can also be used for drawing a light plot.

Elaborate set designs are always drawn to scale, such as the common ¼ inch = 1 foot. There are templates with in-scale cutouts for typical set pieces, such as tables, sofas, chairs, beds, and dressers. You can also use one of the many computer programs on the market for architectural layouts or interior design.

If the setup is relatively simple, the art director may make only a rough sketch that shows the background scenery, set props, and approximate location of the set, leaving it up to the floor manager to place the set in the most advantageous spot in the studio. **SEE 14.14** The floor plan should indicate all scenery, including doors and windows, as well as the type and the location of set props and major hand props. **SEE 14.15**

14.14 SIMPLE FLOOR PLAN SKETCH
The floor plan grid (often the lighting grid) helps locate the positions of scenery and set props.

© Cengage Learning 2011

14.15 FLOOR PLAN WITH SET AND HAND PROPS
Elaborate floor plans indicate the type and the position of set props (furniture, lamp, sculpture, and paintings) and major hand props (newspaper, tea set, and magazines).

When drawing a floor plan, keep in mind that the set must be workable for the cameras—it must provide adequate backing for different camera angles. A common mistake of inexperienced set designers is to show inadequate backing for the set props and the talent action. Another frequent mistake is a set that exceeds the floor area actually available. As mentioned earlier, the cyc and the items stored in the studio can radically reduce the usable floor space. To help the lighting people direct the back lights at the performance areas at not too steep an angle and avoid unwanted shadows on the background flats, all active furniture (furniture used by the talent) must be placed at least 6 to 8 feet from the background flats, as shown in figure 14.15.

Some floor plans indicate a generic set. **SEE 14.16** This set design has all the typical ingredients of a situation comedy: a living area with the inevitable couch in the middle of the room, a door to a second active set area (in this case, the kitchen), another door to an imaginary area (hallway or front yard), and a staircase in the back, leading to yet another imaginary room—usually a bedroom. In a generic set, the

Escape Stairs

Backdrop

Backdrop

Kitchen Dining room Living room

14.16 GENERIC SITCOM RESIDENCE

This set is designed so that four cameras, situated side-by-side in front, can pick up the action. It can be easily changed to other environments by using different set props.

basic setup remains the same but can be individualized by different props and set dressings. Note the "escape" behind the stairs, which helps the actors get back down to the studio floor, and the two backdrops on either side that display the imaginary extended space, such as a hallway or front yard on the right and a patio on the left.

Prop List

Even if the floor plan shows some of the major set and hand props, all props must be itemized on a prop list. Some prop lists itemize set props, set dressings, and hand props separately, but you can combine them on a single list, provided you don't forget anything. Assuming that you are the floor manager, confirm with the property manager that the props you requested are actually available when you need them, and inspect each one to see whether it fits the intended scene design. For example, a Victorian chair would certainly look out of character in an otherwise modern office set, unless it is to suggest an eccentric office manager. Verify that all listed props are delivered to you and that they are not damaged in any way before taking them into the studio.

Using the Floor Plan for Setup

A floor plan is useless if you can't translate it into an actual set and performance environment. You must acquire some of the skills of an architect or builder, who can look at a blueprint of a building and visualize what it will look like when erected and how people will move through and function in it. The following figure shows how a simple floor plan translates into the corresponding setup. **SEE 14.17**

The ability to read a floor plan is a necessary skill for all production personnel. A good floor plan helps the floor manager and the crew put up and dress the set fairly accurately, independent of the designer. The director can map out the major talent positions and blocking and also design the principal camera shots, positions, and

© Cengage Learning 2011

Herbert Zettl

14.17 FLOOR PLAN AND ACTUAL SETUP
The floor plan on the left translates into the simple set in the photo on the right.

movements before setting foot in the studio. The lighting director can lay out the basic light plot, and the audio engineer can determine mic placement. Also, by knowing how to read a floor plan, you can catch and often solve production problems before they occur. Because the floor plan is such a critical factor in production efficiency, you should insist on having one drawn even if the new set and the production are relatively simple.

M A I N   P O I N T S

▶ **Video Production Studio**

Video production studios are designed for multicamera productions and teamwork. Important features include sufficient floor space, a smooth floor for camera travel, adequate ceiling height so that the lights can be suspended, large doors, acoustically treated walls, and relatively quiet air-conditioning.

▶ **Major Studio Installations**

The major studio installations include a lighting grid or movable battens, adequate electrical outlets, an intercommunication system between the studio and the control room, studio video monitors, and studio speakers.

▶ **Studio Control Room**

The studio control room is designed and arranged to coordinate the total production process. It usually comprises the image control—with the switcher, CG (character generator), monitor banks, intercom lines, and sometimes the lighting control board—and the sound control, which contains an audio console and recording and playback equipment.

▶ **Director and TD**

The director and the technical director (TD) must sit next to each other to share the monitors and react quickly to physical signals.

▶ **Master Control**

Master control is the nerve center for television stations. Its basic functions are overseeing the automated workflow and the technical quality of all program material slated for transmission, the content ingest from various internal and external program sources, and the storage and archiving of recorded content. Much of such program acquisition and control is automated.

▶ **Studio Support Areas**

Studio support areas include the scenery and property storage and the makeup and dressing rooms.

▶ **_Scenery, Properties, and Set Dressings_**

Scenery consists of softwall and hardwall flats, a cyclorama and various drops, set pieces, platforms, and wagons. Properties include set props (such as furniture), hand props (items actually used by the talent), and set dressings (artwork, lamps, and decorative plants). Scenery must convey a certain environment and allow for optimal lighting, audio pickup, and talent and camera movement.

▶ **_Floor Plan_**

The floor plan is a diagram of scenery and set props that facilitates the setup of scenery, set decoration, and lighting and the preplanning of shots.

For your reference or to track your work, the *Zettl's VideoLab* program cue in this chapter is listed here with its corresponding page number.

ZVL1 SWITCHING→ Switching introduction   **304**

VI

Production Control: Talent and Directing

Now that you have acquired the basics of video production, you need to learn more about the people who work in front of the camera—the talent—and what they must do to convey the intended message. It is, after all, the people who appear on-camera who do the communicating with the viewers, not the ones who work behind the scenes to make the communication possible. Once you work as a video professional, you are bound to be asked to appear on-camera from time to time, as either a guest or a host. And, as a director, before you can tell the talent what to do, you must have some idea of what to expect from a good performer or actor.

Part VI explains what you need to know about performing in front of the camera—whatever your focus in video production—and prepares you for the culminating experience of multicamera directing from the control room and for single-camera film-style directing.

KEY TERMS

actor A person who appears on-camera in dramatic roles. The actor always portrays someone else.

blocking Carefully worked-out positioning, movement, and actions by the talent and for all mobile video equipment used in a scene.

cue card A large hand-lettered card that contains copy, usually held next to the camera lens by floor personnel.

foundation A makeup base, normally done with water-soluble cake makeup; it is applied with a sponge or sprayed on the face and sometimes all exposed skin areas.

IFB Stands for *interruptible foldback* or *feedback*. A prompting system that allows communication with the talent while on the air. A small earpiece worn by on-the-air talent carries program sound (including the talent's voice) or instructions from the producer or director.

moiré effect Color vibrations that occur when narrow, contrasting stripes of a design interfere with the scanning lines of the video system.

performer A person who appears on-camera in nondramatic shows. The performer does not assume someone else's character.

talent Collective name for all performers and actors who appear regularly in video.

teleprompter A prompting device that projects moving copy over the lens so that the talent can read it without losing eye contact with the viewer.

Talent, Clothing, and Makeup

The incredible amount of equipment and effort that goes into making even a relatively simple production, such as somebody's announcing on-camera the latest company news, is generally lost on viewers. All they judge the show by is whether the person on-screen is likable and whether he or she is doing a credible job. Similarly, viewers attribute the success of a talk show primarily to the host, not to how the show is lighted, how the cameras are handled, or whether the director shows a reaction shot at the right moment.

Video *talent* refers (not always accurately) to all people performing in front of the camera. We divide talent into two groups: performers and actors. **Performers** are primarily engaged in nondramatic activities. They portray themselves and do not assume the role of other characters; they are aware of the viewers and usually communicate directly with them by addressing the camera lens. **Actors**, on the other hand, always portray someone else; they assume a character role, even if the role is close to their own personality. They normally do not acknowledge the presence of the viewers but interact with other actors. Because performance and acting requirements differ in several major ways, they are discussed separately here. Specifically, this chapter focuses on the techniques of appearing in front of the camera, what to wear, and how to do basic makeup for the television camera.

> **KEY CONCEPT**
>
> Talent refers to video performers and actors. Performers portray themselves; actors portray someone else.

▶ **PERFORMING TECHNIQUES**
Performer and camera, audio and lighting, and timing and prompting

▶ **ACTING TECHNIQUES**
Environment and audience, close-ups, and repeating action

▶ **AUDITIONS**
How to prepare

▶ **CLOTHING**
Texture, detail, and color

▶ **MAKEUP**
Technical requirements and materials

■ PERFORMING TECHNIQUES

As a performer you are always aware of the viewers. Your goal is to establish as much rapport as possible with them and to have them share in what you do and say. Because video is normally watched by individuals or small groups of people who know one another, your performance techniques must be adjusted to this kind of communication intimacy. Always imagine that you are looking at and talking with someone you know, seated a comfortably short distance from you. Some performers prefer to imagine that they are talking to a small group or family; in any case, don't envision yourself at a mass rally, addressing "millions of viewers out there in videoland." When viewers watch you at home, it is you who is "out there"—not they. They are not visiting you; you are visiting them.

To help you establish this intimate viewer contact and perform effectively in front of the camera, you need to familiarize yourself with some production aspects of performer and camera, audio and lighting, and timing and prompting.

Performer and Camera

As a performer you have a communication partner—the video camera. It represents the viewer with whom you are talking. You may find it difficult at first to consider the camera your communication partner, especially when all you actually see while talking is the camera and the red tally light or the screen of the prompting device, some lights shining in your eyes, and perhaps the dim outlines of a few production people who are more interested in operating the equipment than in what you have to say.

Eye contact   To establish eye contact with the viewer, you need to look at the lens, not at the camera operator or the floor manager. In fact, good performers keep constant eye contact with the lens and seem to look *through* it rather than merely at it. When pretending to look through the lens, you will more readily extend your glance through the screen—toward the viewer—than if you simply stare at the camera. Also, you must maintain eye contact with the lens much more directly and constantly than when engaged in a real interpersonal conversation. Even a small glance away from the lens will be highly distracting for the viewer; it will not be seen as a polite relief from your stare but as an impolite loss of concentration or interest on your part.

If two or more cameras are used while you demonstrate a product, you need to know which of the two will remain on you and which will take the close-up of the product. Keep looking at the camera (or, rather, through the camera lens) that is focused on you, even when the director switches to the close-up camera that is focused on the product. This way you will not get caught looking in the wrong direction when your camera is switched back on the air.

If both cameras are on you and switched according to the director's cues, you must shift your view from one camera to the other to maintain eye contact. A good floor manager will assist you greatly in this task. He or she will warn you that a switch is coming up by pointing on the director's "ready" cue to the camera you are addressing and then motioning you over to the other camera on the "take" cue. On the floor manager's cue, shift your glance quickly but smoothly in the new direction. Unless told otherwise, always follow the floor manager's cues (shown in figure 16.1) and not the tally light that indicates the hot camera.

If you discover that you are talking to the wrong camera, look down as if to collect your thoughts, then look up into the on-the-air camera. Such a shift works especially well if you use notes or a script as part of your on-camera performance. You can simply pretend that you are consulting your notes while changing your view from the wrong camera to the correct one.

Close-ups   On video you will be shown more often in a close-up (CU) than in a medium or long shot. The camera scrutinizes and magnifies your expressions and your every move. It does not politely look away when you scratch your ear or touch your nose; it reveals faithfully the nervous twitch or mild panic when you have forgotten a line. The close-up also does not give you much room to maneuver. In a tight CU, a slight wiggle of the product you are holding will look as though an earthquake has struck. The close-up also accelerates your actions. If you lift up a book at normal speed to show its cover, you will most certainly yank it out of the close-up camera's view. Here are a few important rules for working with close-ups:

- When on a close-up, do not wiggle—remain as steady as possible.

- Keep your hands away from your face, even if you feel your nose itching or perspiration collecting on your forehead.

- Slow down all movements.

- When demonstrating small objects, keep them as steady as possible in one position. Better yet, keep them on a display table.

- If they are arranged on a table, do not pick them up. You can point to them or tilt them a little to give the camera a better view.

There is nothing more frustrating for the camera operator, the director, and especially the viewer than when a performer snatches the object off the table just as the camera is getting a good close-up of it. A quick look at the studio monitor will tell you whether you are holding or tilting the object for maximum visibility.

Also, don't ask the camera to come a little closer to get a better look at what you are demonstrating. As you well know, the camera operator can get a close-up not just by dollying in with the camera but much more quickly and easily by zooming in. You will not make the director very happy by asking for specific shots when the shot is already on the air or when there are technical problems that prevent the director from calling up the desired material. Talent—however eager they may be to look good on the air—should not try to outdirect the director.

Audio and Lighting

A clear, resonant voice alone will not make you a good performer. Besides having something to say and saying it clearly and convincingly, you need to be aware of the more technical audio requirements.

Microphone techniques   At this point you should briefly review the use of microphones in chapter 7. Here is a short recap of the basic mic techniques of concern to you as a performer:

■ Treat all microphones gently. They are not props but highly sensitive electronic devices that respond to minute vibrations of air.

■ If you work with a lavalier microphone, don't forget to put it on. If not assisted by the floor manager, run the cable underneath your jacket or shirt and fasten the mic to the outside of your clothing. Unless you are wearing a wireless lavalier, once "wired" you have a highly limited action radius. Don't forget to remove the mic and lay it gently on the chair before walking off the set. When using a wireless mic, check the power switch on the transmitter belt pack. It should be on when going on the air but off whenever you are on a break.

■ When using a wired hand mic, see how far the mic cable will let you move. In normal situations hold the hand mic chest high and speak *across* it, not into it. In noisy surroundings hold it closer to your mouth. When interviewing a guest with a hand mic, hold it near you when speaking and toward the guest when he or she responds. Gently pull the mic cable with your free hand when moving around. If you need both hands for something else, tuck the mic under your arm. A wireless hand mic will make your movements less restricted but adds the liability of losing the mic signal on its way to the receiving station.

■ Once a desk mic has been placed by the audio engineer, don't move it. Check with the engineer if you think it should be closer to you or pointing more toward you. Talk toward it, not away from it.

■ When using a stand mic, adjust the height of the stand so that the mic is a little below your chin, pointing toward your mouth.

■ When a fishpole or boom mic is used, be aware of where the mic is when you are moving, but don't look at it. Move slowly and avoid fast turns. If you see that the boom operator can't follow you with the mic, stop, then move on when the problem is fixed.

KEY CONCEPT

When taking a level, speak at the volume you will actually use during the performance, and speak long enough to set the optimal level on the audio console.

Taking a level   When asked to test the mic or to take a level, don't blow into it; say your opening remarks at the volume you will use when on the air. Performers who rapidly count to 10 or speak with a low voice off the air and then blast their opening remarks when on the air will not win points with the audio engineer.

Do not speak louder simply because the camera moves farther away from you. Although you correctly assume that the camera is the viewer with whom you are communicating, the camera distance has nothing to do with how close the shot actually is. More importantly, the distance of the camera has nothing to do with how close the mic is. If you wear a lavalier, you are heard at the same level and with the same presence regardless of whether the camera is 2 or 200 feet away from you.

Checking lighting   Although as a performer you need not be concerned with lighting, it doesn't hurt to quickly check the lighting on the monitor before going on the air. When outdoors, don't stand against a brightly lighted background unless you want to be seen in silhouette. When in the studio, if there is no light hitting your eyes, you are not in the lighted area. Ask the director where you should stand so that you will be properly lighted. In a play, when you happen to get off the rehearsed blocking into a dark area, move a little until you feel the heat of the lights or see the lights hitting you. Such concern for lighting should not encourage you to take over the director's function. Always check with the director if you have any questions about the technical setup and your activities within it.

Timing and Prompting

As a performer you need to be acutely aware of time, whether or not you are on the air. Even nonbroadcast video programs are packaged according to a rigid time frame. Because the audience has no idea about your time restrictions, you need to appear relaxed and unhurried when you have only 2 seconds left or you have to fill unexpectedly for an additional 15 seconds. Experienced performers can accurately judge a 10-second or 30-second duration without looking at a clock or stopwatch. Radio professionals can teach you a lot in this respect. They seem to be totally relaxed and never hurried, even when working up to the last second of the segment. Such timing skills are not inborn but acquired through practice. Don't put too much trust in your instincts; use a clock or stopwatch for precise timing. In any case, respond immediately to the floor manager's time cues.

IFB system   As a performer you must rely on—or put up with—a variety of prompting devices. The most direct prompting device is the ***IFB***—interruptible foldback or, as it is also called, interruptible feedback—system. You have probably seen performers or interview guests in remote locations touch their ear as though they were adjusting a hearing aid. That is exactly what they are doing.

When using interruptible foldback, you wear a small earpiece that carries the total program sound, including your own remarks, unless the producer or director (or some other production member connected to the IFB system) interrupts the program sound with specific instructions. For example, if you interview the CEO of a new Internet company, the producer may cut in and tell you what question to ask next, to slow down, to speed up, or to tell the guest that she has only 15 seconds to explain the latest multiplatform software. The trick is to not let the viewer know that you are listening to somebody other than the guest.

If you conduct an interview long-distance, with the guest in a remote location, he or she may also wear an IFB earpiece that transmits your questions on a separate IFB channel. You may find that guests may experience some problem with the IFB system, especially when the location is relatively noisy. Try to test the IFB system in advance to make sure the guest is comfortable using it.

Floor manager's cues   The time, directional, and audio cues are usually given by the floor manager. As a performer you will quickly learn that the floor manager is your best friend during the production. A good floor manager will always be in your vicinity, telling you whether you are too slow or fast, whether you are holding the product correctly for the close-up camera, and whether you are doing a good job. Unlike prompting devices, the floor manager can react immediately to your needs and to unforeseen performance problems. Normally, the floor manager cues you with a system of hand signals. **SEE 16.1**

16.1 FLOOR MANAGER'S CUES

Because the microphone is live during production, the talent must rely on visual time cues, directional cues, and audio cues from the floor manager.

CUE	SIGNAL	MEANING	SIGNAL DESCRIPTION
TIME CUES			
Standby		Show about to start.	Extends hand above head.
Cue		Show goes on the air.	Points to performer or live camera.
On time		Go ahead as planned (on the nose).	Touches nose with forefinger.
Speed up		Accelerate what you are doing. You are going too slowly.	Rotates hand clockwise with extended forefinger. Urgency of speed-up is indicated by fast or slow rotation.
Stretch		Slow down. Too much time left. Fill until emergency is over.	Stretches imaginary rubber band between hands.

16.1 FLOOR MANAGER'S CUES *(continued)*

CUE	SIGNAL	MEANING	SIGNAL DESCRIPTION
TIME CUES			
Wind up		Finish up what you are doing. Come to an end.	Similar motion to speed-up, but usually with arm extended above head. Sometimes expressed with raised fist, good-bye wave, or hands rolling over each other as if wrapping a package.
Cut		Stop speech or action immediately.	Pulls index finger in knifelike motion across throat.
5 (4, 3, 2, 1) minute(s)		5 (4, 3, 2, 1) minute(s) left until end of show.	Holds up five (four, three, two, one) finger(s) or small card with number on it.
30 seconds (half minute)		30 seconds left in show.	Forms a cross with two index fingers or arms. Or holds card with number.
15 seconds		15 seconds left in show.	Shows fist (which can also mean wind up). Or holds card with number.
Roll VR or server (and countdown) 2, 1, take VR or server		VR is rolling. VR or server insert is coming up.	Holds extended left hand in front of face, moves right hand in cranking motion. Extends two, one finger(s); clenches fist or gives cut signal.

Edward Aiona

16.1 FLOOR MANAGER'S CUES *(continued)*

CUE	SIGNAL	MEANING	SIGNAL DESCRIPTION
DIRECTIONAL CUES			
Closer		Performer must come closer or bring object closer to camera.	Moves both hands toward self, palms in.
Back		Performer must step back or move object away from camera.	Uses both hands in pushing motion, palms out.
Walk		Performer must move to next performance area.	Makes a walking motion with index and middle fingers in direction of movement.
Stop		Stop right here. Do not move anymore.	Extends both hands in front of body, palms out.
OK		Very well done. Stay right there. Do what you are doing.	Forms an *O* with thumb and forefinger, other fingers extended, motioning toward talent.

Edward Aiona

16.1 FLOOR MANAGER'S CUES *(continued)*

CUE	SIGNAL	MEANING	SIGNAL DESCRIPTION
AUDIO CUES			
Speak up		Performer is talking too softly for current conditions.	Cups both hands behind ears or moves hand upward, palm up.
Tone down		Performer is too loud or too enthusiastic for the occasion.	Moves both hands toward studio floor, palms down, or puts extended forefinger over mouth in *shhh*-like motion.
Closer to mic		Performer is too far away from mic for good audio pickup.	Moves hand toward face.
Keep talking		Keep on talking until further cues.	Extends thumb and forefinger horizontally, moving them like a bird's beak.

Edward Aiona

As a performer you must react to the floor manager's cues immediately, even if you think that a cue is inappropriate. Good performers don't try to run the show all by themselves: they react to the floor manager's cues quickly and smoothly.

Don't look around for the floor manager when you think that you should have received a time cue; he or she will make sure that you see the signal without having to break eye contact with the lens. As you just learned, even a brief glance away from the lens will tend to interrupt the connection you have established with the viewer. Once you have seen a cue, don't acknowledge it in any way. The floor manager can tell by your subsequent actions whether you received the cue.

KEY CONCEPT

Always respond promptly to the floor manager's cues.

16.2 TELEPROMPTER

The teleprompter consists of a small video display that reflects the copy onto a slanted glass plate directly in front of the lens. The talent can see the copy clearly while it remains invisible to the camera.

Glass plate reflecting image from monitor

Copy as it appears to talent

Flat-panel monitor displaying copy

Teleprompter   The ***teleprompter*** enables you to read copy without taking your eyes off the lens. The teleprompter projects the copy off a small, usually flat-panel monitor or computer screen (such as an iPad) onto a slanted glass plate mounted directly in front of the lens. **SEE 16.2** While you read the copy on the glass plate, the lens can view the scene through the plate without seeing the lettering. All newscasters and hosts of shows with a newslike format use teleprompters, as do people who deliver on-camera speeches. The copy itself is normally generated by a word-processing program and sent by a desktop computer to the teleprompter monitor on each camera that focuses on you. The computer scrolls the copy from the bottom of the teleprompter screen to the top exactly at your reading speed. If you have to change your pace to stay within the allotted time, the scrolling speed can be adjusted accordingly by the floor manager or the teleprompter operator.

When you are using a teleprompter, the camera should be far enough away that the viewers don't see your eyes moving back and forth while reading yet close enough that you can clearly see the copy. Experienced performers still manage to look through the lens and make eye contact with the viewer even while reading the copy in front of the lens. Not an easy job by any means!

For the small teleprompters that can be used in the field, the copy originates from a laptop computer that also controls the speed of the scroll. Simple field prompters use a paper roll that projects hand-lettered copy over a glass plate in front of the lens. On some field prompters, the paper roll is mounted below or to the side of the lens. The roll is battery-powered and can operate at various speeds. If nothing else is available, read the copy off your script or notebook.

Cue cards   One of the simplest yet most highly effective cueing devices is ***cue cards***—sheets of paper or posterboard on which the copy is hand-lettered with a marker. The size of the cards depends on how well you can see and how far away the camera is when you're reading the copy. A floor person must hold the cards as close to the lens as possible so that you don't have to glance too far away and thereby lose eye contact with the viewer. You must read the copy out of the corner of your

Edward Aiona

16.3 HANDLING CUE CARDS

A This is the wrong way to hold cue cards. The card is too far away from the lens. The floor person is also covering part of the copy, is not reading along with the talent, and is therefore unable to change cards when necessary.

B This is the correct way to hold cue cards. The cards are as close to the lens as possible, and the floor person reads along with the talent to facilitate smooth card changes.

eye while looking through the lens. Decide on an optimal distance, then check that the cards are in the right order and that the floor person holds them close to the lens without covering the copy. **SEE 16.3** Ask the floor person to practice changing cards with you. A good floor person will change the card while you are reading the last few words and have the new card up while you are still delivering the last word from the previous card. He or she will not dump the used cards on the floor but put them quickly and quietly on a nearby chair.

◼ ACTING TECHNIQUES

To become a good video or television actor, you must first learn the art of acting. Whereas performers always portray themselves, actors assume somebody else's character and identity. Even the best stage and film actors must adjust their acting style and methods to the requirements of the video medium. Some of the major requirements are working in a technical environment without an audience, adjusting to the relatively small video screen and the frequent use of close-ups, and repeating the action.

Environment and Audience

As a video actor, you will be surrounded by much more technical equipment than if you were on-stage. Worse, you do not have an audience whose reaction you can see, hear, and feel. Unless there is a studio audience, all you see are lights, cameras, and production people who do not pay much attention to you. In fact, you will often feel neglected even by the director. But realize that, in a multicamera production, the director has to coordinate numerous pieces of equipment and a great many personnel and that some of the technical operations may need more of the director's attention than you do.

You may feel even more abandoned because of the lack of a live audience. Unlike in the theater, where the audience remains in a fixed place and gives you direct and indirect feedback, the camera does not respond to your performance but stares at you impassively and moves quietly all around you. It may look at your eyes, your back, your feet, your hands, or whatever the director chooses for the viewer to see. It is a little like acting for theater-in-the-round, except that in video all viewers, as represented by the cameras, sit at arm's length and even join you on-stage to get a better look at you.

Because the viewer is in such close virtual proximity, you need not, and should not, project your actions and emotions to somebody sitting in the last row. The camera, which is doing the projecting for you, can convert a small gesture into a grand act. When on a close-up, there is no need for you to act out your role; instead you must feel it. Internalizing your role is a key factor in acting for video.

The intimacy of video also influences the way you speak. You must reduce the customary stage declamation and voice projection to clear but normal speech. Good writers help you in this task. Instead of having you, as Oedipus, dramatically request, "Who planned the crime, aye, and performed it, too?" on video you would simply ask, "Who did it?" Exaggerated voice projection is one of the hardest things for stage actors to unlearn when switching over to the video medium. In video (as in radio) precise enunciation is more important than volume and projection.

Most importantly, you must be able to memorize your lines quickly and accurately. Although there may be a variety of prompting devices available (mainly cue cards), you cannot and should not rely on them if you want to be convincing in your role. Because many of your lines serve as important video and audio cues that trigger all sorts of production activity, you cannot afford to ad-lib. Ad-libbing a cue line will inevitably cause chaos in the control room and prompt a retake of the scene.

Close-Ups

The frequent use of close-ups does not give you much wiggle room. Sometimes you must stand uncomfortably close to other actors or move much more slowly than normal without appearing to do so to stay within camera range. The close-up also limits your gestures. If, when seated, you lean back or move forward unexpectedly, you may fall out of focus, and weaving sideways just a little may take you right out of the frame.

The close-up shots require that you be extremely exact in following the rehearsed *blocking*—the carefully worked-out stage positions, movements, and actions relative to other actors and the camera. If you stray even a few inches from the rehearsed blocking, you may be out of camera range or obstructed by another actor. To help you remember the critical blocking positions, the floor manager will usually mark the floor with chalk or masking tape.

If you or another actor is off the mark in an over-the-shoulder shot, you may be obstructed from camera view by the other actor. You can tell whether the camera sees you simply by looking for the camera lens. If you see the lens, the camera can see you; if you don't see the lens, you aren't being seen. If you can't see the lens, inch to one side or the other without obviously searching for it. Although the camera can be adjusted to get the proper over-the-shoulder shot, it is usually easier to adjust your position than the camera's.

To remember blocking, you may want to establish a mental road map that has prominent landmarks, for example: "First stop, the left corner of the table. Second landmark, couch. Move to the couch and sit on the right. Third landmark, telephone. Get up and move behind the telephone table facing the center camera. Pick up the phone with the left hand."

Although good directors will block you as much as possible so that your movements are natural, you will occasionally be in a position that seems entirely wrong to you. Do not try to correct this position until you have consulted the director. A certain shot or special effect may very well warrant such blocking.

Repeating Action

Unlike the theater, where your performance is continuous and according to plot progression, video acting—like acting for digital cinema—is usually done piecemeal. You may have to switch from the happy opening scene to the intensely sad closing scene, merely because both play in the friend's living room. By remembering the exact blocking, you can also help preserve continuity. For instance, if you held the telephone receiver in your left hand during the medium shots, don't switch it to your right hand for the close-ups.

In single-camera productions, it is normal to repeat the same scene over and over again. Such repetitions are done to get a variety of camera angles or close-ups or to correct major or minor technical problems. In repeats not only must you duplicate exactly the lines and the blocking for each take, you must also maintain the same energy level throughout. You cannot be "on" during the first takes and "off" during the later close-ups.

▐ AUDITIONS

Auditions are a test of your ability as a performer—and of your self-confidence. Not getting the part does not mean that you gave an inferior performance but that somebody else was thought to be more suitable. Take all auditions equally seriously, whether you are trying out for a starring role in a big television drama or for a one-line off-camera utterance for a product demonstration; but don't take them so seriously that you begin to suffer from depression because you didn't get the part.

Although you may not know beforehand what will be asked of you in an audition, you can still prepare for it. Be properly groomed and wear something that's appropriate and that looks good on-camera. Arrive on time, bring your résumé, and don't be intimidated by either the number or the caliber of people auditioning with you. You all have an equal chance; otherwise you would not have been called to try out for the part. Have a brief monologue ready that shows your range of ability. Keep your energy up even if you have to wait half a day before being asked to perform.

If you get a script beforehand, study it carefully. If the script calls for you to talk about or demonstrate a specific product, such as a new computer, familiarize yourself with the product ahead of time. The more you know about the product, the more confidence shows in your delivery. Ask the person conducting the audition what shots the camera will take. If close-ups predominate, slow down your actions and avoid excessive movements. Remember that you are not addressing a large audience but an individual or a small family seated near you.

As an actor be sure that you understand the character you are to portray. If you are not sure what the segment you are to read or the character you are to portray is all about, ask the person conducting the audition (casting director or producer)—but don't ask for the proper motivation. As a professional actor, you are expected to motivate yourself. Be inventive but don't overdo it. When working in video, little mannerisms, such as a specific way of keeping your eyeglasses from slipping down your nose, playing with keys, or using a slightly rusty fingernail clipper while engaged in a serious conversation, tend to sharpen your character more readily than simply working up to a high emotional pitch.

■ CLOTHING

What you wear depends not only on your preference and taste but also on how the camera sees your clothing. Because the camera can look at you from extremely close range or from a distance, you need to consider the overall line of your clothes as well as the texture and the accessories.

The video camera has a tendency to add a few pounds. Clothing that is cut to a slim silhouette usually looks more favorable than something loose and baggy. Avoid horizontal stripes; they emphasize width instead of length and make you look wider around the middle.

Texture and Detail

Because of the frequent close-ups in video and the extremely sharp image of the high-definition television (HDTV) camera, you need to pay special attention to texture and detail. Textured material and ties look better than plain so long as the texture is not too busy or contrasting. Even the best video cameras have a difficult time handling closely spaced and highly contrasting patterns, such as black-and-white herringbone weaves or checks. The electronic scanning of the video image can't accommodate the frequency of the high-contrast pattern, causing the camera to create a new, highly distracting frequency that shows up on-screen as vibrating rainbow colors and patterns, called a ***moiré effect***. **SEE 16.4**

Prominent, high-contrast horizontal stripes may also extend beyond the clothing fabric and bleed through surrounding sets and objects as though you were superimposing venetian blinds. On the other hand, extremely fine detail in a pattern will either look busy or, more likely, show up on-screen as smudges even in high-definition video.

You can always provide the necessary texture by adding such details as jewelry or a tie or scarf. Although you will undoubtedly prefer wearing jewelry that you like, refrain from overly large or too many pieces. Too much tends to look gaudy on a close-up, even if the jewelry is of high quality.

Color

Again, the colors you select are not entirely up to you but must fulfill certain technical requirements. If the set you work in is primarily beige, a beige dress or suit will certainly get lost in it. Avoid wearing blue if you are part of a chroma-key effect that uses blue as the backdrop. The chroma-key process renders transparent everything

Elizabeth von Radics

16.4 MOIRÉ EFFECT
The vibrating rainbow colors on the white shirt and gray tie of this performer were caused by narrow rows of reflective dots that crashed with the scanning of the video image.

blue and lets the background show through. If you wear a tie or suit whose blue color is similar to that of the chroma-key backdrop, you will see the keyed background image in place of the clothing. Of course, if the chroma-key color is green, you can wear blue but not green.

Although you may like red, most video small cameras—and some home television sets—don't. Even fairly good video cameras may show highly saturated reds as vibrating and bleeding into other areas. Such video problems, called artifacts, are especially noticeable in low-light conditions. But even if the camera can handle the brilliant red of your dress or sweater, your home receiver is apt to display vibration or bleeding effects.

Most high-quality cameras, especially HDTV cameras, can tolerate a relatively high brightness contrast. But, again, you will make the lives of the lighting director and the VO (video operator) much easier if you reduce the contrast of your clothing.

You should therefore avoid wearing colors of high-contrast brightness, such as dark blue and white, or black and white. If you wear a black jacket over a reflecting white shirt, the camera or the VO does not know whether to adjust for the high brightness values of the white or the low values of the black. If the VO tries to lighten the black areas to see some shadow detail, the white areas become overexposed and begin to "bloom." If the VO tries to control the overly bright areas to show more picture detail, the shadows become uniformly dense. Your skin tones will also get a few shades darker. Obviously, if you are a dark-skinned performer, you should not wear a starched white shirt (unless the occasion demands it). If you wear a dark suit, reduce the brightness contrast by wearing a pastel shirt rather than a white one.

As you remember from chapter 4, this contrast problem is especially noticeable when the camcorder is on automatic iris. The auto-iris will seek out the brightest spot in the picture and close down the aperture to bring this excess light under control. As a consequence all other picture areas darken accordingly. If, for example, you wear a brilliantly white jacket while standing in a relatively dark restaurant set, the auto-iris will close to darken the brightness of the jacket and, unfortunately, the already dark set as well. What you will get is a properly exposed jacket in front of an underlighted set.

■ MAKEUP

All makeup is used for three reasons: to enhance appearance, to correct appearance, and to change appearance.

Most video productions require makeup that accentuates the features rather than changes them. For female performers, normal makeup does just fine on-camera; male performers may need some makeup primarily to reduce light reflections off the forehead or bald spots and perhaps to cover some wrinkles and skin blemishes. In both cases, makeup must be adjusted to the technical requirements of the HDTV camera and the scrutiny of the close-up.

Technical Requirements

The video camera prefers warmer (more reddish) makeup colors over cooler (more bluish) ones. Especially under high-color-temperature lighting (outdoor or fluorescent lighting, which is bluish), bluish red lipsticks and eye shadow look unnaturally blue. Warm makeup colors, with their reddish tint, look more natural and provide sparkle, especially on dark skin.

Regardless of whether you are a dark-skinned or light-skinned performer, you should use *foundation* makeup that matches your natural skin color. This foundation is available in various types of cake or spray-on makeup. If you perspire readily, you should use a generous amount of foundation; although it won't prevent your perspiration, it will make it less visible to the camera.

Because you will be seen in close-ups, your makeup must be smooth and subtle. This requirement is the reverse of theatrical makeup, which you need to exaggerate as much as possible for the spectators sitting some distance from the stage. Good video makeup should accentuate your features but remain invisible, even on an HDTV close-up. Most talent who appear on high-definition shows prefer spray-on make-up. This make-up comes in liquid form that is applied to the face with an airbrush (an atomizer using compressed air). Be careful, however, that you don't spray too much on your face. Too much foundation makeup will make your face look pasty or even mask-like, especially when the lighting is rather flat (slow falloff).

Always apply makeup under the lighting conditions of the performance area. If you apply your makeup in a room that has bluish fluorescent (high-color-temperature 5,600K) lights and then perform under normal studio lights (with a lower color temperature of 3,200K), your makeup will be excessively reddish and your face will look pink. The opposite is true if you apply your makeup under lights with the indoor standard of 3,200K and then move into a location that is illuminated with the outdoor standard of 5,600K: your makeup will look unnaturally bluish.

If possible, check your makeup on-camera: have the camera take a close-up of you in the performance area. You may consider this method a frivolously expensive mirror, but it will benefit you during the performance.

If you need to use makeup to change your appearance, enlist the services of a professional makeup artist.

Materials

You can easily find a great variety of excellent makeup materials for video. Most large drugstores carry the basics for improving a performer's appearance. Women performers are generally experienced in using cosmetic materials and techniques; men may, at least initially, need some advice.

The most basic makeup item is the foundation that covers minor skin blemishes and cuts down light reflections from oily skin. Water-based cake makeup foundations are preferred over the more cumbersome grease-based foundations. The Max Factor or Kryolan pancake series is probably all you need for most makeup jobs. The colors range from a warm light ivory for light-skinned performers to a very dark tone for dark-skinned performers. For critical HDTV makeup, you may try the Dinair Airbrush Foundation, or Kryolan's HD micro foundation, which is sprayed on and looks smooth even in an extreme CU with a digital cinema camera.

Women can use their own lipsticks or rouge, so long as the reds do not contain too much blue. Other materials, such as eyebrow pencils, mascara, and eye shadow, are generally a part of every performer's makeup kit. Additional materials, such as hairpieces and even latex masks, are part of the professional makeup artist's inventory. They are of little use in most nondramatic productions.

Regardless of whether you will be on-camera as a reporter, a performer, or an actor, a solid knowledge of basic video production techniques will aid you greatly not only when working behind the camera but also when working in front of it. In fact, talent who know basic production techniques seem more relaxed in front of the camera and more prepared to cope gracefully with the technical commotion and the unexpected problems while on the air than performers who know little or nothing about video production. Likewise, knowing how to perform and act in front of the camera will make you a better behind-the-camera production person. As a director, such knowledge is essential.

M A I N   P O I N T S

▶ **Talent**
Talent are people who work in front of the camera. Talent include performers, who are primarily engaged in nondramatic activities, and actors, who portray someone else.

▶ **Performing Techniques**
The performer must imagine the video camera as his or her communication partner, keep eye contact with the lens when addressing the viewer directly, handle the microphone for optimal sound pickup, and use prompting devices discreetly, without making the viewer aware of it.

▶ **Close-Ups**
When on a close-up (CU), move slowly and keep all gestures small.

▶ **Prompting Devices**
In addition to the floor manager's cues, the major prompting devices are the IFB (interruptible foldback or feedback) system, the studio or field teleprompter, and cue cards.

▶ **Cues**
Always respond promptly to the floor manager's cues.

▶ **Acting Techniques**
Good video actors learn how to work well within a highly technical environment, adjust to frequent close-ups, and repeat certain actions in the same way and with the same intensity.

▶ **Blocking**
Meticulously follow the rehearsed blocking during each take. If you can't see the camera lens, you won't be in the shot.

▶ **Clothing**
On-camera clothing should have a slim silhouette, with textures and colors that are not too busy or contrasting. The camera does not like closely spaced, high-contrast herringbone weaves or checks because they cause the camera to produce moiré effects. Try to avoid highly saturated reds, especially if you're using small camcorders.

▶ **Makeup**
Makeup is used to enhance, correct, and change appearance. Always apply makeup under lights that have the same color temperature as those in the performance area.

KEY TERMS

angle The particular approach to a story—its central theme.

blocking Carefully worked-out positioning, movement, and actions by the talent and for all mobile video equipment used in a scene.

camera rehearsal Full rehearsal with cameras and other pieces of production equipment. Often identical to the dress rehearsal.

dry run Rehearsal without equipment, during which the basic actions of the talent are worked out. Also called *blocking rehearsal*.

fact sheet Script format that lists the items to be shown on-camera and their main features. May contain suggestions of what to say about the product. Also called *rundown sheet*.

multicamera directing Simultaneous coordination of two or more cameras for instantaneous editing (switching). Also called *control room directing* and *live-switched directing*.

news script Fully scripted text with video information on page-left and news copy on page-right. The copy (spoken text) can also be in a large center column that contains some additional information.

program objective The desired effect of the program on the viewer. The defined process message.

script Written document that tells what the program is about, who says what, what is supposed to happen, and what and how the audience will see and hear the event.

shot The smallest convenient operational unit in video and film, usually the interval between two transitions. In cinema it may refer to a specific camera setup.

shot sheet A list of every shot a particular camera has to get. It is attached to the camera to help the camera operator remember a shot sequence.

single-camera directing Directing a single camera (usually a camcorder) in the studio or field for takes that are recorded separately for postproduction.

single-column drama script Traditional script format for television plays. All dialogue and action cues are written in a single column.

take Any one of similar repeated shots taken during video-recording and filming.

time line A breakdown of time blocks for various activities on the actual production day, such as crew call, setup, and camera rehearsal.

trim handles Recording additional footage before and after the major shot content for precise editing. Also called *edit margins* and *pads*.

two-column A/V script Traditional script format with video information (V) on page-left and audio information (A) on page-right for a variety of video scripts, such as for interviews, documentaries, and commercials. Also called *two-column documentary script*.

visualization The mental image of a shot. May also include the imagining of verbal and nonverbal sounds. Mentally converting a scene into a number of key video images and their sequence.

walk-through/camera rehearsal A combination of an orientation session for talent and crew and a follow-up rehearsal with full equipment. This combination rehearsal is generally conducted from the studio floor.

Putting It All Together: Directing

irecting is where everything you have learned so far comes together. The job description is relatively simple: all you need to do is tell people behind and in front of the camera what to do and how to do it. The difficulty is that you must know exactly what you want them to do before you can direct them to do it.

Of course, reading about directing or listening to somebody explain it can take you only so far. The real test is when you sit in the studio control room and literally call the shots. Once you feel comfortable with directing multiple cameras from the control room, you can adjust relatively easily to single-camera directing—in the studio or in the field.

Before you dash into directing by reserving cameras, drawing a storyboard, and marking up a script, you must ask yourself what the intended program is all about. Recall the discussion from chapter 1 about the production model: moving from the idea to **program objective**—the desired effect on the viewer, then backing up to the specific medium requirements to achieve the process message—the actual effect. Fortunately, most scripts and program proposals state the program objective or purpose on the cover page or in the general introduction to the project.

You should also be clear about the angle with which the topic is approached. The **angle** of the program—its central theme and major storytelling approach or framework—is often buried in the script itself. The angle is usually provided by the writer or producer, but sometimes it is up to you, the director, to find one. The angle will then dictate your visual approach to the program.

Now it is time to learn about the various script formats, how to visualize and "hear" the scripted information as audio and video images, and finally how to coordinate your team to accomplish the actual production steps efficiently and reliably.

▶ **SCRIPT FORMATS**
   Fact, or rundown, sheet; news script; two-column A/V script; and single-column drama script

▶ **VISUALIZATION**
   Visualization of image, sound, context, and sequence

▶ **PREPARING FOR A MULTICAMERA STUDIO PRODUCTION**

Floor plan, talent blocking, camera positions, and script marking

▶ **CONTROL ROOM DIRECTING**

Terminology, time line, rehearsals, and directing the multicamera show

▶ **SINGLE-CAMERA DIRECTING**

Differences between multicamera and single-camera studio directing, and directing a single-camera production in the field

■ SCRIPT FORMATS

The **script** interprets the show idea into what the viewers should actually see and hear when watching the program. It is similar to a recipe in that it lists the major ingredients of the program and how they must be mixed to get the desired result. In the language of the production model, the script helps you translate the program objective into specific medium requirements. As a director you must know the basic script formats used in video production so that you can make this translation process as efficient and effective as possible.

Despite considerable variations, there are four basic script formats for video productions: the fact, or rundown, sheet; the news script; the two-column A/V script; and the single-column drama script.

Fact, or Rundown, Sheet

The **fact sheet** format is used for simple demonstrations by a show host. Also called a rundown sheet, it normally lists the major features of a product that the host should mention, although the presentation itself is ad-libbed. The director may write in the cameras used for the demonstration, but the cutting from one to the other depends on the host's actions. The rundown script format may also be used for routine shows, such as the morning show sequence of program segments that repeat Monday through Friday. **SEE 17.1**

News Script

The only thing that news scripts from different newsrooms have in common is that they are, more or less, two-column. In a **news script** format, every word spoken by the anchorperson is fully scripted. You may find news scripts that have two equally sized columns: The right column contains the spoken news copy plus the out-cues of the words of prerecorded segments, called packages. The left column contains cues to who is talking; the name, number, and length of the prerecorded clips, CG (character generator) copy, and effects; some shot designations; and whether the prerecorded insert is to be played with a voice-over (V/O) of the anchor describing what is happening on the video insert or with SOS (sound on source) or SOT (sound on tape)—the actual sounds that are recorded on the sound track of the news package. At other times the news copy takes center-stage and is written as a single-column text, with the nontext information squeezed into a narrow left-margin column or

```
Zettl's VideoLab 4.0 DVD-ROM COMMERCIAL
SHOW:
DATE:

PROPS:
Laptop computer running Zettl's VideoLab 4.0.
VideoLab package with disc as hand props.

FEATURES TO BE STRESSED:

1.  New multimedia product by Wadsworth/Cengage Learning.

2.  Sensational success.

3.  Was nominated for prestigious Codie Award.

4.  Designed for both the production novice and the video
    professional.

5.  Truly interactive. Provides users with a video studio in
    their own home. Easy to use.

6.  Users can proceed at their own speed and test their progress
    at any time.

7.  Will operate on both Windows and Macintosh platforms.

8.  Special introductory offer. Expires Oct. 20. Hurry. Available
    from all major software and bookstores. For more information
    or the dealer nearest you, visit www.academic.cengage.com.
```

17.1 FACT SHEET

The fact, or rundown, sheet lists the major points of what the talent is to do and show. The talent ad-libs the demonstration, and the director follows the talent's actions. No specific audio or video cues are listed.

embedded in the center column. In the latter case, the nontext information is clearly separated from the spoken copy by lines and/or a different typeface. **SEE 17.2**

A news package is a brief, prerecorded, self-contained story by the field reporter that is inserted into the newscast after the news anchor's lead-in. There are usually several packages in a newscast.

What news writers don't seem to agree on is just how to format the audio column. Many use uppercase letters for the spoken words, but some prefer upper- and lowercase letters; others use a combination of both. Reading from a printed page seems easier when the copy is in upper- and lowercase letters; when using a teleprompter, however, all-caps copy seems easier to read. In fact, some of the larger news services change all types of news scripts into an all-caps format when used as teleprompter copy.

Two-Column A/V Script

The two-column A/V (audio/visual) script is also called the two-column documentary script or, simply, documentary format, although it may be used for a variety of nondramatic programs, such as interviews, cooking shows, and commercials. In a

```
KHZV NOON NEWS 04/16


SFX bumper

JODEE O/C (on-camera)     IS SILICON VALLEY IN TROUBLE? YESTERDAY
CU                        PROFESSOR JOSEPH ALEXANDER OF THE UNIVERSITY
                          OF CALIFORNIA AT BERKELEY UNVEILED HIS
                          SUPERCOMPUTER IN HIS PHYSICS LAB. INSTEAD
                          OF SILICON CHIPS, ITS PROCESSOR IS BUILT
                          ENTIRELY OF NANOTUBES. NONOTUBES WILL MAKE
                          OUR FASTEST COMPUTERS SEEM LIKE DINOSAURS,
                          SAYS ALEXANDER.


Server 04                 TEN YEARS OF INTENSIVE RESEARCH HAVE FINALLY
File 147   (1:02)         PAID OFF FOR THE ALEXANDER RESEARCH TEAM AT
JODEE VO                  BERKELEY. THEIR NEW SUPERCOMPUTER IS ABOUT THE
                          SIZE OF A MATCHBOX AND A THOUSAND TIMES FASTER
                          THAN THE BEST THAT SILICON VALLEY CAN MUSTER.
------------------------------------------------------------------
Package 1                 IN-CUE: "The secret is nanotubes . . ."
Sound on source
Server 02                 OUT-CUE: ". . . will make silicon chips
File 12   (0:27)          totally obsolete."
------------------------------------------------------------------
JODEE O/C                 PROFESSOR ALEXANDER THINKS THAT THIS IS ONLY
                          THE BEGINNING . . .


                          (more--more--more)
```

17.2 NEWS SCRIPT

In this two-column news script format, the left margin contains such production information as who is on-camera, the type and the length of the video inserts, and special effects. The right or center column shows every word to be spoken by the newscaster as well as the audio in- and out-cues of the video-recorded inserts.

two-column A/V script, the left column contains all of the video information, and the right column lists all of the audio information. **SEE 17.3** Review the content of the script in figure 17.3, as well, as it is the basis of your control room directing assignment later in this chapter. **ZVL1** PROCESS→ Ideas→ scripts

Note that all audio cues in the audio column, including the names of the talent speaking the lines, are in uppercase letters. All spoken words are in upper-/lowercase style. The instructions in the video column use both upper- and lowercase. Some

LIGHT AND SHADOWS Series
Program No. 4: High- and Low-Key Lighting

VIDEO	AUDIO
VR standard opening	SOS
Mary on camera	MARY
	Hi, I'm Mary, your LD. Today I will show the differences between high-key and low-key lighting. No, high-key and low-key has nothing to do with how high or low the key light hangs but rather with how much light is on the scene. High-key has plenty of light on the scene. Low-key uses only a few instruments to illuminate specific areas. But high- and low-key make us feel differently about a situation. Let's watch.
Susan sitting on bench waiting for bus	OPEN MICS. SFX: DISTANT TRAFFIC SOUNDS. OCCASIONAL CARS GOING BY.
Key titles	
John walks to telephone	
Freeze-frame	SFX OUT - MARY (VO)
	This is a high-key scene. It is obviously daylight. There is plenty of light on the set with fairly prominent shadows. But the faces of the people have enough fill light to slow down the falloff and make the attached shadows transparent. Now let's see what John and Susan are up to.

17.3 TWO-COLUMN A/V SCRIPT

In the two-column A/V (audio/video) script format, the left column contains all of the video information, and the right column shows all of the audio information. The dialogue or narration is fully scripted.

VIDEO	AUDIO
John by the phone, looking for change	SFX: DISTANT TRAFFIC SOUNDS. OCCASIONAL CARS GOING BY.
John approaches bench	JOHN Excuse me. Could you please change a five-dollar bill? I need to make a call and . . .
Susan gets up and walks toward curb	SUSAN No!
Freeze-frame	MARY (VO) Oops. They don't seem to be hitting it off too well. In the meantime, note that the high light level helps give the scene a great depth of field. Although Susan and John are relatively far apart on the z-axis, they are both in sharp focus. Sorry about the interruption. Let's see how this plot develops.
CU John	JOHN I didn't mean to startle you. But I really need to make this call. You wouldn't have a cell phone I could borrow?
Susan studies the bus schedule; she looks through her purse	SUSAN No, I am sorry.

17.3 TWO-COLUMN A/V SCRIPT *(continued)*

VIDEO   AUDIO

CU John   JOHN
                               You wouldn't use pepper spray on me,
                               would you?

Susan moves to the lamp
post; John steps closer
                               SFX: BUS APPROACHES AND STOPS
                               POLICE SIREN COMING CLOSER

                               SUSAN
                               I'm not so sure . . .

Susan boards the bus   SFX: BUS PULLS AWAY

                               JOHN
                               Thanks a lot.

> The scene will be repeated under low-key lighting. Mary now comments over the
> freeze-frames on the specifics of low-key lighting. She emphasizes the change in how
> we feel about the situation under high-key and low-key lighting.

Mary O/C   MARY
                               I would certainly prefer to have John
                               ask me for change in the high-key scene
                               than in this low-key scene. Wouldn't
                               you? With all those ominous cast shadows
                               around and such sparse street lighting,
                               I wouldn't have taken a chance with him
                               either. Poor John!

Freeze-frame of   MUSIC
low-key scene

Closing credits

Fade to black

17.3 TWO-COLUMN A/V SCRIPT *(continued)*

scriptwriters maintain the all-caps convention because these words are not spoken. Because upper-/lowercase lettering is much easier to read, however, you will find that most scripts use that style for the video column.

Partial two-column A/V script If there is considerable ad-libbing to be done by the talent, the audio column indicates only who is speaking and the general topic; such a script is generally called a partial two-column A/V script. **SEE 17.4** This partial A/V script format is often used for instructional shows, even if they contain some dramatic scenes.

VIDEO	AUDIO
CU of Katy	KATY But the debate about forest fires is still going on. If we let the fire burn itself out, we lose valuable timber and kill countless animals, not to speak of the danger to property and the people who live there. Where do you stand, Dr. Hough?
CU of Dr. Hough	DR. HOUGH (SAYS THAT THIS IS TRUE BUT THAT THE ANIMALS USUALLY GET OUT UNHARMED AND THAT THE BURNED UNDERBRUSH STIMULATES NEW GROWTH.)
MS of Katy and Dr. Hough	KATY Couldn't this be done through controlled burning? DR. HOUGH (SAYS YES BUT THAT IT WOULD COST TOO MUCH AND THAT THERE WOULD STILL BE FOREST FIRES TO CONTEND WITH.)

© Cengage Learning 2011

17.4 PARTIAL TWO-COLUMN A/V SCRIPT

The partial two-column A/V script format shows all of the video information in the left column but only partial dialogue or narration in the right column. The questions are usually fully scripted, but the answers are paraphrased.

Single-Column Drama Script

The **single-column drama script** format contains the complete dialogue, narration over video, and all major action cues in one column. **SEE 17.5** As you can see, all names of characters ("ALAN" and "VICKY") and audio cues ("THEME #2") are in uppercase letters. All spoken dialogue (or narration over a scene) is in upper-/lowercase. Specific delivery cues ("surprised") and directions ("getting an extra chair for Alan") are also in upper-/lowercase but are clearly isolated from the dialogue either by double-spacing or by parentheses or brackets. You will, however, find scripts in which these instructions are in all-caps. If you aspire to be a scriptwriter, don't ever include camera instructions. Specific descriptions of shots should always be omitted and left for the director to add in the visualization and script preparation phases.

> **KEY CONCEPT**
>
> The four basic script formats are the fact, or rundown, sheet; the news script; the two-column A/V script; and the single-column drama script.

▆ VISUALIZATION

Take just a moment and pretend that you see your mother on television. Just how do you picture her? In a close-up (CU) or a medium shot (MS)? Seated or moving around? Do you see her indoors or out? What is she wearing? What is she doing? Reading? Getting ready for work? Cooking? Sweeping the front steps? Now imagine your dream car. What color is it? Is it parked in your garage or tearing up a winding country road? What sounds do you hear in these scenes?

What you just did is called visualization. In video production **visualization** means creating a mental image of a shot or a sequence of shots. A **shot** is the smallest convenient operational unit in video and film, usually the interval between two transitions. In a wider sense, visualization also includes imagining the sounds that go with the pictures. For the director visualization is an indispensable preproduction tool.

Image If the script gives you only general visualization cues, such as "young woman waiting at the bus stop" or "bus stop in an isolated part of town," you need to fill in the details to make a specific person out of the "young woman" and to give the bus stop a certain look (refer to the script in figure 17.3). You would certainly have different visualizations if the scene were to take place at midday than if it were played on a deserted street late at night. Providing such details is an important part of the director's job.

Sound Though you may find it difficult at first, you should always try to "hear" the sounds simultaneously with the pictures you are visualizing. For example, what sounds do you imagine at a brightly lit bus stop scene and at a dimly lit one? You probably think of different sounds in the two scenes. Assuming that you will support the lighting shifts with audio, we should probably hear more traffic sounds in the daytime scene than in the nighttime one. But the few traffic sounds in the low-key scene should be more penetrating. Similarly, we should hear the steps of the person approaching the young woman much more distinctly (higher volume) in the nighttime scene than in the daytime one. If music is used, the nighttime scene should have ominous music and, for good measure, be mixed with a faint police siren. It is usually easier to establish the emotional context of a shot or scene with the sound track than with the pictures.

```
SCENE 6

SKY ROOM. TABLE BY THE BANDSTAND.

THEME #2

We hear the last bars of dance music. The band is taking a break.
ALAN and YOLANDA are coming back to their table to join STUART, who
has been watching them dance. During their dance, VICKY joined STUART
and is now sitting in ALAN'S chair.

                         ALAN
                      (surprised)
                 You're sitting in my chair.


                         VICKY
         Oh, it's YOUR chair? No wonder it felt so good.
         But I didn't see any name on it. You know--reserved
              for . . . what's your name again?


                         ALAN
                         Alan.


                         VICKY
                       Alan who?


                         ALAN
                 Alan Frank . . . like in frank!


                         VICKY
                Reserved for Mr. Alan Frank!


                        STUART
                   Dr. Alan Frank.


                         VICKY
           Oh, DOCTOR! What are you a doctor of?


                        STUART
             (getting an extra chair for Alan)
                 He's a doctor of philosophy.


                         VICKY
                       (laughing)
           A doctor of philosophy? You look like one!
```

17.5 SINGLE-COLUMN DRAMA SCRIPT

The single-column drama script format contains every word of characters' dialogue and occasional descriptions of their major actions.

Context   Besides the program objective and the angle, your visualization is ultimately determined by the prevailing context in which a scene plays. For example, in the nighttime scene you would probably work with more tight close-ups of the young woman and have the man approach her more aggressively. But even if you kept the shots pretty much the same for both lighting scenes, the sound tracks could readily establish their different contexts.

Sequence   Your visualization must include not only the key shots but also a shot sequence. Unless you are dealing with a static setup and little camera movement, such as in news or studio interviews, your visualization must include how to get from one shot to the next. This is where your knowledge of vectors and the mental map comes in handy. A good storyboard can also be of great help in planning shots and sequencing. As you recall from chapter 12, the storyboard shows a number of carefully framed shots and their sequence (see figure 12.15). Such a sequence illustration is especially important for maintaining shot continuity when shooting out of sequence for postproduction editing.

But even in seemingly simple directing assignments, such as video-recording the monthly campus report by the college president, shot continuity must be foremost in your mind. Recall from chapter 13 how to preserve continuity when somebody misreads a word during a recording session. This advice is important enough to repeat here. If, for example, the college president mispronounces a name, stop the video recorder (VR) or camcorder and inform her of the problem. Do not resume the recording just before the mistake was made; ask her to go back to a point where a new idea—a new paragraph—is introduced. You can then start with a different camera angle or a tighter or looser shot, or have her look up from her notes, thus making the edit look natural and properly motivated.

A good rule is to keep your visualization simple. Don't be afraid to use conventional approaches; they are conventions because they have proved effective. As pointed out earlier, there is nothing wrong with a steady close-up of a "talking head" so long as the head talks well and has something worthwhile to say. Using conventional approaches is different from stereotyping, which deliberately seeks out event details that reinforce prejudices. Creativity in directing does not mean doing everything differently from all other directors; it means adding subtle touches that intensify the message and that give your visualization personality.

■ PREPARING FOR A MULTICAMERA STUDIO PRODUCTION

With your understanding of the program objective and the angle, you must now interpret the script for its medium requirements. This implies visualizing the shots; working out major talent and equipment positions and moves, or ***blocking***; and marking the script with cues to the talent and the crew.

Unless you are directing soap operas or dramatic specials right away, most of your initial directing assignments will not involve complicated shots or the blocking of complex scenes. More often you will have to coordinate where an interview

© Cengage Learning 2011

17.6 BUS STOP FLOOR PLAN
This floor plan shows the principal scenery and props for simulating a bus stop.

set should be located for optimal lighting, making sure that the audio is functioning properly and that the cameras are positioned for the best shots. Nevertheless, let's revisit the lighting-show script of the bus stop scene (figure 17.3); it is a bit more complicated than setting up an interview, but it will help you learn to read a floor plan, block talent and cameras, and mark a script.

Reading the floor plan   A floor plan will greatly assist you in visualizing key shots, determining the lighting and audio requirements, and blocking the talent and the cameras. Let's take a brief look at the floor plan sketch for the bus stop scenes. **SEE 17.6**

This bus stop floor plan will make your job relatively easy. You have four major action areas: Susan's bench, John's telephone, the bus stop sign and schedule, and the streetlight. Both cameras can be positioned for z-axis blocking of John and Susan in the bench and streetlight areas. The four areas offer a good opportunity for demonstrating selective low-key lighting. The audio is best handled by two wireless lavaliers, which eliminates any problems with unwanted shadows during the low-key scene.

Blocking the talent   Although the script has already given you basic visualization and action cues, such as "Susan sitting on bench" and "John walks to telephone," you need to be specific about exactly where on the bench Susan will sit and just where John will be at the pay phone. You can probably come up with several blocking ideas, but try to keep them simple. According to the program objective, you are not demonstrating clever blocking but the difference between high-key and low-key lighting. **SEE 17.7**

17.7 TALENT BLOCKING AND CAMERA POSITIONS
With a floor plan, the director can block the major moves of the talent and the cameras.

Positioning the cameras Note that whenever possible you should block the talent first, then place the available cameras in optimal shooting positions. This will achieve a more natural flow than if you move the talent to accommodate the cameras. Of course, there are many circumstances in which camera positions are established before you can do any talent blocking. Don't forget that you are essentially blocking for the cameras, not for a stage performance. In this directing assignment, two cameras should be sufficient. Both are positioned to cover z-axis blocking and effective over-the-shoulder shots (see figure 17.7). With minor reblocking you could even do this scene with a single camera.

Marking the script Unless you have a photographic memory, you need to mark your script for multicamera directing. Although there is no universal standard for marking a script, over the years certain conventions have been developed that make the job easier. The key to good script marking is to keep it consistent and to a minimum. Because every command should have a ready or standby cue preceding it, you don't need to mark the ready cues. A circled number 2 not only designates camera 2 but also implies the "Ready 2" cue. The worst thing you can do is overmark your script: While you are trying to read all your scribbles, you won't be able to watch the preview monitors or listen to the audio. Before you know it, the talent is a page or two ahead of you. As you can see in the next figure, some of the cues that were included in the script are reinforced, but most of the other essential cues are marked by the director. **SEE 17.8**

LIGHT AND SHADOWS Series
Program No. 4: High- and Low-key Lighting

VIDEO	AUDIO
(VR) standard opening	SOS
Mary on camera	Q MARY ⎣_____ / MS (2)

Hi, I'm Mary, your LD. Today I will
show the differences between high-key
and low-key lighting. No, high-key and
low-key has nothing to do with how
high or low the key light hangs but
rather with how much light is on the
scene. High-key has plenty of light on
the scene. Low-key uses only a few
instruments to illuminate specific
areas. But high- and low-key make us
feel differently about a situation.
Let's ⎣watch.   2 Susan cu (1)

Susan sitting ⎣on bench | OPEN MICS. SFX: DISTANT TRAFFIC SOUNDS.
waiting for bus | OCCASIONAL CARS GOING BY.   ZOOM OUT

(Key titles)

John walks to telephone ⎣_____   Q John walk

(Freeze-frame) | SFX OUT - (MARY (VO))

This is a high-key scene. It is obviously
daylight. There is plenty of light on
the set with fairly prominent shadows.
But the faces of the people have enough
fill light to slow down the falloff and
make the attached shadows transparent.
Now let's see what John and Susan are
up to.

17.8 MARKED SCRIPT

This script has been marked by the director. Note that the markings for the field of view (how close a shot appears) are written by the director, not the scriptwriter. Many script-marking symbols have become standardized, but you can use your own system so long as you are consistent. The ready cues are not written but implied.

VIDEO	AUDIO	
John by the phone, looking for change	(SFX:) DISTANT TRAFFIC SOUNDS. OCCASIONAL CARS GOING BY.	*3 John CU ②*
John approaches bench	JOHN	*4 z-axis ①*
	Excuse me. Could you please change a five-dollar bill? I need to make a call and . . .	
Susan gets up and walks toward curb	SUSAN No!	
(Freeze-frame)	☿ MARY (VO) Oops. They don't seem to be hitting it off too well. In the meantime, note that the high light level helps give the scene a great depth of field. Although Susan and John are relatively far apart on the z-axis, they are both in sharp focus. Sorry about the interruption. Let's see how this plot develops.	*5 John CU ②*
CU John	JOHN I didn't mean to startle you. But I really need to make this call. You wouldn't have a cell phone I could borrow?	*6 follow ① Susan*
Susan studies the bus schedule; she looks through her purse.	SUSAN No, I am sorry.	*7 CU Purse ②* *8 John CU ①*

17.8 MARKED SCRIPT *(continued)*

VIDEO	AUDIO
CU John	JOHN You wouldn't use pepper spray on me, would you?
Susan moves to the lamp post; John steps closer	(SFX:) BUS APPROACHES AND STOPS POLICE SIREN COMING CLOSER SUSAN L̲_____9_____ ② I'm not so sure . . .
Susan boards the bus *Walks past C-2*	(SFX:) BUS PULLS AWAY L̲ *10* ① JOHN Thanks a lot. L̲____*11*____ *Zoom out* *FREEZE*

> The scene will be repeated under low-key lighting. Mary now comments over the
> freeze-frames on the specifics of low-key lighting. She emphasizes the change in how
> we feel about the situation under high-key and low-key lighting.

VIDEO	AUDIO
Mary O/C	ⓠ MARY L̲____*12*____ *Mary Ms* ② I would certainly prefer to have John ask me for change in the high-key scene than in this low-key scene. Wouldn't you? With all those ominous cast shadows around and such sparse street lighting, I wouldn't have taken a chance with him either. Poor John! *13 DISS* ① *FREEZE*
Freeze-frame of low-key scene	(MUSIC)
(Closing credits)	
(Fade to black)	

17.8 MARKED SCRIPT (continued)

17.9 **SHOT SHEET**
This shot sheet shows the shot sequence for camera 2.

© Cengage Learning 2011

Make the markings big enough that you can see them clearly in the dark control room. Try to keep all of the camera markings in one row so that you can easily grasp the sequencing cues without having to read all of the lines. If there are many shots, you should number them in ascending order as they occur in the script. You can then prepare a ***shot sheet*** for each camera. **SEE 17.9** Don't number the shots for each camera with 1, 2, 3, etc. Rather, copy the shot number that you assigned each camera in the script.

> **KEY CONCEPT**
> Keep your script marks to a minimum and make them big enough for easy recognition.

■ CONTROL ROOM DIRECTING

Now you are ready to step into the studio to rehearse before going into the control room and video-recording the show. To communicate effectively with talent and crew and to make efficient use of your assigned time, you now must learn about the director's terminology, the time line, directing rehearsals, standby procedures, and on-the-air procedures.

Terminology

Most of the director's commands and cues have become pretty well standardized. The following five tables introduce you to the basic visualization, sequencing, special-effects, audio, and video-recording cues. **SEE 17.10–17.14**

> **KEY CONCEPT**
> Keep your terminology consistent.

Time Line

All studio productions must be done within a tight time frame. The overall production schedule, which lists the deadlines for the production, is usually prepared by

17.10 DIRECTOR'S VISUALIZATION CUES

The visualization cues are directions for the camera to achieve certain shots. Some of these visualizations can be achieved in postproduction (such as an electronic zoom through digital magnification), but they are much more easily done with proper camera handling.

ACTION	DIRECTOR'S CUE
To reveal what is in the upper off-screen space or to increase headroom	**Tilt up.**
To reveal what is in the lower off-screen space or to decrease headroom	**Tilt down.**
To center an object	**Center it.**
To reveal right off-screen space	**Pan right.**
To reveal left off-screen space	**Pan left.**
To raise the camera height	**Pedestal up.** *or:* **Boom up.** [with a jib or crane]
To lower the camera height	**Pedestal down.** *or:* **Boom down.** [with a jib or crane]
To move the camera closer	**Dolly in.**
To move the camera farther away	**Dolly out.**
To move the camera in a slight left curve	**Arc left.**
To move the camera in a slight right curve	**Arc right.**
To zoom to a tighter shot	**Zoom in.** *or:* **Push in.**
To zoom to a looser shot	**Zoom out.** *or:* **Pull out.**
To move the camera to the left with the lens pointing at the scene	**Truck left.**
To move the camera to the right with the lens pointing at the scene	**Truck right.**
To tilt the camera sideways to the left	**Cant left.**
To tilt the camera sideways to the right	**Cant right.**

17.11 DIRECTOR'S SEQUENCING CUES

The sequencing cues help get from one shot to the next. They include the major transitions.

ACTION	DIRECTOR'S CUE
Cut from camera 1 to camera 2	**Ready two — take two.**
Dissolve from camera 3 to camera 1	**Ready one for dissolve — dissolve.**
Horizontal wipe from camera 1 to camera 3	**Ready three for horizontal wipe** [over 1] **— wipe.** *or:* **Ready effects number *x*** [the number being specified by the switcher program] **— effects.**
Fade in camera 1 from black	**Ready fade in one — fade in one.** *or:* **Ready up on one — up on one.**
Fade out camera 2 to black	**Ready black — go to black.**
Short fade to black between cameras 1 and 2	**Ready cross-fade to two — cross-fade.**
Cut between camera 1 and clip 2 from server	**Take clip two.** [Sometimes you simply call the server number. If , for example, the server is labeled 6, you say: **Ready six — take six.**]
Cut between VR and CG	**Ready CG — take CG** *or:* **Ready effects on CG — take effects.**
Cut between CG titles	**Ready change page — change page.**

© Cengage Learning 2011

17.12 DIRECTOR'S SPECIAL-EFFECTS CUES

Special-effects cues are not always uniform, and, depending on the complexity of the effect, directors may invent their own verbal shorthand. Whatever cues are used, they need to be standardized among the production team.

ACTION	DIRECTOR'S CUE
To super camera 1 over camera 2	**Ready super one over two — super.**
To return to camera 2	**Ready to lose super — lose super.** *or:* **Ready to take out one — take out one.**
To go to camera 1 from the super	**Ready to go through to one — through to one.**
To key the CG over the base picture on camera 1	**Ready key CG** [over 1] **— key.**
To key the studio card title on camera 1 over the base picture on camera 2	**Ready key one over two — key.**
To have a wipe pattern appear over a picture, such as a scene on camera 2, and replace a scene on camera 1	**Ready two diamond wipe — wipe.**

Many complicated effects are preset and stored in the computer. The retrieval goes by numbers. All you do to activate a whole effects sequence is call for the number: **Ready effects eighty-seven — take effects.**

© Cengage Learning 2011

17.13 DIRECTOR'S AUDIO CUES

Audio cues involve cues for microphones, starting and stopping audio sources such as CD players, and integrating or mixing those sources.

ACTION	DIRECTOR'S CUE
To activate a microphone in the studio	**Ready to cue talent.** [Or something more specific, like **Mary** — **cue her.** The audio engineer will automatically open her mic.] *or:* **Ready to cue Mary** — **open mic, cue her.**
To start music	**Ready music** — **music.**
To bring the music under for an announcer	**Ready to fade music under** — **music under, cue announcer.**
To take the music out	**Ready music out** — **music out.** *or:* **Fade music out.**
To close the microphone in the studio (announcer's mic) and switch over to the sound on source, in this case, a clip from the server	**Ready SOS** [sound on source] — **close mic, track up.** *or:* **Ready SOS** — **SOS.**
To roll an audio recording (such as a clip or CD)	**Ready audio recorder, clip two** [or **CD two**]. **Roll audio.** *or:* **Ready audio clip two** — **play.**
To fade one sound source under and out while simultaneously fading another in (similar to a dissolve)	**Ready cross-fade from** *[source]* **to** *[other source]* — **cross-fade.**
To go from one sound source to another without interruption (usually two pieces of music)	**Ready segue from** *[source]* **to** *[other source]* — **segue.**
To increase program speaker volume for the director	**Monitor up, please.**
To play a sound effect from a CD	**Ready CD cut** *x* — **play.** *or:* **Ready sound effect** *x* — **play.**
To put slate information on the recording media (either open floor manager's mic or talkback patched to the VR)	**Ready to read slate** — **read slate.**

17.14 DIRECTOR'S VIDEO-RECORDING CUES

These cues are used to stop or start the recording mechanism (VR, optical disc, hard drive, or video server), to slate a video recording, and to switch to the recording output.

ACTION	DIRECTOR'S CUE
To start recording a program	**Ready to roll VR one — roll VR one.** [Now you have to wait for the "in-record" or "speed" confirmation from the VR operator.]
To "slate" the program after the VR is in the record mode. The slate is on camera 2 or on the CG; the opening scene is on camera 1. (We are assuming that the color bars and the reference level audio tone are already on the recording media.)	**Ready two [or CG], ready to read slate — take two [or CG], read slate.**
To put the opening 10-second beeper on the audio track and fade in on camera 1. (Do not forget to start your stopwatch as soon as camera 1 fades in.)	**Ready black, ready beeper — black, beeper.** **Ten — nine — eight — seven — six — five —** **four — three — two — cue Mary — up on one.** [Start your stopwatch.]
To stop the recording on a freeze-frame	**Ready freeze — freeze.**
To roll the recording out of a freeze-frame	**Ready to roll VR three — roll VR three.**
To roll the recording for a slow-motion effect	**Ready VR four slo-mo — roll VR four.** *or:* **Ready VR four slo-mo — slo-mo four.**
To roll a VR as a program insert while you are on camera 2; sound is on source. Assuming a 2-second roll.	**Ready to roll VR three, SOS — roll VR three.** **Two — one, take VR three, SOS.** If you do not use a countdown because of instant start, simply say: **Ready VR three, roll and take VR three.** [Start your stopwatch for timing the VR insert.]
To return from VR to camera and Mary on camera 1. (Stop your watch and reset it for the next insert.)	**Ten seconds to one, five seconds to one.** **Ready one, ready cue Mary — cue Mary, take one.**

the producer. The ***time line*** for the single production day is your—the director's—responsibility; it assigns each production activity a block of time in which the specific job must be accomplished. Initially, you will feel that the allotted time is much too short to even get through the basic rehearsals, or you may allocate too much time for one activity and too little for another. With some experience, however, you will quickly learn how long the individual production activities take and what you can accomplish in a certain period. The time line in the following figure allows generous time blocks for your lighting-show assignment. **SEE 17.15**

17.15 TIME LINE
The time line shows a breakdown of the major activities on the production day.

6:45 a.m.	Crew call
7:00–10:00 a.m.	Setup and lighting; dry run in rehearsal room
10:00–10:30 a.m.	Talent and crew meeting; trim lighting
10:30–11:30 a.m.	Camera and talent blocking in studio
11:30–11:45 a.m.	Notes and reset (correction of minor problems)
11:45 a.m.–12:15 p.m.	Lunch
12:15–1:15 p.m.	Camera (dress) rehearsal
1:15–1:30 p.m.	Notes and reset
1:30–1:35 p.m.	Break
1:35–3:00 p.m.	Recording
3:00–3:30 p.m.	Spill (grace period to fix whatever needs fixing)
3:30–4:00 p.m.	Strike

Once you have a realistic time line, you must stick with it. Novice directors tend to spend an inordinate amount of time polishing the first takes and then have to rush through the better part of the show before having to clear the studio. (Recall that a *take* is any one of similar repeated shots during video-recording and filming.) When rehearsing, good directors move on to the next activity according to the time line, even if they are not quite done with the current one. They usually gain enough time to pick up the skipped part at the end of the rehearsal.

Rehearsals

For most nondramatic shows, you probably need only two rehearsal methods: the dry run and the walk-through/camera rehearsal combination. The best way to explain these two methods is to apply them to your lighting-show assignment.

Dry run   You use the ***dry run***, or blocking rehearsal, to work out the basic actions of the talent—where they stand and walk and what they do. If you have worked out such blocking on the floor plan, you simply test your blocking schematic in a real situation. For the dry run of your lighting show, any room will do because you don't need an actual set. You can use masking tape on the floor to indicate the sidewalk and use three chairs for the bus stop bench, another chair for the pay phone, a fifth chair for the sign with the bus schedule, and a trashcan for the streetlight. Your eyes will substitute for the cameras.

Watch the blocking first from camera 1's point of view (POV), then from camera 2's POV. In a complicated scene, you may want to use a director's viewfinder (an optical device that is similar to a monocular with which you can set aspect ratios and zoom lens positions) or a small camcorder to check the approximate shot framing. Effective dry runs usually include some or all of the following points:

- Start with the more complicated blocking, but don't get hung up on details. In the lighting show, you can block Susan first, then John, then both of them. If time is limited, you can block both talent simultaneously. Have Susan seated on the bench, anxiously looking for the bus. Enter John from camera-right and have him go to the pay phone and look for change. Susan gets up and walks toward camera 1, and so forth. Check especially the z-axis positions so that the camera can get good over-the-shoulder shots.

- Be as precise with your cues as possible. Don't just say, "Susan, sit on the bench," but, "Susan, sit on the left side—your left—of the bench." Your cue to the floor manager would be: "Have Susan sit on the camera-right side of the bench."

- Whenever possible, run through the scenes in the order they will be recorded. This will help the talent prepare for the sequence. More often than not, the scene sequence is dictated by location and necessary talent rather than narrative development.

- Call out the cues, such as, "Ready two, cue John—take two," and so on. This will enable you to get used to the cues and will help the talent anticipate them.

- If timing is critical, do a rough timing for each scene.

Walk-through/camera rehearsal   To rehearse a routine show, such as a standard interview in a permanent set, you can go straight to the control room. From there you ask the cameras to line up their shots, ask the audio engineer to check the audio levels of host and guest, have the video-record operator calibrate the VR with the audio console, and ask the CG operator to run through the titles and the credits for a final check of proper sequence and correct spelling of names.

If the show is a special event, you need to do a walk-through and a separate camera rehearsal. If you have enough time (a rare occurrence), you can do one after the other. In a walk-through you have the talent repeat the rehearsed blocking on the actual set, and you give the technical people some idea of what you expect them to do during the show. Then you go to the control room and conduct a ***camera rehearsal***, which should approximate the on-the-air or recording sessions as closely as possible except that the signal goes only as far as the line-out monitor.

More often than not, you won't have time for separate walk-throughs and camera rehearsals, so you must combine them to stay within the allotted rehearsal time. Here are some recommendations for conducting a ***walk-through/camera rehearsal*** combination:

- Always conduct such a rehearsal from the studio floor, not the control room. To change some minor blocking or camera positions, you can simply walk to the spot where you want the talent or camera to be. Explaining such corrections over the intercom would take up too much valuable rehearsal time. Use a headset or a wireless lavalier to communicate with the control room.

- If possible, have the technical director (TD) show a split feed of all cameras used on the studio monitor. (You may have to discuss such a split-screen display with the TD prior to the rehearsal.) This way you can preview the cameras from the studio floor. If this is not practical, have the TD switch as usual and feed the line-out signal to the studio monitor.

- Have all talent and crew who are actively involved in the rehearsal take their positions. On the studio floor, this includes the floor manager and the floor persons, all camera operators, and the fishpole mic operator. In the control room, you should have the TD, the audio engineer, and, if necessary, the LD (lighting director), standing by to adjust the lighting.

- Give all cues as you would in the control room. The TD will execute your switching calls and feed them to the studio monitor (assuming you don't have a split-screen setup).

- Have the floor manager do all the cueing, as though you were giving the instructions from the control room. The more you involve the floor manager in the walk-through/camera rehearsal, the better prepared he or she will be when you give the cues from the control room during the actual recording.

- Once the talent has moved into a new position or you are satisfied with an especially demanding camera maneuver, skip to the next section. Do not get hung up on a minor detail while neglecting to rehearse more important parts. For example, in the lighting show, don't waste time rehearsing John standing at the pay phone, looking for change. Instead, rehearse his walk from the phone to the bench while Susan walks to the curb.

- If you encounter some minor problems, don't stop the rehearsal. Have the AD (associate director) or the PA (production assistant) take notes. The time line should have notes and reset time scheduled at least twice for this rehearsal (see chapter 2).

- Allow some time for yourself in the control room to rehearse the most critical parts of the show. At least go through the opening of the show and the opening cues to the talent.

- Stay calm and be courteous to everyone, even if things don't go as well as expected. Give the talent and the crew a brief break before the video recording. Rehearsing right up to airtime rarely contributes to a better performance.

KEY CONCEPT

All but routine multicamera shows require a dry run and a walk-through/camera rehearsal combination.

Directing the Multicamera Show

You are finally ready to undertake **multicamera directing**, also known as control room directing and live-switched directing; that is, to use switching to coordinate two or more cameras from the control room and edit their output while the show is in progress. Live recording does not necessarily mean that you must do the entire show in a single take but that you video-record fairly long, uninterrupted sequences that require no, or only minor, postproduction editing. Normally, such editing consists of joining the video-recorded segments in their correct sequence.

Once you are in the control room, your directing job becomes largely a matter of coordinating and cueing the production crew to instantly execute their assigned tasks. The following lists give some pointers about standby and on-the-air procedures. Of course, such lists are no substitute for actual control room experience, but they can help avoid common mistakes when first sitting in the director's chair.

Standby procedures   Use these procedures immediately preceding the on-the-air or live-recorded show. Use the SA (studio address) system and have every crewmember put on a PL (private line) headset. Call on each crewmember and ask whether he or she is ready. This includes the TD, audio technician, VR operator, CG operator, teleprompter operator (if necessary), floor manager, camera operators, audio boom or fishpole operator, and lighting technician (if light changes occur during the segment).

- Ask the floor manager whether the talent and the rest of the floor crew are ready. Tell the floor manager who gets the opening cue and which camera will be on first. The floor manager is now your essential link between the control room and the studio.

- You can save time by having the TD and the VR operator prepare the video leader. Have the VR operator do a test recording, including a brief audio feed of the talent's opening remarks.

- Announce periodically the time remaining until the telecast or recording.

- Alert everyone to the first cues and shot sequence. Ready the VR operator to start the recording, the CG operator to bring up the opening titles, the audio engineer to fade in the opening music, and the TD to fade in the opening shot.

- Have the floor manager get the talent into position.

On-the-air procedures   You now need to use the director's terminology as explained in figures 17.10 through 17.14. When giving standby and on-the-air cues, speak clearly and precisely. Do not chatter on the intercom to show how relaxed you are; you will only encourage the crew to do the same. Don't shout, even if something goes terribly wrong. Keep your cool and pay particular attention to these matters:

- Call for the VR start and wait for the confirmation that the VR is actually in the record mode. A VTR (videotape recorder) needs a few seconds to reach full tape speed so that you won't experience picture breakup for the first few frames. The VR operator will call out "speed" or "in-record" when the system is ready.

- Unless done by the AD or TD, start the recording with the leader information. Otherwise, start with the recording of the program.

- Fade in the camera that has the opening shot and key the opening titles.

- Cue talent by name. Don't just say, "Cue her"; say, "Cue Susan."

- Cue the talent *before* you fade in the camera. By the time the floor manager has relayed your cue to the talent and the talent begins to speak, the TD will have faded in the picture.

- Talk to the cameras by number, not by the name of the operator.

- First call the camera before you give the instructions: "Three, when we come to you, dolly in. One, stay on the close-up."

- Do not pause too long between your ready and take cues. The TD may no longer be ready by the time you get to the action cue.

- Do not pause between the "take" and the number of the camera. Do not say, "Take [pause] one." The TD may punch up your camera at the take cue.

- If you change your mind after your ready cue, cancel the cue by saying, "No" or "Cancel" or "Change that." Then give the correct ready cue.

- Try to watch the camera preview monitors as much as possible while reading the script. Large but clear script markings make this juggling act easier.

- Do not do one take after another to get the first scene right at the expense of the rest of the show. Realize that the crew and the talent may lose energy and interest if you require too many takes.

- If you must stop the recording because of a technical problem, ask the floor manager to inform the studio crew and the talent of the nature of the problem. If solving the problem takes more than a few minutes, have the crew and the talent relax until you call for the video-recording to resume.

- If timing is critical, keep an eye on the clock and the stopwatch.

- After fading to black at the end of the show, call for a "Stop VR" and give the all-clear signal. Have the VR operator spot-check the recording before dismissing the talent and calling for a scenery strike.

But we are not there yet. It's time to go into the control room and do the show.

Standby. Ten seconds to VR one roll. Ready VR. Roll VR [if using a VTR, wait for the in-record confirmation]. Bars and tone. Ready slate. Take slate. Read slate [done by the AD or audio technician; this will give you an additional audio slate]. Black. Countdown [done by the AD or audio technician; the numbers from 10 to 2 flash by each second]. Ready server 2.12. Roll it, take it, sound up. Two on Mary. One on Susan. Ready two. Cue Mary. Take two. Ready one. Take one. Cue Susan [this is strictly an action cue]. Traffic sounds. Open mics. Ready key. Key. Change page [new title from CG]. Lose key. Cue John [action cue for John to walk]. Ready freeze-frame. Ready to cue Mary voice-over . . .

You are on your way. Don't bury your face in the script; by now you are pretty familiar with it. As much as possible, keep your head up and watch the preview monitors. Listen to what is being said but especially to the cue lines. Unless something went wrong, stop the recording only after the daylight segment is finished. You can use this break for a brief notes session, and the lighting people can use the opportunity to fine-tune the nighttime lighting. Give everyone a short break before recording the nighttime scene, but tell them the exact time to be back in the studio.

This time around you don't need a new VR leader, but you should have a new slate indicating that you are now doing the low-key scene. Before you restart the VR, make sure that Mary's V/O script includes the commentary for the low-key lighting segment. Fade in camera 1 (with Susan sitting on the bench), key the low-key scene titles, cue John to walk to the phone, freeze the long-shot frame, and cue Mary for her voice-over segment.

When you have about one minute left, get ready for the closing (shot 9, two-shot on C2):

Thirty seconds. Ready bus effect [sound effect of the bus pulling up]. Ready to cue Susan. Bus effect one. Cue Susan [she delivers her last line, turns, and walks past C2]. SFX police siren low under. Bus effect two [sound effect of bus closing door and driving off]. Ready one on John. Cue John. Take one. Zoom out. Slowly. Freeze. Ready two on Mary. Cue Mary. Take two. Ready dissolve to one. Ready CG credits and music. Dissolve. Music. Roll credits. Key. Lose key. Fade music. Fade to black. Stop VR. Hold everything. Check tape. All clear. Thank you all. Good job.

> **KEY CONCEPT**
>
> When in the control room, give all your calls with clarity and precision.

If everything goes that smoothly, you have indeed done a superior job. But don't be discouraged if you need to stop down to repeat a portion of the scene or even reblock a shot. Just don't spend an inordinate amount of time polishing a specific shot while the clock ticks right into the next time line segment. If you have postproduction time and a good editor, you can have the editor add all sound effects (traffic, bus, police siren), do the freeze frame and titles, and insert a few segment you had to retake. **ZVL2** SWITCHING→ Advanced lab→ try it #1 | try it #2 | try it #3 | quiz

■ SINGLE-CAMERA DIRECTING

In *single-camera directing*, you need to observe all the continuity principles of multicamera directing except that you are video-recording the shots piecemeal and not necessarily in the order of the script. Let's first look at some of the more obvious differences between single-camera (film-style) and multicamera directing and then demonstrate these differences briefly with the lighting-show example.

Major Differences

When switching from multicamera to single-camera directing, you will find major differences in the way you conduct rehearsals and in how and when to engage performers and actors. Continuity becomes a prime consideration, as well.

Rehearsals   Single-camera scenes are easier to rehearse than multicamera scenes because you can walk through and rehearse the talent and the crew immediately before the actual video recording. The performers can quickly review their lines, and you can give detailed instructions to the crew as to the nature of the upcoming shot and the specific lighting and audio requirements. Because of the short time lapse between rehearsal and recording, your directions will be fresh in the minds of talent and crew for each take.

Rehearsing single-camera scenes can also be more difficult, however, because you need to reconstruct the preceding and following shots for each take to maintain continuity of action, emotion, and aesthetic energy. This is why many movie directors like to work from carefully worked-out storyboards. The storyboard helps them recall what happened before and should happen after the specific shot they are rehearsing.

Performing and acting   Single-camera production puts an added strain on the performers. Because the video-recording sequence is not governed by the narrative continuity of the script, the talent cannot build or maintain a specific emotional level but must often switch from one extreme to another. Also, many repetitions of a single take to get a variety of camera angles and close-ups require the actors to deliver identical performances each time. As a director you need to make sure that the talent not only repeat the same blocking and actions but also maintain the same rhythm and energy level during each subsequent take.

Continuity   One of the major challenges for the director in single-camera shooting is maintaining continuity from shot to shot. Because the shots are almost always video-recorded out of sequence, you need to maintain a mental map of how they will cut together for good continuity. In the absence of a detailed storyboard, marking the field log with principal vector symbols can greatly facilitate your lining up shots for proper continuity. For example, if in the lighting show you want to imply in a CU that Susan is watching John walk to the phone, Susan's index vector must converge with John's screen-left motion vector. The field log would simply show $i\rightarrow$ (for Susan's CU) and $\leftarrow m$ (for John's walk). This notation will be enough for you to remember John's shot even if the actual takes are fairly far apart.

An experienced director of photography (DP), who might also be operating the camera, or the AD can be of great assistance in continuity matters, such as continuity of vectors, sound, and general aesthetic energy. Don't be afraid to ask them if you are not sure whether your next shot will provide the necessary continuity. To make the editor's job a little easier, ask the camera operator to start the camera before you call for action and to let it run for a few seconds after the action is finished. These ***trim handles*** (ample "leaders" and "tails") will give the editor some wiggle room to

> **KEY CONCEPT**
>
> In single-camera directing of out-of-sequence shots, watch for continuity of vectors, action, sound, and aesthetic energy.

cut precisely on action and dialogue. At this point it might be worthwhile for you to revisit the discussion of field production in chapter 15.

Single-Camera Studio Directing

Most directors do single-camera directing from the studio floor, similar to a walk-through/camera rehearsal. If you direct the single-camera production from the studio floor, you can have the AD in the control room, handling all the operational activities such as rolling the VR, putting on the leader, calling for the slate, and key-ing the titles. The AD or the PA can also keep the field log. You, as the director, are then free to watch the line monitor on the studio floor and call for action to get the first take recorded.

For practice, let's direct the first three "scenes" of the lighting show. Strictly defined, they are actually shots, but for logging they count as scenes. The first scene in the lighting program is Mary's intro: "Hi, I'm Mary . . ."

The AD rolls the VR and calls for the slate: *Scene 1, take 1 (Mary)*. After Mary says, "Let's watch," have her stand there quietly for a moment before calling "cut"—to stop the action. This will make the exact edit-out point more flexible. "Cut" in this context means to stop the action and the camera.

Because Mary did such a good job, you can now move on to the next scene, John's walk to the pay phone. The slate should now read: *Scene 2, take 1 (J walk)*. On your "action" call, John walks to the phone and the camera pans with him. John stops at the phone and waits for your "cut." Both John and the camera operator did a great job, but you must call for another take. Why? Because your cut to a CU of John looking for change would not allow the editor to cut on action—a fundamental requirement for smooth continuity in postproduction editing. John must start to reach into his pocket while still on the wide or medium shot and then repeat the action on the close-up. The editor can now cut from an LS to a CU *during* the action, not before or after it. This way the cut will remain virtually invisible to the audience. For the second take of John's walk, the slate now reads: *Scene 2, take 2 (J walk)*.

Next you can line up the camera on the z-axis shot that includes Susan in the foreground and rehearse John's approach to the bench. Now the slate should read: *Scene 3, take 1 (J and S)*. Again, start the scene with John looking for coins before ap-proaching Susan, to give the editor the necessary trim handles and the opportunity to cut on action. Susan blocks John while he's walking to the curb, so you need to retake the scene. The slate now reads: *Scene 3, take 2 (J and S)*.

Although not in the script, an essential shot would be a CU of Susan watching John walk to the phone. You decide to do this reaction shot, so the slate reads: *Scene 3, take 3 (S CU)*.

What happened to the traffic sounds, the occasional cars going by, and the police siren? Shouldn't the AD have cued the sound engineer to mix John's walking sounds and the brief dialogue between John and Susan with the traffic sounds? No. That audio will be laid in later in postproduction mixing. That way you can keep the background sounds continuous through John's walk, fishing for coins, and talking to Susan.

Single-Camera Field Production

Your single-camera production changes radically if you were to take the lighting show on-location—to an actual bus stop. In effect, you would now be directing a single-camera electronic field production (EFP). The major change would be in the script breakdown, that is, how the scenes are arranged for video recording.

The order of the shooting script is no longer determined by narrative progression (Susan waiting for the bus and John walking to the phone) but by location. Location here refers to the action areas of the bus stop. All shots are exterior—outdoors and, in this case, at a real bus stop. This is how the script might read:

Daytime Shot Breakdown

1. **Location:** *Bus stop. Bus pulls up. Susan boards bus. Bus drives off.* This shot is listed first because you need to adhere to the bus schedule to get a variety of angles. The timing of all the other shots is under your control.

2. **Location:** *Pay phone and bench. John walks to phone and bench.* Show John walking to the phone and to the bench from several angles. Get CUs of him looking for change and glancing at Susan. Ordinarily, you would do a pickup of close-ups after shooting most of the long shots and medium shots. In this case, however, the continuity of lighting is crucial, so you should get the close-ups right away.

3. **Location:** *Bench. Susan sitting on the bench.* Susan performs moves 1 through 4 in combination with John's blocking and, depending on the angle, without John (seated on the bench, looking for the bus, and watching John; walking toward the curb and looking back at John; looking at the bus schedule, looking through her purse, moving to the lamp post, and talking to John; and moving toward the curb to board the bus).

4. **Cutaways:** *Bus pulling up and departing, the bus schedule, the pay phone, the newspaper rack, and the bench.* Shoot additional cutaways of whatever other event details could serve as transitions and intensifiers.

5. **Audio:** You will have ample background sounds of traffic and cars going by whether you like it or not, but this can be a disadvantage, especially if the street noise overpowers the talent's lines. Wind noise is always a potential hazard. Be sure to audio-record a generous amount of such sounds after you are done with the actual production. This will help the postproduction editor establish shot continuity through ambient sound. The police siren can be supplied by the sound-effects (SFX) library.

The real problem is that all of these shots must now be repeated as closely as possible for the nighttime scene. Night shooting is always difficult because of the additional lighting requirements. Also, as pointed out earlier, the audio requirements change (fewer traffic sounds). In this case the postproduction sound manipulation is becoming more difficult.

As you can see, the single-camera EFP of the lighting show is getting more complicated. What at first glance seemed to be the easier aspect of the production assignment turns out to be a much more formidable job than the multicamera studio production.

Isn't shooting on-location a rather clumsy way of doing the lighting show, especially if it can be done more efficiently with multiple cameras in the studio? Yes, in a way, it is. This is where the producer's judgment comes in. A relatively simple production, such as the lighting show, is much more efficiently done as a multicamera studio production than a single-camera EFP. But bigger projects are often more easily and effectively done film-style with a single camera, even if it doesn't seem that way considering the many takes it may require just to get a simple action right. Fortunately, neither video production nor filmmaking is locked into one or the other approach.

Many digital cinema productions use multiple cameras simultaneously, not just for spectacular one-time-only shots—like blowing up a building—but also for ordinary scenes. Video too uses both approaches, depending on the nature of the production. There are two EFP formats that are almost always produced with a single-camera setup: the interview with a single guest and various forms of documentary.

Interview The standard formula for setting up an interview for a host and a guest is to position the camera next to the host (interviewer), pointed at the guest (interviewee), who is sitting or standing opposite the host. **SEE 17.16** If the emotional context requires a close-up, zoom in. You can replace the zoom later in postproduction with a reaction shot of the interviewer. If you interrupt the interview, start the next take with a different angle or field of view (a tighter or looser shot). At the end of the interview, place the camera next to the guest's chair or where the guest was standing and get some reaction shots of the host.

In this reaction shot session, watch that you don't cross the vector line with the camera in the new setup. If the host sports an automatic smile when on-camera, be

Interviewer (host)

Interviewee (guest)

Camera

© Cengage Learning 2011

17.16 STANDARD SINGLE-CAMERA INTERVIEW SETUP
In the standard single-camera interview setup, the interviewer (host) sits opposite the interviewee (guest). The camera is placed next to the interviewer.

careful that he or she doesn't smile in all reaction shots, especially when the interview had some serious moments. To show the host asking some of the questions, you can have him or her repeat them. Try to match the CU sizes of guest and host—don't make one or the other CU noticeably larger. The editor will insert the reaction and question shots in the spots you designate.

Because camcorders have become smaller and less expensive while maintaining high quality, you should try to use two cameras in over-the-shoulder setups on the same side of the vector line. In this way you will have one recording of the guest and another recording of the host; you can then mix the source material in various ways in postproduction, provided you have striped both media with identical time codes.

Documentary   When shooting a documentary, you cannot and should not direct the event itself but simply the coverage of it. Although you usually have a basic objective or angle in mind before you start recording, don't try to predetermine shots before you see the actual event. Directors who draw up detailed scripts and story-boards before they have seen at least part of the event they are to document often fail to see the event essences but instead seek shots that fit their preconception of what the event should look like. Ultimately, they document their prejudices rather than the true event.

A good initial approach is to "take notes" with the camera before doing the actual EFP. If you are open-minded and sensitive to what is going on, you may not only refine your initial objective but also develop an idea for an effective angle.

In any case, get some shots that best express the essence of the event; then get some environmental shots that establish the location and the atmosphere, as well as plenty of cutaways. Remind the camera operator or DP to shoot tight: inductive sequencing with plenty of close-ups packs a more powerful punch than a series of medium and long shots, regardless of screen size.

Your real directing skills may have to come into play during postproduction, when you work with the video and sound editors. If you have a specific idea of what the show should look like, do a paper-and-pencil rough-cut for the editor that will help communicate your idea.

M A I N   P O I N T S

▶ *Script Formats*
   The fact, or rundown, sheet simply lists the major points to be covered by the talent and the director. The news script and the two-column A/V (audio/video) script contain the video and some directing information on page-left and all spoken words and additional audio information on page-right. The single-column drama script contains all spoken dialogue, major character behaviors, and action cues in a single column.

▶ *Visualization*
   A principal task of the director is translating the script into video images and sound. Visualization is one of the techniques employed. It means creating a mental image of a shot or a series of shots. It also includes the mental imaging of sound, context, and sequence.

▶ *Floor Plan*

A floor plan can help the director visualize key shots, determine lighting and audio requirements, and decide on blocking for talent and cameras.

▶ *Script Marking, Director's Terminology, and Time Line*

Easy-to-read script markings, consistent terminology, and a realistic time line are essential to successful multicamera directing.

▶ *Rehearsals*

A dry run, or blocking rehearsal, is used to block the movements of the talent—where they stand and walk and what they do. In a walk-through/camera rehearsal, the director explains to talent and crew what is happening on the set before doing a run-through with full equipment. The initial walk-through/camera rehearsal should be conducted from the studio floor.

▶ *Multicamera Directing*

When directing from the control room, the director communicates all major cues to the crew via PL (private line) headset. The director's cues and procedures must be consistent.

▶ *Single-Camera Directing*

In single-camera directing, production efficiency rather than script narrative dictates the order of shots. Utmost care must be taken that the out-of-order shots will enable seamless continuity in postproduction editing. Always provide the editor with usable cutaways and trim handles.

ZETTL'S VIDEOLAB

For your reference or to track your work, the *Zettl's VideoLab* program cues in this chapter are listed here with their corresponding page number. ZVL2 is designed as an advanced switching exercise; however, you will benefit from hearing a director call shots.

ZVL1 PROCESS→ Ideas→ scripts   364

ZVL2 SWITCHING→ Advanced lab→ try it #1 | try it #2 | try it #3 | quiz   387

Glossary

480i/480p A scanning system of digital television. The *i* stands for *interlaced,* and the *p* stands for *progressive.* Each complete television frame consists of 480 visible lines, usually in the 4 × 3 aspect ratio, that are scanned as two interlaced fields (480i) or one after the other (480p). This system is generally referred to as *digital SDTV* (standard-definition television).

720p A scanning system of digital television. The *p* stands for *progressive,* which means that each complete television frame consists of 720 visible lines that are scanned one after the other. An HDTV (high-definition television) standard.

1080i A scanning system of high-definition television. The *i* stands for *interlaced,* which means that each complete television frame consists of two interlaced scanning fields. A high-end HDTV system.

1080p A scanning system of high-definition television. The *p* stands for *progressive,* which means that each complete television frame consists of 1,080 visible lines that are scanned one after the other. A high-end HDTV system.

above-the-line personnel *See* **nontechnical production personnel**

AB-roll editing Creating an edit master tape from two source VTRs, one containing the A-roll and the other containing the B-roll. Transitions other than cuts, such as dissolves and wipes, are possible.

academy leader *See* **video leader**

actor A person who appears on-camera in dramatic roles. The actor always portrays someone else.

AD Stands for *associate* or *assistant director.* Assists the director in all production phases.

additive primary colors Red, green, and blue. Ordinary white light (sunlight) can be separated into the three primary light colors. When these three colored lights are combined in various proportions, all other colors can be reproduced.

address code An electronic signal that marks each frame with a specific address. *See* **SMPTE time code**.

advanced television (ATV) *See* **digital television**

AGC Stands for *automatic gain control.* Regulates the volume of the audio or video levels automatically, without using pots.

ambience Background sounds.

analog A signal that fluctuates exactly like the original stimulus.

angle The particular approach to a story—its central theme.

aperture Iris opening of a lens; usually measured in *f*-stops.

arc To move the camera in a slightly curved dolly or truck.

aspect ratio The ratio of the width of the television screen to its height. In STV (standard television), it is 4 × 3 (4 units wide by 3 units high); for HDTV (high-definition television), it is 16 × 9 (16 units wide by 9 units high). Mobile media devices have various aspect ratios, including vertical ones.

assemble editing In linear editing, adding shots on videotape in consecutive order without first recording a control track on the edit master tape.

ATR Stands for *audiotape recorder.*

attached shadow Shadow that is on the object itself. It cannot be seen independent of (detached from) the object.

ATV Stands for *advanced television. See* **digital television**.

audio track The area of the videotape used for recording the audio information.

auto-focus Automatic focusing system on most consumer camcorders and some ENG/EFP cameras.

auto-iris Automatic control of the aperture (lens opening).

background light Illumination of the set pieces and the backdrop. Also called *set light.*

back light Illumination from behind the subject and opposite the camera; usually a spotlight.

barn doors Metal flaps in front of a lighting instrument that control the spread of the light beam.

baselight Even, nondirectional (diffused) light necessary for the camera to operate optimally. Refers to the overall light intensity.

beam splitter Optical device within the camera that splits the white light into the three additive primary light colors: red, green, and blue.

below-the-line personnel *See* **technical production personnel**

big remote A production outside the studio to televise live and/or live-record a large scheduled event that has not been staged specifically for television. Examples include sporting events, parades, political gatherings, award ceremonies, and government hearings. Also called *remote.*

binary digit (bit) The smallest amount of information a computer can hold and process. A charge is either present, represented by a 1, or absent, represented by a 0. One bit can describe two levels, such as on/off or black/white. Two bits can describe four levels (2^2 bits); 3 bits, eight levels (2^3 bits); 4 bits, 16 (2^4 bits); and so on. A group of 8 bits (2^8) is called a *byte.*

blocking Carefully worked-out positioning, movement, and actions by the talent and for all mobile video equipment used in a scene.

blocking rehearsal *See* **dry run**

book *See* **twofold**

boom (1) *Audio:* microphone support. (2) *Video:* part of a camera crane. (3) To move the boom of the camera crane up or down; also called *crane.*

bump-down Copying a videotape to a lower-quality tape format. Also called *dub-down.*

bump-up Copying a videotape to a higher-quality tape format. Also called *dub-up.*

calibrate the zoom lens To preset a zoom lens to stay in focus throughout the zoom.

camcorder A portable camera with the video recorder built into it.

camera chain The camera and the associated electronic equipment, consisting of the power supply, sync generator, and camera control unit.

camera control unit (CCU) Equipment, separate from the actual camera, that allows the video operator to adjust the color and brightness balance before and during the production.

camera rehearsal Full rehearsal with cameras and other pieces of production equipment. Often identical to the dress rehearsal.

cant To tilt the camera sideways.

cap (1) Lens cap: a rubber or metal cap placed in front of the lens to protect it from light, dust, and physical damage. (2) Electronic device that eliminates the picture from the camera CCD.

capture Moving video and audio from the recording media to the hard drive of a computer with a nonlinear editing program. Analog video signals must be converted to digital before they can be imported by a computer.

cardioid Heart-shaped pickup pattern of a unidirectional microphone.

cast shadow Shadow that is produced by an object and thrown (cast) onto another surface. It can be seen independent of the object.

CCD Stands for *charge-coupled device.* One of the popular imaging devices in a studio camera or camcorder. *See* **sensor**.

C channel *See* **chrominance channel**

C-clamp A metal clamp with which lighting instruments are attached to the lighting batten.

CCU *See* **camera control unit**

CD Stands for *compact disc.* A recording media that contains audio and/or video information in digital form.

CG *See* **character generator**

character generator (CG) A computer dedicated to the creation of letters and numbers in various fonts. Its output can be directly integrated into video images.

chip *See* **CCD** and **sensor**

chroma key Key effect that uses a color (usually blue or green) for the key source backdrop. All blue or green areas are replaced by the base picture during the key.

chrominance channel Contains the RGB video signals or some combination thereof. Also called *color,* and *C, channel.*

close-up (CU) Object or any part of it seen at close range and framed tightly. The close-up can be extreme (extreme or big close-up) or rather loose (medium close-up).

closure *See* **psychological closure**

CMOS Stands for *complementary metal-oxide semiconductor.* A high-quality imaging device similar to a CCD. *See* **sensor**.

codec Stands for *compression-decompression.* Can be one of several compression systems of digital video, graphics, and audio files.

coding To change the quantized values into a binary code, represented by 0's and 1's. Also called *encoding.*

color bars A color standard used in video production for the alignment of cameras and videotape recordings. Color bars can be generated by most professional portable cameras.

color channel *See* **chrominance channel**

color media *See* **gel**

color temperature Relative reddishness or bluishness of white light, as measured on the Kelvin (K) scale.

The norm for indoor video lighting is 3,200K; for outdoors, 5,600K.

complexity editing Building an intensified screen event from carefully selected and juxtaposed shots. Does not have to adhere to the continuity principles.

component system *See* **RGB component video, Y/C component video**, and **Y/color difference component video**

composite video A system that combines the Y (luminance, or black-and-white) and C (color—red, green, and blue) video information into a single signal. Also called *NTSC.*

compression The temporary rearrangement or elimination of redundant picture information for easier storage and signal transport.

condenser microphone A high-quality, sensitive microphone for critical sound pickup.

contact person A person who is familiar with, and can facilitate access to, the remote location and the key people. Also called *contact.*

continuing vectors Graphic vectors that extend each other, or index and motion vectors that point and move in the same direction.

continuity editing Preserving visual continuity from shot to shot.

contrast The difference between the brightest and the darkest spots in a video image.

control room directing *See* **multicamera directing**

control track The area of the videotape used for recording synchronization information.

control track system *See* **pulse-count system**

converging vectors Index and motion vectors that point toward each other.

crane To move the boom of the camera crane up or down. Also called *boom.*

cross-shot (X/S) Similar to the over-the-shoulder shot except that the camera-near person is completely out of the shot.

CU *See* **close-up**

cue card A large hand-lettered card that contains copy, usually held next to the camera lens by floor personnel.

cut (1) The instantaneous change from one shot (image) to another. (2) Director's signal to interrupt action (used during rehearsal).

cutaway A shot of an object or event that is peripherally connected with the overall event and that is relatively static. Commonly used between two shots that do not provide good continuity.

cyc See **cyclorama**

cyc light See **strip light**

cyclorama A U-shaped continuous piece of canvas or muslin for backing of scenery and action. Also called *cyc*. Hardwall cycs are permanently installed in front of one or two of the studio walls.

delegation controls Controls that assign a specific function to a bus on a switcher.

depth of field The area in which all objects, located at different distances from the camera, appear in focus. Depends primarily on the focal length of the lens, its *f*-stop, and the distance from the camera to the object.

diffused light Light that illuminates a relatively large area and creates soft shadows.

digital Pertaining to data in the form of binary digits (on/off pulses).

digital television (DTV) Digital systems that generally have a higher image resolution than standard television. Sometimes called *advanced television (ATV)*.

digital versatile disc (DVD) The standard DVD recording media can store 4.7 gigabytes of video and/or audio information.

digital video effects (DVE) Video effects generated by an effects generator in the switcher or by a computer with effects software. The computer system dedicated to DVE is called a *graphics generator*.

digitize Necessary step with analog source material whereby the analog signals are converted to digital signals prior to capture.

dimmer A device that controls the intensity of light by throttling the electric current flowing to the lamp.

directional light Light that illuminates a relatively small area and creates harsh, clearly defined shadows.

diverging vectors Index and motion vectors that point away from each other.

documentary script See **two-column A/V script**

dolly To move the camera toward (dolly in) or away from (dolly out) the object.

downstream keyer (DSK) A control that allows a title to be keyed (cut in) over the picture (line-out signal) as it leaves the switcher.

dress (1) What people wear on-camera. (2) Decorating a set with set properties. (3) Set dressing: set properties. *See also* **dress rehearsal**.

dress rehearsal Final rehearsal with the cast fully dressed and all facilities operating. The dress rehearsal is often video-recorded.

drop Heavy curtain suspended from a track (usually in front of the cyc). A painted drop is a large piece of canvas with a background scene painted on it.

dry run Rehearsal without equipment, during which the basic actions of the talent are worked out. Also called *blocking rehearsal*.

DSK See **downstream keyer**

DSLR camera Stands for *digital single-lens reflex camera*. Basically a still-photo camera that can also produce video footage. It has an optical viewfinder that permits viewing through the lens for still pictures. In the video mode, it switches to an electronic image.

DTV See **digital television**

dub The duplication of an electronic recording. The dub is always one generation away from the recording used for dubbing. In analog systems, each dub shows increased deterioration.

dub-down See **bump-down**

dub-up See **bump-up**

DVD See **digital versatile disc**

DVE See **digital video effects**

DVR Stands for *digital video recorder*.

dynamic microphone A relatively rugged microphone. Good for outdoor use.

edit controller A machine that assists in various linear editing functions, such as marking edit-in and edit-out points, rolling source and record VTRs, and integrating effects. It can be a desktop computer with editing software. Also called *editing control unit*.

edit decision list (EDL) Consists of edit-in and edit-out points, expressed in time code numbers, and the nature of transitions between shots.

editing control unit *See* **edit controller**

editing log *See* **VR log**

edit master The videotape or disc that contains the final version of an edited program. Subsequent copies are struck from the edit master.

EDL *See* **edit decision list**

effects bus Row of buttons on the switcher that can select the video sources for a specific effect. Usually the same as a mix bus that has been switched to an effects function.

effect-to-cause model *See* **production model**

EFP *See* **electronic field production**

EFP team Usually a three-person team consisting of the talent, a camcorder operator, and a utility person who handles lighting, audio, and/or video recording, and, if necessary, the microwave transmission back to the studio.

electron beam A thin stream of electrons, which is generated by the electron gun in back of the video tube and strikes the photosensitive color dots at the face of the tube.

electronic field production (EFP) Video production done outside the studio that is usually shot for postproduction (not live).

electronic news gathering (ENG) The use of portable camcorders, lights, and sound equipment for the production of mostly unscheduled daily news events. ENG is usually done for live transmission or immediate postproduction.

electronic still store (ESS) system Stores still video frames in digital form for easy random access.

encoding *See* **coding**

ENG *See* **electronic news gathering**

ENG/EFP camera Highly portable, high-end self-contained camera for electronic field production.

ESS *See* **electronic still store (ESS) system**

essential area The section of the television picture that is seen by the home viewer, regardless of minor loss during signal transmission or signal processing by the television receiver. Also called *safe title area*.

establishing shot *See* **long shot**

fact sheet Script format that lists the items to be shown on-camera and their main features. May contain suggestions of what to say about the product. Also called *rundown sheet*.

fade The gradual appearance of a picture from black (fade-in) or disappearance to black (fade-out).

fader A volume control that works by sliding a button horizontally along a scale. Identical in function to a pot. Also called *slide fader*.

fader bar A lever on the switcher that activates buses and can produce superimpositions, dissolves, fades, keys, and wipes of different speeds. Also called *T-bar*.

falloff The speed (degree) with which a light picture portion turns into shadow areas. *Fast falloff* means that the light areas turn abruptly into shadow areas and there is a great difference in brightness between light and shadow areas. *Slow falloff* indicates a very gradual change from light to dark and a minimal brightness difference between light and shadow areas.

fast lens A lens that permits a relatively great amount of light to pass through at its largest aperture (lowest *f*-stop number). Can be used in low-light conditions.

fc *See* **foot-candle**

field One-half of a complete scanning cycle, with two fields necessary for one television picture frame. In analog (NTSC) television, there are 60 fields, or 30 frames, per second.

field dolly A plywood platform supported by four wheels with pneumatic tires. Used for moving a tripod-mounted camera on a rough surface.

field log A record of each take during the video recording.

field of view The portion of a scene visible through a particular lens; its vista. Expressed in symbols, such as CU for close-up.

field production Production activities that take place away from the studio.

fill light Additional light on the opposite side of the camera from the key light to illuminate shadow areas and thereby reduce falloff; usually done with floodlights.

film-style *See* **single-camera production**

fishpole A suspension device for a microphone; the mic is attached to a pole and held over the scene for brief periods.

flash drive *See* **memory card**

flat A piece of standing scenery used as a background or to simulate the walls of a room. There are hardwall and softwall flats.

floodlight A lighting instrument that produces diffused light.

floor director *See* **floor manager**

floor manager In charge of all activities on the studio floor, such as setting up scenery, getting talent into place, and relaying the director's cues to the talent. In the field, basically responsible for preparing the location for the shoot and for cueing all talent. Also called floor director and *stage manager.*

floor plan A diagram of scenery, properties, and set dressings drawn on a grid.

focal length With the lens set at infinity, the distance from the iris to the plane where the picture is in focus. Normally measured in millimeters or inches.

foldback The return of the total or partial audio mix to the talent through headsets or IFB channels. *See* **IFB**.

foot-candle (fc) The unit of measurement of illumination, or the amount of light that falls on an object. One foot-candle is 1 candlepower of light (1 lumen) that falls on a 1-square-foot area located 1 foot away from the light source. *See also* **lux**.

foundation A makeup base, normally done with water-soluble cake makeup; it is applied with a sponge or sprayed on the face and sometimes all exposed skin areas.

fps *See* **frame rate**

frame A complete scanning cycle of the electron beam. In interlaced scanning, two partial scanning cycles (fields) are necessary for one frame. In progressive scanning, each scanning cycle produces one complete frame. *See* **interlaced scanning** and **progressive scanning**.

frame rate The time it takes to scan a complete frame; usually expressed in frames per second (fps). In analog (NTSC) television, there are 60 fields, or 30 frames, per second. HDTV can have variable frame rates for acquisition, editing, and delivery.

frame store synchronizer Image stabilization and synchronization system that has a memory large enough to store and read out one complete video frame. Used to synchronize signals from a variety of video sources that are not locked to a common sync signal.

Fresnel spotlight One of the most common spots, named after the inventor of its lens, which has steplike concentric rings.

f-stop The scale on the lens, indicating the aperture. The larger the *f*-stop number, the smaller the aperture; the smaller the *f*-stop number, the larger the aperture.

gel Generic name for color filter put in front of spotlights or floodlights to give the light beam a specific hue. *Gel* comes from *gelatin,* the filter material used before the invention of much more heat- and moisture-resistant plastic material. Also called *color media.*

generation The number of dubs away from the original recording. A first-generation dub is struck directly from the source media. A second-generation tape is a dub of the first-generation dub (two steps away from the original media), and so forth. The greater the number of nondigital generations, the greater the loss of quality.

graphics generator A computer specially designed for creating a variety of images and colors. Also called *paint box. See also* **digital video effects**.

hand props Objects, called *properties,* that are handled by the performer or actor.

HDTV *See* **high-definition television**

headroom The space between the top of the head and the upper screen edge.

high-definition television (HDTV) Includes the 720p, 1080i, and 1080p scanning systems.

high-key lighting Light background and ample light on the scene. Has nothing to do with the vertical positioning of the key light.

hundredeighty *See* **vector line**

hypercardioid Very narrow unidirectional pickup pattern with a long reach. The mic is also sensitive to sounds coming directly from the back.

IFB Stands for *interruptible foldback* or *feedback.* A prompting system that allows communication with the talent while on the air. A small earpiece worn by on-the-air talent carries program sound (including the talent's voice) or instructions from the producer or director.

imaging device In a video camera, converts the optical image into electric energy—the video signal. Also called *chip, pickup device,* and *sensor.*

incident light Light that strikes the object directly from its source. To measure incident light, point the light meter at the camera lens or into the lighting instruments.

ingest The selection, coding, and recording on a large server of various program feeds.

insert editing Produces highly stable edits for linear editing. Requires the prior laying of a continuous control track by recording black on the edit master tape.

instantaneous editing *See* **switching**

interactive video A computer-driven program that gives the viewer some control over what to see and how to see it. It is often used as a training device.

intercom Short for *intercommunication system.* Used for all production and engineering personnel involved in a show. The most widely used system has telephone headsets to facilitate voice communication on several wired or wireless channels. Includes other systems, such as IFB and cellular telephones.

interlaced scanning The scanning of all the odd-numbered lines (first field) and the subsequent scanning of all the even-numbered lines (second field). The two fields make up a complete television frame. *See also* **frame**.

iris Adjustable lens-opening mechanism. Also called *lens diaphragm.*

jack (1) *Audio:* a socket or receptacle for a connector. (2) *Scenery:* a brace for a flat.

jib arm A small camera crane that can be operated by the cameraperson.

jogging Frame-by-frame advancement of a recorded shot sequence, resulting in a jerking motion.

jump cut An image that jumps slightly from one screen position to another during a cut. Also, any gross visual discontinuity from shot to shot.

Kelvin (K) The standard scale for measuring color temperature, or the relative reddishness or bluishness of white light.

key An electronic effect in which the keyed image (figure— usually letters) blocks out portions of the base picture (background) and therefore appears to be layered on top of it.

key bus Row of buttons on the switcher used to select the video source to be inserted into the background image.

key light Principal source of illumination; usually a spotlight.

lavalier A small microphone that is clipped to clothing. Also called *lav.*

leadroom The space in front of a laterally moving object or person.

LED lights *LED* stands for *light-emitting diodes.* A solid-state device that changes electric energy into light energy. Most computer screens use LEDs as the light source.

lens Optical lens, essential for projecting an optical image of the scene onto the front surface of the camera imaging device. Lenses come in various fixed focal lengths or in a variable focal length (zoom lenses) and with various maximum apertures (lens openings).

lens diaphragm *See* **iris**

level (1) *Audio:* sound volume. (2) *Video:* video signal strength.

light intensity The amount of light falling on an object that is seen by the lens. Measured in lux or foot-candles. Also called *light level. See* **foot-candle** and **lux**.

light level *See* **light intensity**

light plot A plan, similar to a floor plan, that shows the type, size (wattage), and location of the lighting instruments relative to the scene to be illuminated and the general direction of the light beams.

lighting triangle *See* **photographic principle**

line *See* **vector line**

line monitor The monitor that shows only the line-out pictures that go on the air or to the video recorder.

linear editing system Uses videotape as the editing medium. It does not allow random access of shots.

line-level input Input channel on a mixer or an audio console for relatively high-level audio sources. *See also* **mic-level input**.

line of conversation and action *See* **vector line**

line-out The line that carries the final video or audio output.

live recording The uninterrupted video recording of a live show for later unedited playback. Also called *live-on-tape* even if other recording media are used.

live-switched directing *See* **multicamera directing**

location sketch A rough, hand-drawn map of the locale for a remote telecast. For an indoor remote, the sketch shows the dimensions of the room and the locations of furniture and windows. For an outdoor remote, the sketch indicates the buildings and the location of the remote truck, power source, and the sun during the time of the telecast.

long-focal-length lens *See* **telephoto lens**

long shot (LS) Object seen from far away or framed very loosely. The extreme long shot shows the object from a great distance. Also called *establishing shot*.

lossless compression Rearranging but not eliminating pixels during digital storage and transport.

lossy compression Throwing away redundant pixels during digital compression. Most compression is the lossy kind.

low-key lighting Fast-falloff lighting with dark background and selectively illuminated areas. Has nothing to do with the vertical positioning of the key light.

LS *See* **long shot**

luma *See* **luminance**

luma channel *See* **luminance channel**

lumen The light intensity power of one candle (light source radiating in all directions).

luminance The brightness (black-and-white) information of a video signal. Also called *luma* to include the gray-scale information.

luminance channel Contains the black-and-white part of a video signal. It is mainly responsible for the sharpness of the picture. Also called *luma,* or *Y, channel*.

lux European standard unit for measuring light intensity. One lux is 1 lumen (1 candlepower) of light that falls on a surface of 1 square meter located 1 meter away from the light source. 10.75 lux = 1 foot-candle. Most lighting people figure roughly 10 lux = 1 foot-candle. *See also* **foot-candle**.

master control Controls the program input, storage, and retrieval for on-the-air telecasts. Also oversees the technical quality of all program material.

matte key The key (usually letters) is filled with gray or a color.

MD *See* **mini disc**

M/E bus Row of buttons on the switcher that can serve mix or effects functions.

medium requirements All personnel, equipment, and facilities needed for a production, as well as budgets, schedules, and the various production phases.

medium shot (MS) Object seen from a medium distance. Covers any framing between a long shot and a close-up.

memory card A read/write solid-state portable storage device that can download, store, and upload a limited amount of digital audio and video information. Also called *flash drive*.

mental map Tells us where things are or are supposed to be in on- and off-screen space.

mic Short for *microphone*.

mic-level input Input channel on a mixer or an audio console for relatively low-level audio sources such as microphones. *See also* **line-level input**.

mini disc (MD) An optical disc that can store one hour of CD-quality audio.

mini plug Small audio connector.

mix bus Row of buttons on the switcher that permits the mixing of video sources, as in a dissolve or a super.

mixing (1) *Audio:* combining two or more sounds in specific proportions (volume variations) as determined by the event (show) context. (2) *Video:* combining two shots as a dissolve or superimposition via the switcher.

moiré effect Color vibrations that occur when narrow, contrasting stripes of a design interfere with the scanning lines of the video system.

monitor High-quality video display used in the video studio and control rooms. Cannot receive broadcast signals. Also refers to flat-panel camera viewfinders.

monochrome One color. In video it refers to a camera or monitor that produces a black-and-white picture.

mounting head A device that connects the camera to its support. Also called *pan-and-tilt head*.

MPEG A digital compression technique developed by the Moving Picture Experts Group for moving pictures.

MPEG-2 A digital compression standard for motion video.

MS *See* **medium shot**

multicamera directing Simultaneous coordination of two or more cameras for instantaneous editing (switching). Also called *control room directing* and *live-switched directing*.

multicamera production The use of two or more cameras to capture a scene simultaneously from different points of view. Each camera's output can be recorded separately (iso configuration) and/or fed into a switcher for instantaneous editing.

multimedia Computer display of text, sound, and still and moving images. Usually recorded on CD-ROM or DVD.

narrow-angle lens *See* **telephoto lens**

news script Fully scripted text with video information on page-left and news copy on page-right. The copy (spoken text) can also be in a large center column that contains some additional information.

NLE *See* **nonlinear editing (NLE) system**

noise (1) *Audio:* unwanted sounds that interfere with the intentional sounds, or unwanted hisses or hums inevitably generated by the electronics of the audio equipment. (2) *Video:* electronic interference that shows up as snow.

nonlinear editing (NLE) system Allows random access of shots. The video and audio information is stored in digital form on computer disks. Usually has two external monitors, small loudspeakers, and an audio mixer.

nonlinear recording media Storage of video and audio material in digital form on a hard drive, memory card, or read/write optical disc. Each single frame can be instantly accessed by a computer.

nontechnical production personnel People concerned primarily with nontechnical production matters that lead from the basic idea to the final screen image. Includes producers, directors, and talent. Also called *above-the-line personnel*.

noseroom The space in front of a person looking or pointing toward the edge of the screen.

NTSC Stands for *National Television System Committee*. Normally refers to the composite video signal, consisting of the Y signal (luminance, or black-and-white information) and the C signal (red, green, and blue color information). *See also* **composite video**.

off-line editing In linear editing it produces an edit decision list or a rough-cut not intended for broadcast. In nonlinear editing the selected shots are captured in low resolution to save computer storage space.

omnidirectional Pickup pattern of a microphone that can hear equally well from all directions.

on-line editing In linear editing it produces the final high-quality edit master for broadcast or program duplication. In nonlinear editing the shots listed on the edit decision list are recaptured at a higher resolution.

over-the-shoulder shot (O/S) Camera looks over the camera-near person's shoulder (shoulder and back of head included in shot) at the other person.

O/S See **over-the-shoulder shot**

PA Production assistant.

P.A. system See **SA**

pads See **trim handles**

paint box See **graphics generator**

pan To turn the camera horizontally.

pan-and-tilt head See **mounting head**

party line See **PL**

patchbay A device that connects various inputs with specific outputs. Also called *patchboard.*

patchboard See **patchbay**

pedestal To move the camera up or down using a studio pedestal.

performer A person who appears on-camera in nondramatic shows. The performer does not assume someone else's character.

photographic principle The triangular arrangement of key, back, and fill lights. Also called *triangle,* or *three-point, lighting.*

pickup device See **imaging device**

pickup pattern The territory around the microphone within which the mic can hear well.

PL Stands for *party line, phone line,* or *private line.* Major intercommunication device in video studios.

pocket recorder Small camcorder, such as a cell phone, that fits into a shirt pocket. Records exclusively on memory cards. Also called *mobile media.*

point of convergence (POC) The point where z-axis vectors of the right and left 3D lenses meet, resulting in a perfect overlap of the right-eye and left-eye images.

polar pattern The two-dimensional representation of the microphone pickup pattern.

pop filter A wire-mesh screen attached to the front of a mic that reduces breath pops and sudden air blasts.

postproduction Any production activity that occurs after the production. Usually refers to video editing and/or audio sweetening.

postproduction editing The assembly of recorded material after the actual production, in contrast to instantaneous editing with the switcher.

postproduction team Normally consists of the director, a video editor, and, for complex productions, a sound designer who remixes the sound track.

pot Short for potentiometer, a sound-volume control. See **fader**.

preproduction The preparation of all production details.

preproduction team Comprises the people who plan the production. Normally includes the producer, writer, director, art director, and technical director. Large productions may include a composer and a choreographer. In charge: producer.

preroll To start a videotape and let it roll for a few seconds before it is put in the playback or record mode to give the electronic system time to stabilize.

preset bus See **preview bus**

preset the zoom lens See **calibrate the zoom lens**

preview bus Row of buttons on the switcher that can direct an input to the preview monitor at the same time another video source is on the air. Also called *preset bus.*

preview monitor Any monitor that shows a video source, except for the line and off-the-air monitors.

process message The message actually perceived by the viewer in the process of watching a video program.

producer Creator and organizer of video programs.

production The actual activities in which an event is recorded and/or televised.

production model Moving from the idea to the program objective and then backing up to the specific medium requirements to achieve the program objective.

production schedule A calendar that shows the preproduction, production, and postproduction dates and who is doing what, when, and where. *See also* **time line**.

production switcher Switcher designed for instantaneous editing, located in the studio control room or remote truck.

production team Comprises a variety of nontechnical and technical people, such as producer and various assistants (associate producer and production assistant), director and assistant director, and talent and production crew. In charge: director.

program bus Row of buttons on the switcher, with inputs that are directly switched to the line-out.

program objective The desired effect of the program on the viewer. The defined process message.

progressive scanning The consecutive scanning of lines from top to bottom. *See also* **frame**.

properties *See* **props**

props Short for *properties*. Furniture and other objects used by talent and for set decoration.

psychological closure Mentally filling in missing visual information that will lead to a complete and stable configuration. Also called *closure*.

pulse-count system An address code that counts the control track pulses and translates that count into time and frame numbers. It is not frame-accurate. Also called *control track system*.

quantizing A step in the digitization of an analog signal. It changes the sampling points into discrete numerical values (0's and 1's). Also called *quantization*.

quick-release plate A mechanism on a tripod that makes it easy to mount and position the camera so that it is perfectly balanced each time.

radio mic *See* **wireless microphone**

RCA phono plug Connector for video and audio equipment.

reflected light Light that is bounced off the illuminated object. To measure reflected light, point the light meter close to the object from the direction of the camera.

refresh rate The number of complete scanning cycles per second. Also expressed in frames per second (fps). *See also* **frame**.

remote A production of a large, scheduled event done for live transmission or live-on-tape recording. *See also* **big remote**.

remote survey An inspection of the remote location by key production and engineering personnel so that they can plan for the setup and the use of production equipment. Also called *site survey*.

remote truck The vehicle that carries the production control room, audio control, video-recording section, video control section, and transmission equipment.

RGB Stands for *red, green,* and *blue*—the basic colors of television.

RGB component video A system in which all three color signals are kept separate and recorded separately on videotape. Often called *RGB system*.

RGB system *See* **RGB component video**

ribbon microphone A high-quality, highly sensitive microphone for critical sound pickup in the studio, usually for recording string instruments.

rough-cut A preliminary edit.

rundown sheet *See* **fact sheet**

SA Stands for *studio address system*. A public address loudspeaker system from the control room to the studio. Also called *studio talkback* and *PA* (public address) *system*.

safe title area *See* **essential area**

sampling Taking a number of samples (voltages) of the analog video or audio signal at equally spaced intervals.

scanning The movement of the electron beam from left to right and from top to bottom on the video screen.

scene Event details that form an organic unit, usually in a single place and time. A series of organically related shots that depict these event details.

scenery Background flats and other pieces (windows, doors, pillars) that simulate a specific environment.

scoop A scooplike floodlight.

scrim A heat-resistant spun-glass material that comes in rolls and can be cut with scissors like cloth; it is attached to a scoop to diffuse the light beam.

script Written document that tells what the program is about, who says what, what is supposed to happen, and what and how the audience will see and hear the event.

sensor A solid-state imaging device in a video or digital cinema camera that converts the optical image into electric energy—the video signal. Also called *CCD, chip,* and *CMOS.*

sequencing The control and the structuring of a shot sequence.

server *See* **video server**

set light *See* **background light**

shader *See* **video operator (VO)**

shot The smallest convenient operational unit in video and film, usually the interval between two transitions. In cinema it may refer to a specific camera setup.

shot sheet A list of every shot a particular camera has to get. It is attached to the camera to help the camera operator remember a shot sequence.

shotgun microphone A highly directional mic with a shotgunlike barrel for picking up sounds over a great distance.

shutter speed A camera control that reduces the blurring of bright, fast-moving objects. The higher the shutter speed, the less blurring occurs but the more light is needed.

single-camera directing Directing a single camera (usually a camcorder) in the studio or field for takes that are recorded separately for postproduction.

single-camera production All of the video is captured by a single camera or camcorder for postproduction editing. Similar to the traditional film approach. Also called *film-style.*

single-column drama script Traditional script format for television plays. All dialogue and action cues are written in a single column.

site survey *See* **remote survey**

slate (1) To identify, verbally or visually, each video-recorded take. (2) A blackboard or whiteboard upon which essential production information is written, such as the title of the show, date, and scene and take numbers. It is recorded at the beginning of each video-recorded take.

slide fader *See* **fader**

slow lens A lens that permits a relatively small amount of light to pass through (relatively high *f*-stop number at its largest aperture). Requires higher light levels for optimal pictures.

SMPTE Stands for *Society of Motion Picture and Television Engineers.*

SMPTE time code A specially generated address code that marks each video frame with a specific number (hour, minute, second, and frame). Named for the Society of Motion Picture and Television Engineers, this time code is officially called *SMPTE/EBU* (for *European Broadcasting Union*).

sound perspective People (or other sound-producing sources) sound farther away in long shots than in close-ups.

source VTR The videotape recorder that supplies the program segments to be edited by the record VTR.

spotlight A lighting instrument that produces directional, relatively undiffused light.

stage manager *See* **floor manager**

Steadicam A camera mount that allows the operator to walk and run, with the camera remaining steady.

sticks *See* **tripod**

storyboard A series of sketches of the key visualization points of an event, with the corresponding audio information given below each visualization.

strike To remove certain objects; to remove scenery and equipment from the studio floor after the show.

strip light Several self-contained lamps arranged in a row. Used mostly for illumination of the cyclorama. Also called *cyc light.*

studio camera Heavy, high-quality camera and zoom lens that cannot be maneuvered properly without the aid of a pedestal or some other type of camera mount.

studio control room A room adjacent to the studio in which the director, producer, production assistants, technical director, audio engineer, and sometimes the lighting director perform their production functions.

studio pedestal A heavy camera dolly that permits raising and lowering the camera while on the air.

studio production Production activities that take place in the studio.

studio talkback *See* **SA**

super Short for *superimposition*. A double exposure of two images, with the top one letting the bottom one show through.

Super Hi-Vision A video system that produces extremely high-resolution video images. Generally used for digital cinema.

S-video *See* **Y/C component video**

sweep Curved piece of scenery, similar to a large pillar cut in half.

sweetening The postproduction manipulation of recorded sound.

switcher (1) A panel with rows of buttons that allow the selection and the assembly of multiple video sources through a variety of transition devices as well as the creation of electronic effects. (2) Production person who is doing the switching.

switching A change from one video source to another and the creation of various transitions and effects during production with the aid of a switcher. Also called *instantaneous editing*.

sync generator Part of the camera chain; produces electronic synchronization pulses.

synthetic environment Electronically generated settings, either through chroma key or computer.

take Any one of similar repeated shots taken during video-recording and filming.

talent Collective name for all performers and actors who appear regularly in video.

tally light Red light on the camera and inside the camera viewfinder, indicating when the camera is on the air (switched to the line-out).

tapeless systems Refers to the recording, storage, and playback of audio and video information via digital storage devices other than videotape.

TBC *See* **time base corrector**

TD Stands for *technical director*. The TD usually operates the switcher.

technical personnel People who operate the production equipment, including camera operators, floor persons, and video and audio engineers. Also called *below-the-line personnel*.

telephoto lens Gives a close-up view of an event relatively far away from the camera. Also called *long-focal-length, and narrow-angle, lens*.

teleprompter A prompting device that projects moving copy over the lens so that the talent can read it without losing eye contact with the viewer.

threefold Three flats hinged together.

three-point lighting *See* **photographic principle**

tilt To point the camera up or down.

time base corrector (TBC) An electronic accessory to videotape recorders that helps make videotape playbacks electronically stable. It keeps slightly different scanning cycles in step.

time code *See* **SMPTE time code**

timeline *Nonlinear editing:* shows all video and audio tracks of a sequence and the clips they contain. Each track has individual controls for displaying and manipulating the clips.

time line *Production:* a breakdown of time blocks for various activities on the actual production day, such as crew call, setup, and camera rehearsal.

tongue To move the boom with the camera from left to right or from right to left.

track *See* **truck**

triangle lighting The triangular arrangement of key, back, and fill lights. Also called *three-point lighting* and *photographic principle. See* **photographic principle**.

triaxial cable Thin camera cable in which one central wire is surrounded by two concentric shields.

trim handles Recording additional footage before and after the major shot content for precise editing. Also called *edit margins* and *pads*.

tripod A three-legged camera mount. Also called *sticks*.

truck To move the camera laterally by means of a mobile camera mount. Also called *track*.

two-column A/V script Traditional script format with video information (V) on page-left and audio information (A) on page-right for a variety of television scripts, such as for interviews, documentaries, and commercials. Also called *two-column documentary script*.

two-column documentary script *See* **two-column A/V script**

twofold Two flats hinged together. Also called *book*.

two-shot Framing of two people in a single shot.

unidirectional Pickup pattern of a microphone that can hear best from the front.

uplink truck The vehicle that sends video and audio signals to a satellite.

variable-focal-length lens *See* **zoom lens**

vector A directional screen force. There are graphic, index, and motion vectors.

vector line An imaginary line created by extending converging index vectors or the direction of a motion vector. Also called the *line of conversation and action,* the *hundredeighty* (for 180 degrees), and, simply, the *line*.

video leader Visual and auditory material that precedes any color videotape recording. Also called *academy leader*.

video operator (VO) In charge of the camera setup and picture control during a production. Also called *shader*.

video-record operator In charge of video recording. Also called *VR operator* and *VTR operator*.

video server A large-capacity hard-drive array that can ingest, store, and play back a great amount of audio and video information. It can be accessed by several users simultaneously.

video track The area of the videotape used for recording the video information.

viewfinder A small video screen or flat-panel display on a camera that shows the black-and-white or color picture the camera generates. The flat-panel displays are also called *monitors*.

virtual reality Computer-simulated environment with which the user can interact.

visualization The mental image of a shot. May also include the imagining of verbal and nonverbal sounds. Mentally converting a scene into a number of key video images and their sequence.

VO *See* **video operator**

volume-unit (VU) meter Measures volume units, the relative loudness of amplified sound.

VR log A record of each take on the source media. Also called *editing log*. When the recording media is videotape, the shot record is also called *VTR log*.

VR operator *See* **video-record operator**

VTR operator *See* **video-record operator**

VU meter *See* **volume-unit (VU) meter**

walk-through/camera rehearsal A combination of an orientation session for talent and crew and a follow-up rehearsal with full equipment. This combination rehearsal is generally conducted from the studio floor.

waveform Graphic representation of a sound that occurs over a period of time.

white-balance To adjust the color circuits in the camera to produce white color in lighting of various color temperatures (relative reddishness or bluishness of white light).

wide-angle lens A short-focal-length lens that provides a large vista.

wind jammer *See* **windsock**

window dub A dub of the source tapes to a lower-quality tape format with the address code keyed into each frame.

windscreen Acoustic foam rubber that is put over the entire microphone to cut down wind noise.

windsock A moplike cloth cover that is put over the windscreen to further reduce wind noise in outdoor use. Also called *wind jammer.*

wipe A transition in which one image seems to "wipe off" (gradually replace) another from the screen.

wireless microphone A system that sends audio signals over the air rather than through microphone cables. The mic is attached to a small transmitter, and the signals are sent to a receiver connected to the audio console or recording device. Also called *radio mic.*

XLR connector Professional three-wire connector for audio cables.

X/S *See* **cross-shot**

Y/C component video A system that keeps the Y (luminance, or black-and-white) and C (color—red, green, and blue) signals separate. Y and C are combined again when recorded on a specific media. Also called *Y/C system* and *S-video.*

Y channel *See* **luminance channel**

Y/color difference component video Video-recording system wherein the three signals—the luminance (Y) signal, the blue signal minus its luminance (B–Y; in digital, Pb), and the red signal minus its luminance (R–Y; in digital, Pr)—are kept separate during the transport and recording process.

Y/C system *See* **Y/C component video**

z-axis Indicates screen depth. In standard two-dimensional video space, it extends from the screen (camera lens) to the background (horizon). In three-dimensional video space, it also extends from the screen to the viewer.

zoom To change the focal length of the lens through the use of a zoom control while the camera remains stationary.

zoom lens Variable-focal-length lens. All video cameras are equipped with a zoom lens.

zoom range How much the focal length can be changed from a wide shot to a close-up during a zoom. The zoom range is stated as a ratio, such as 20:1. Also called *zoom ratio.*

zoom ratio *See* **zoom range**

Index